AF505478

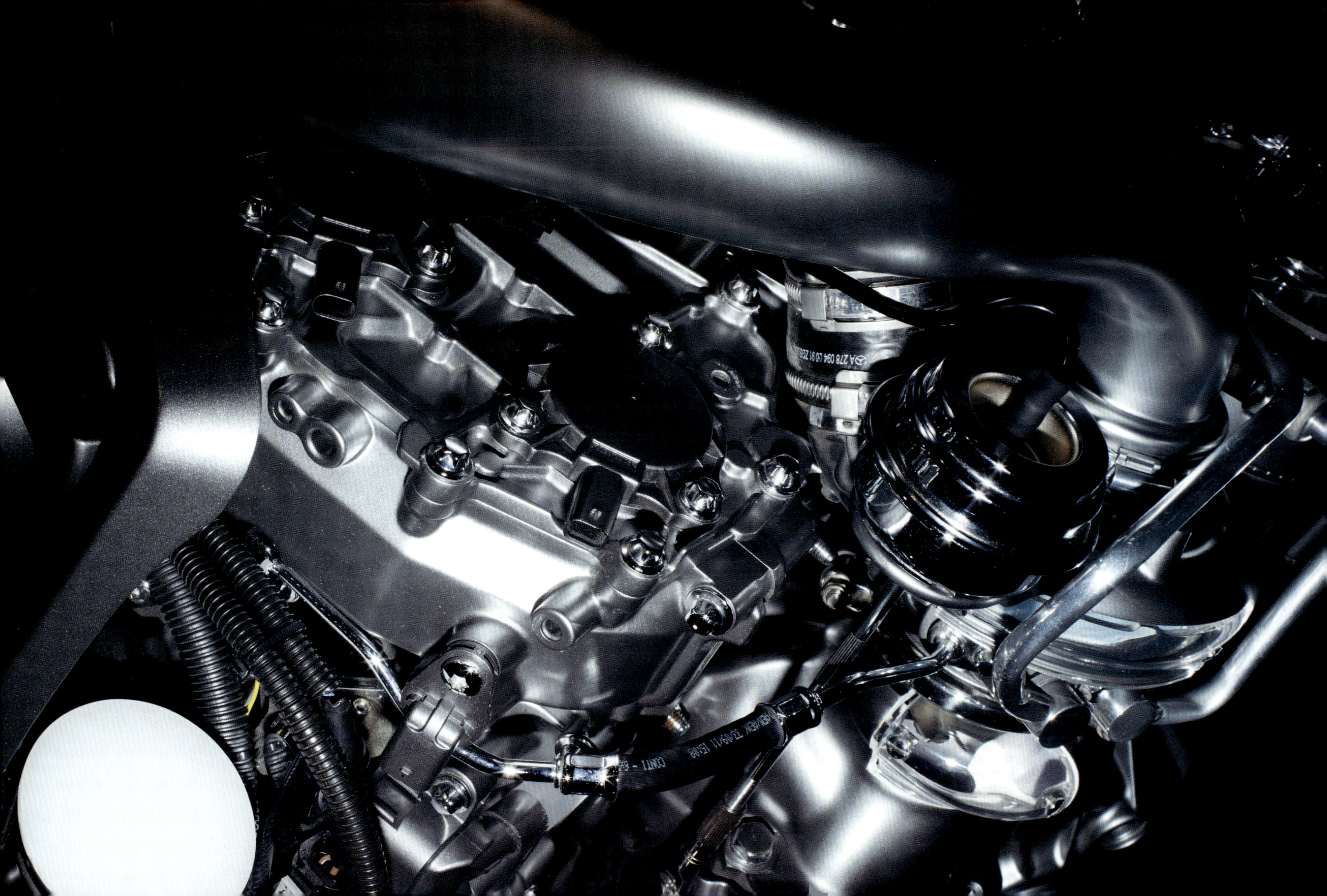

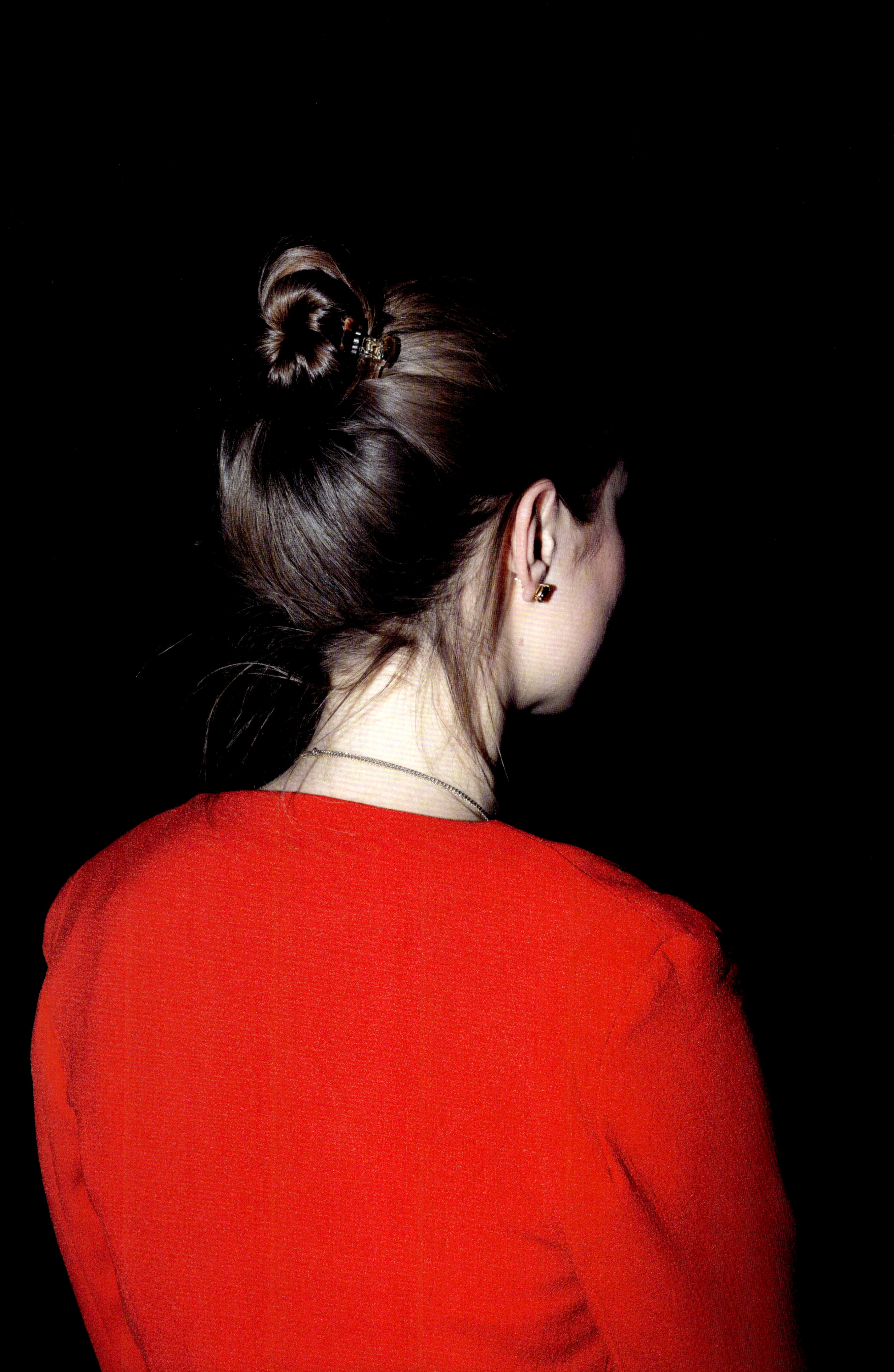

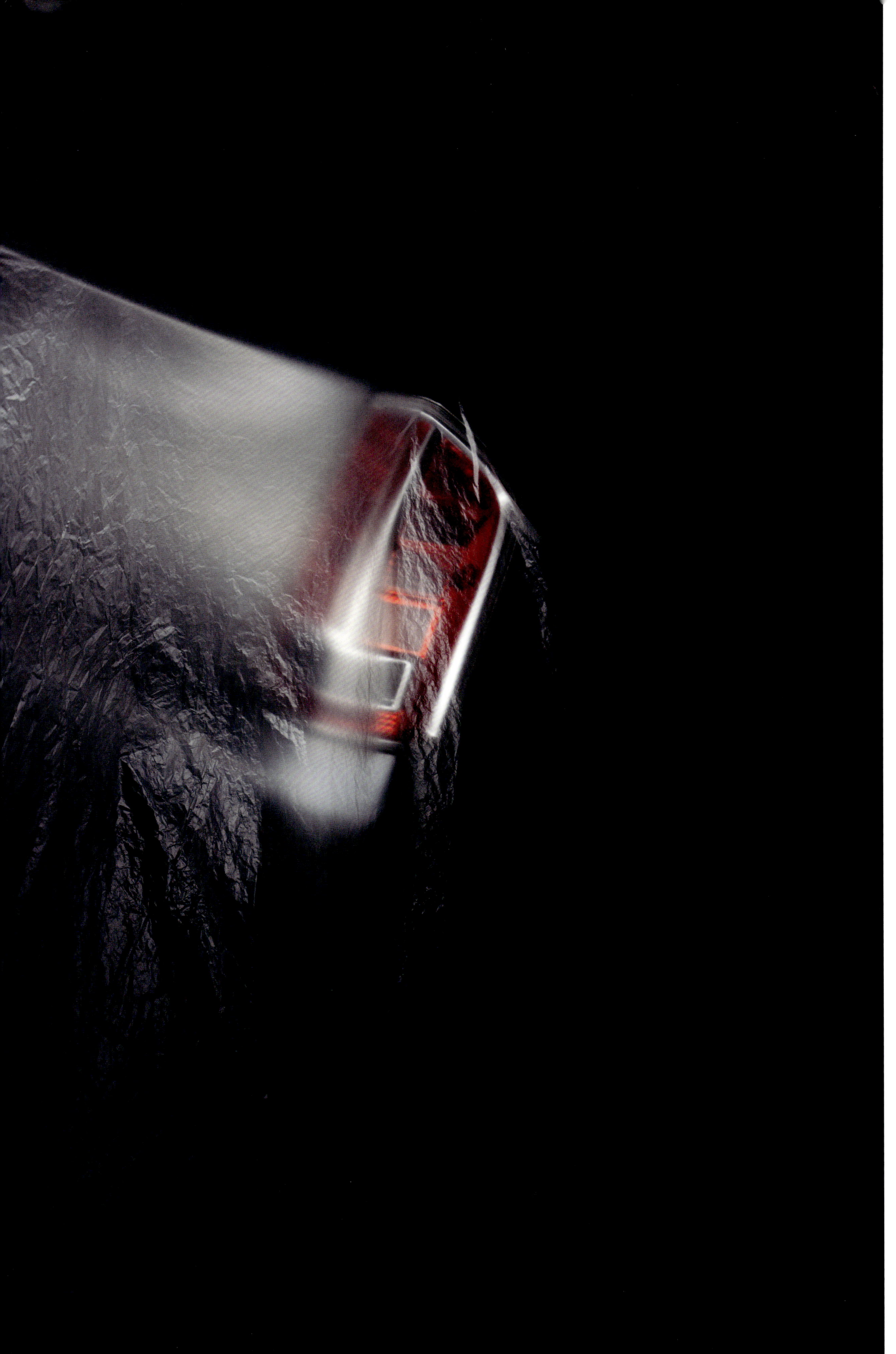

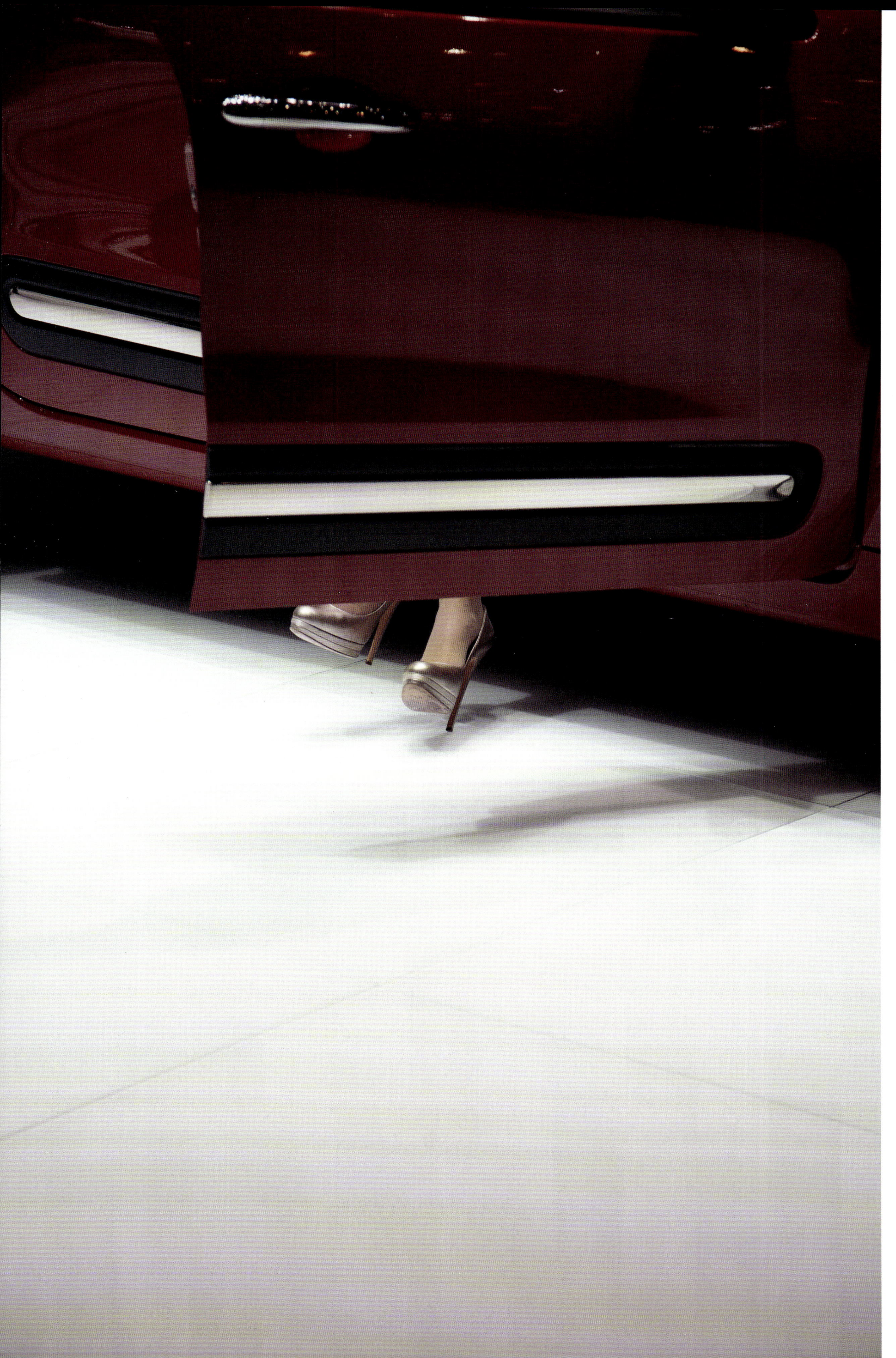

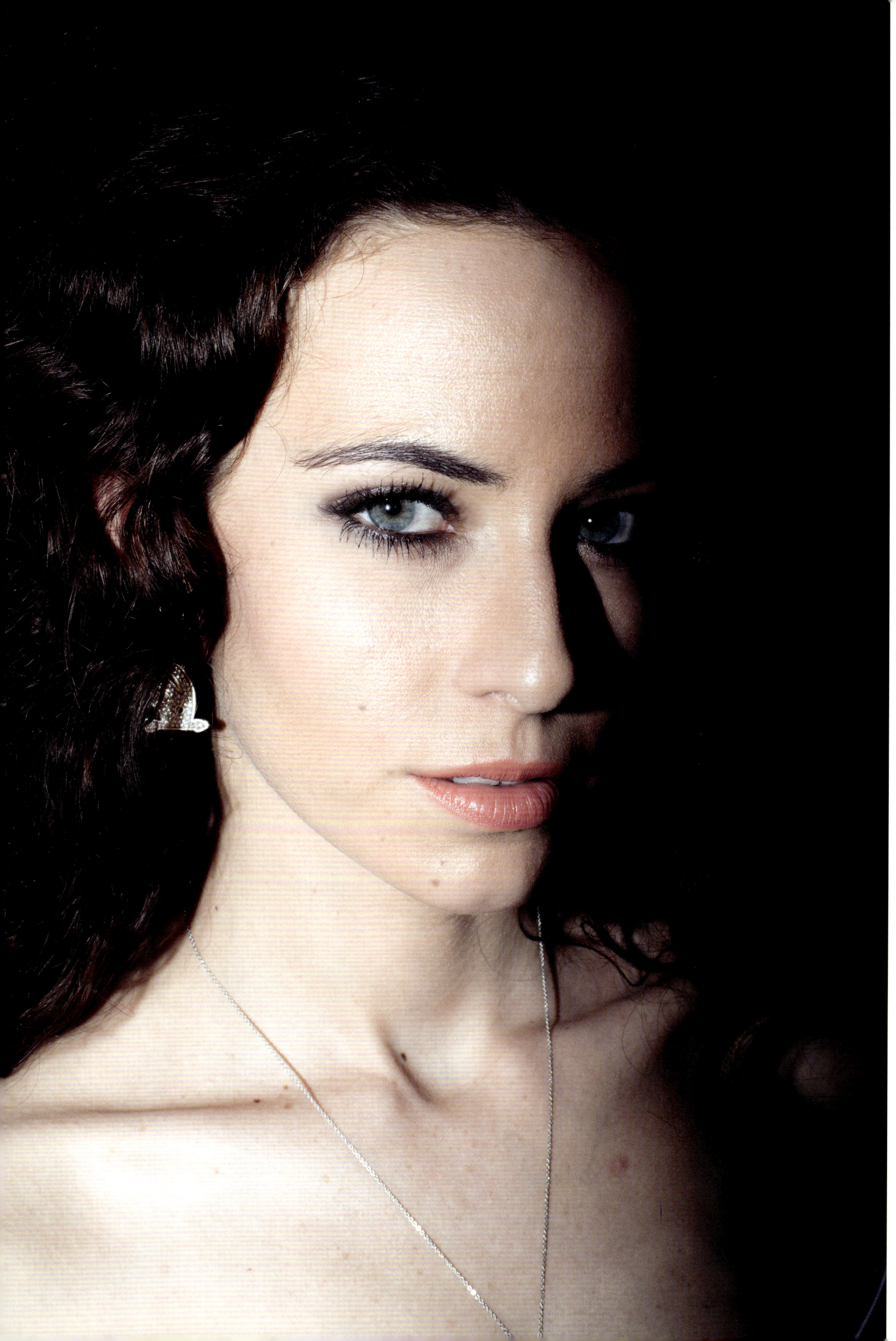

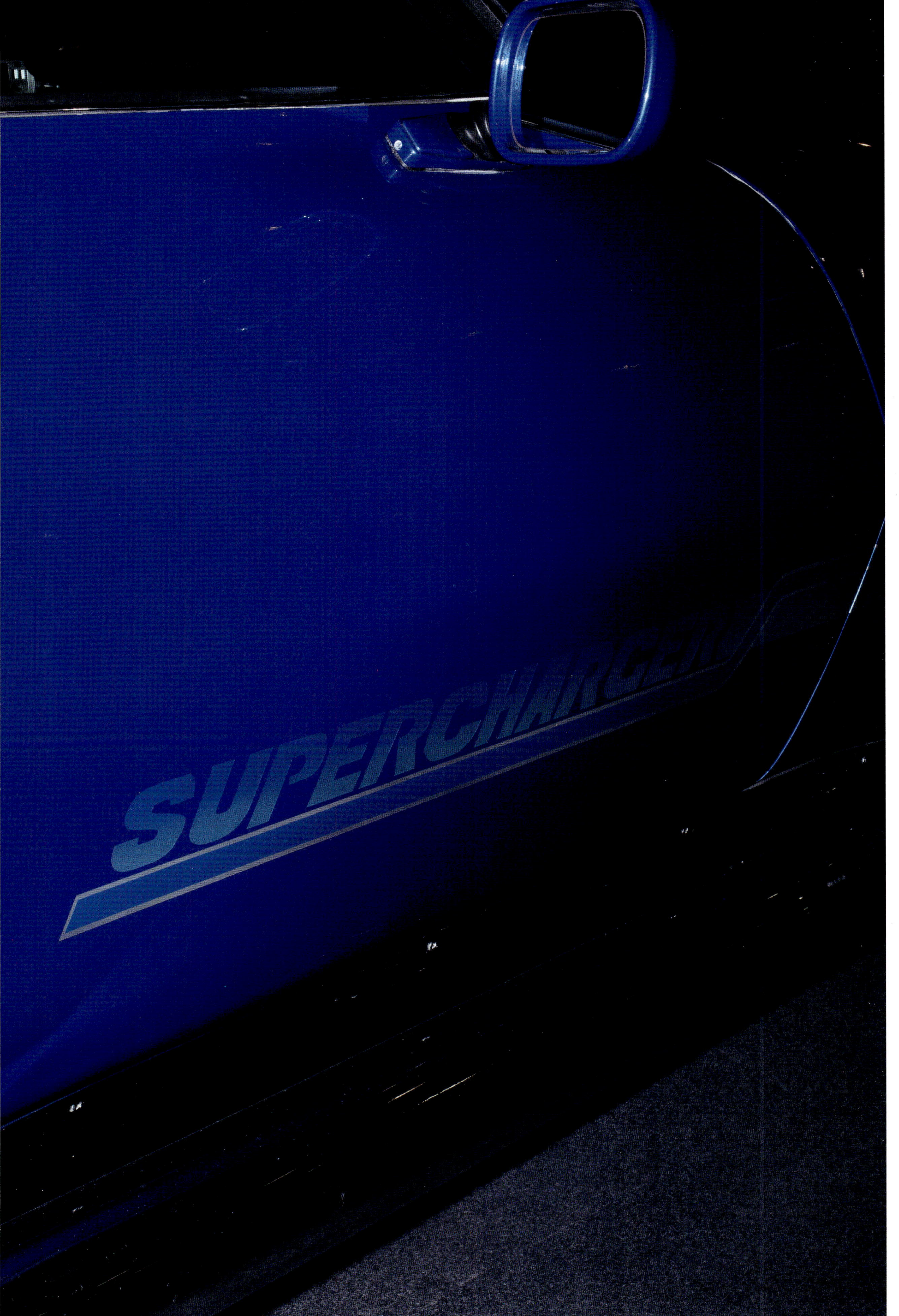
SUPERCHARGED

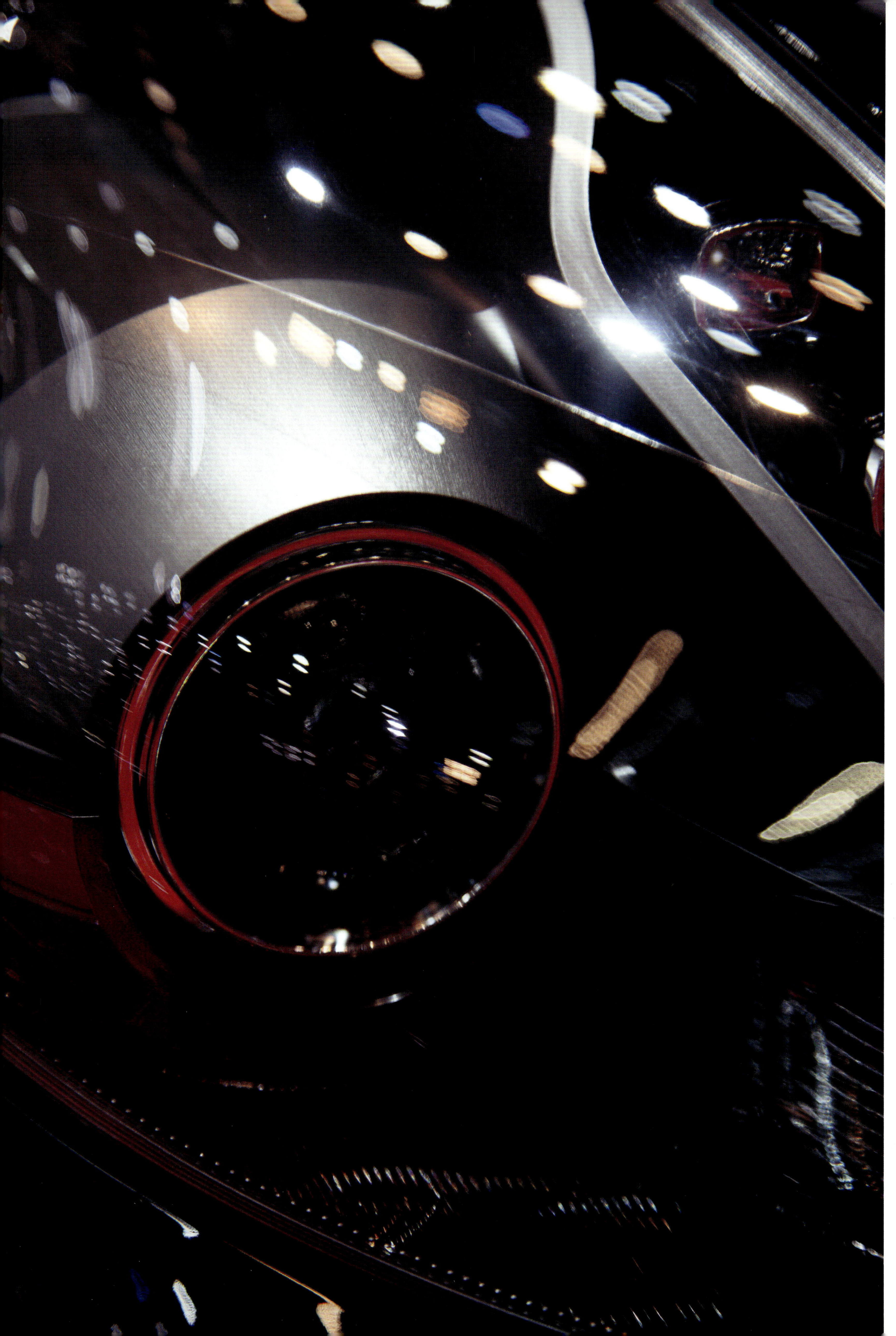

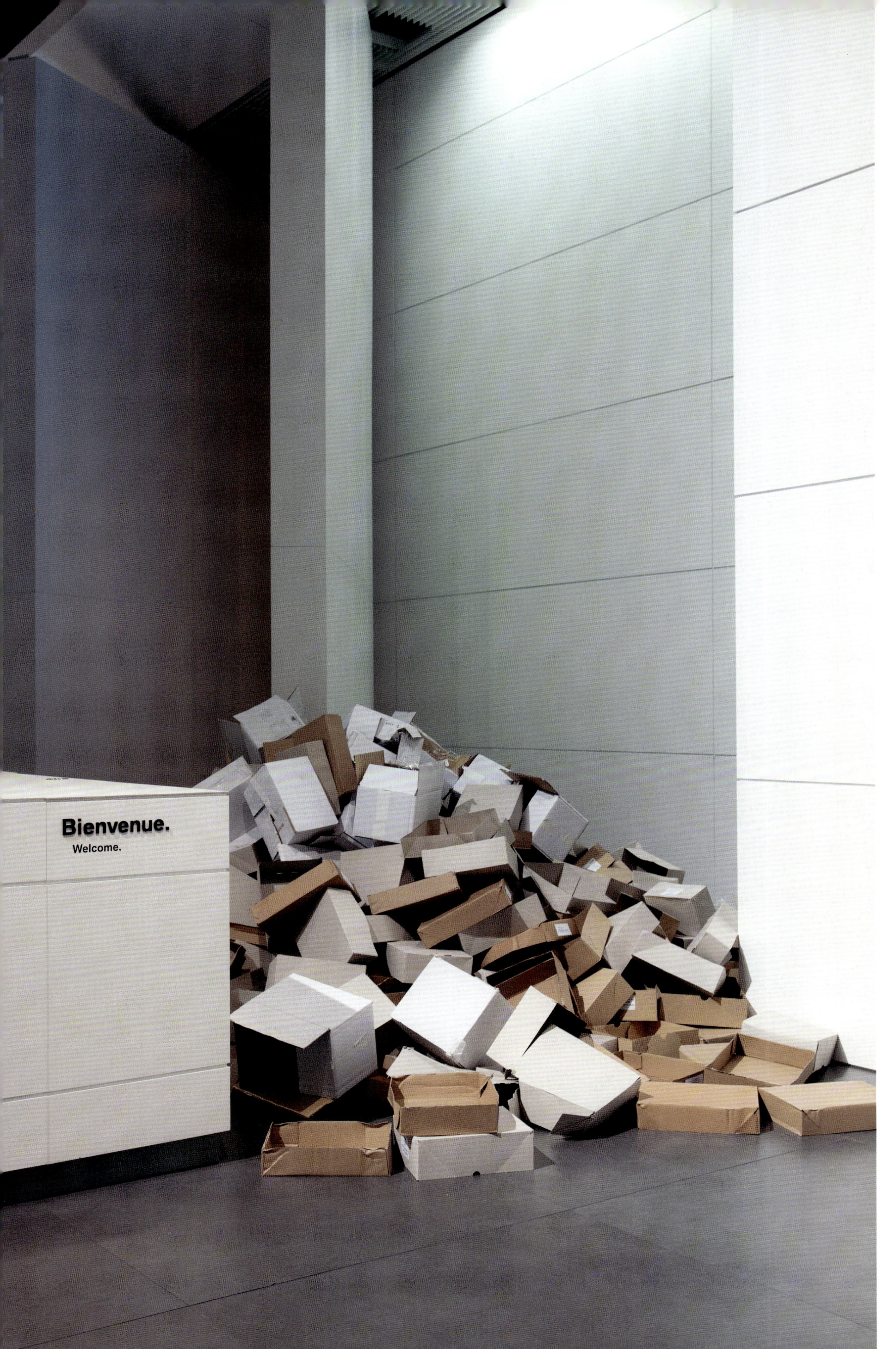
Bienvenue.
Welcome.

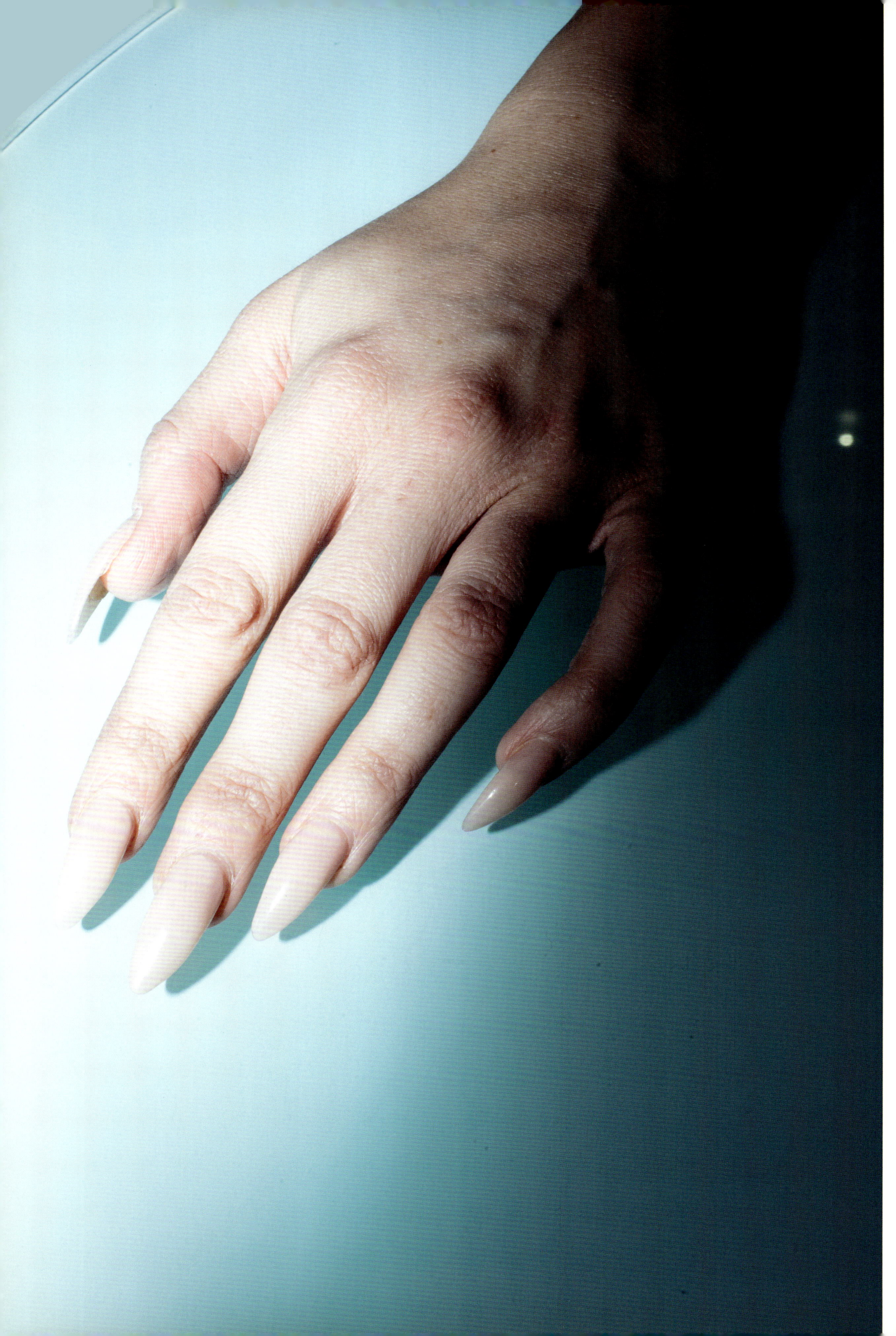

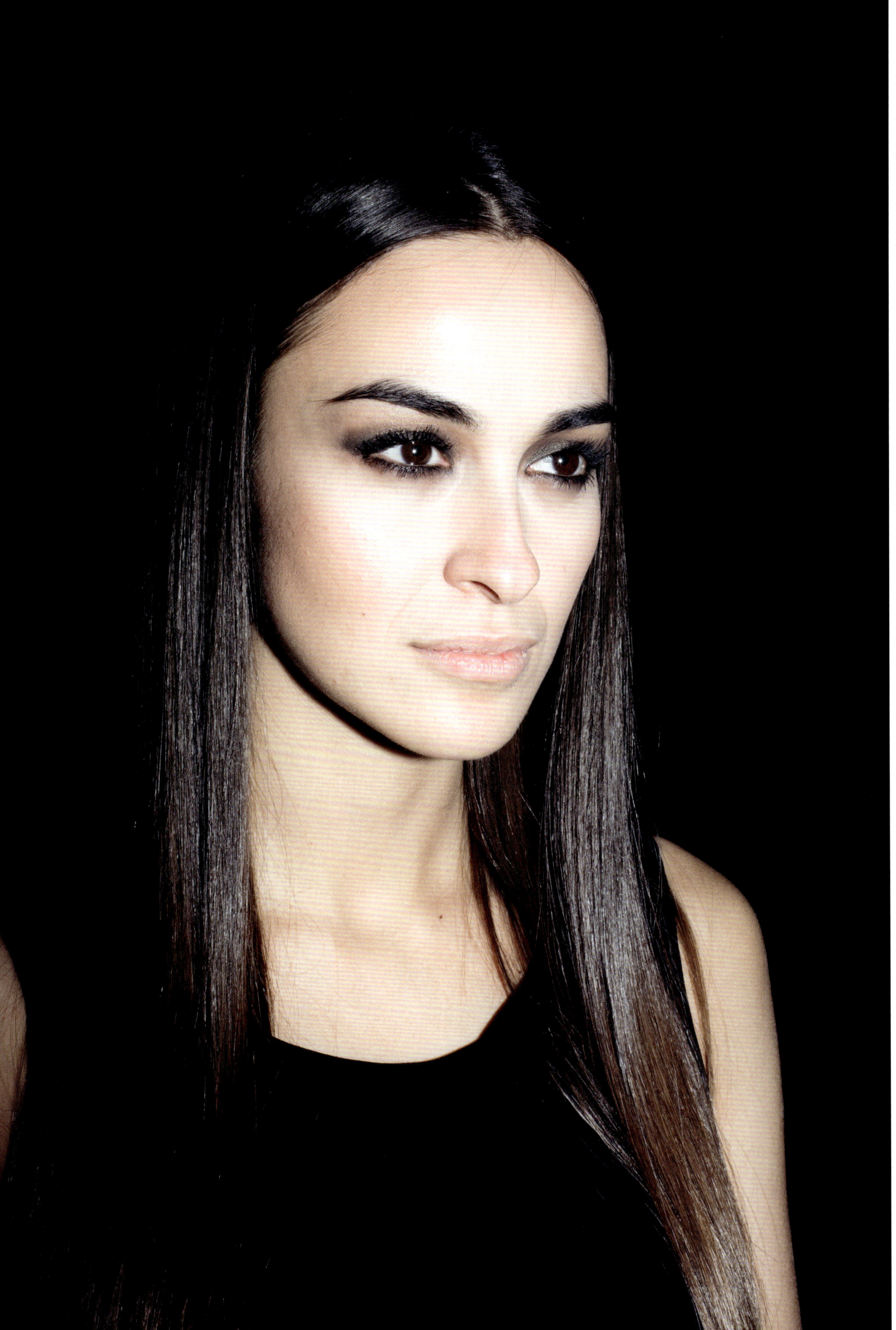

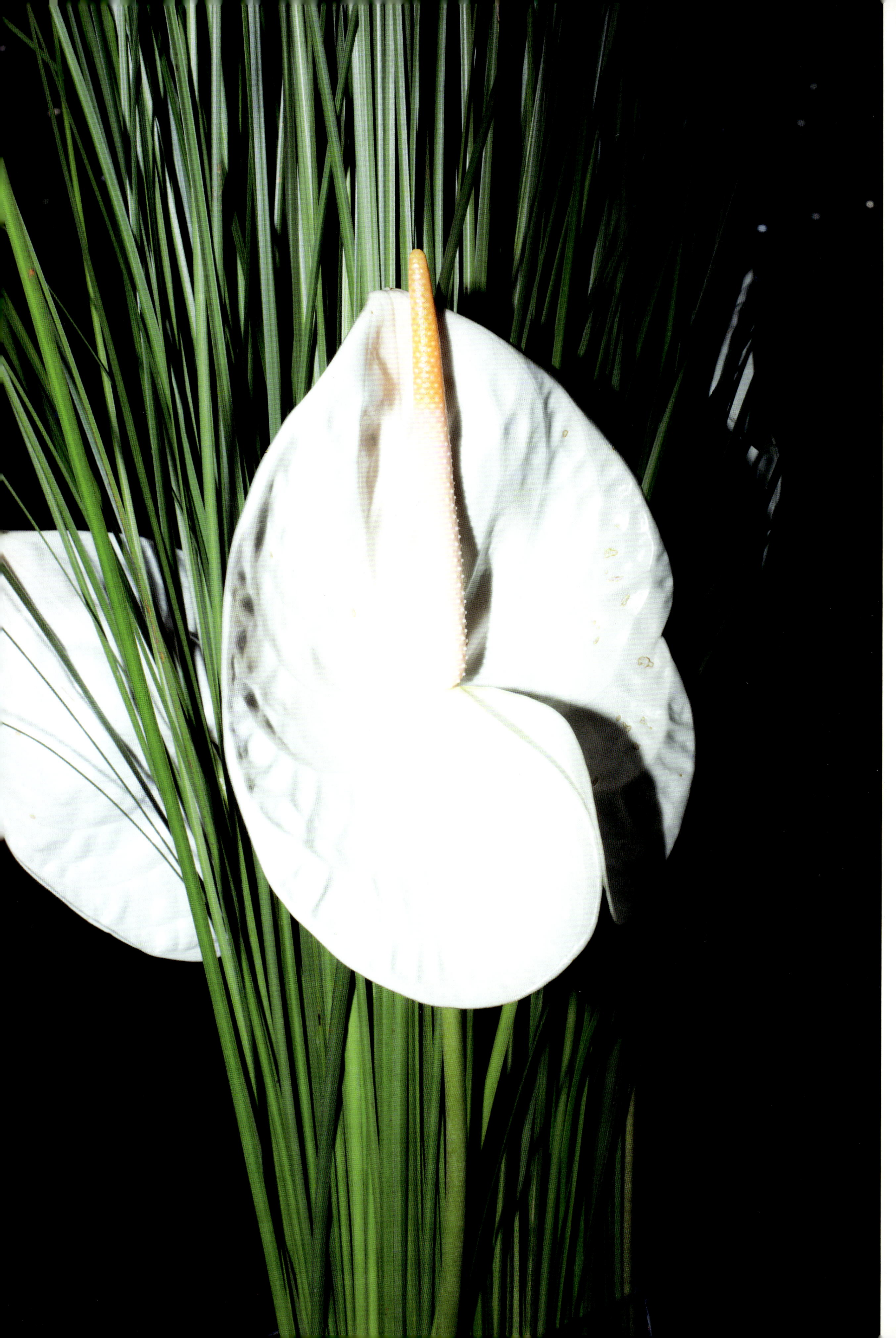

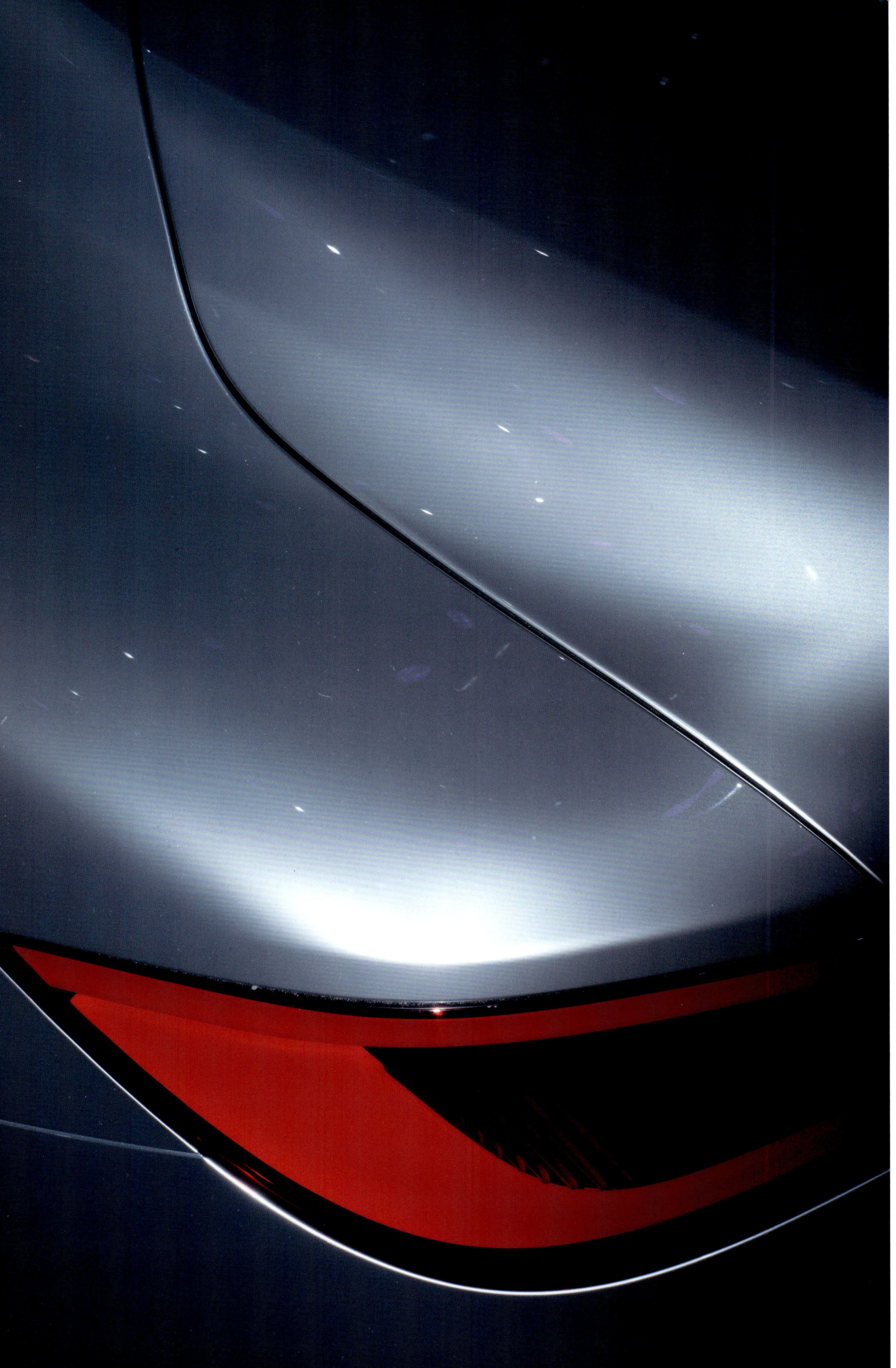

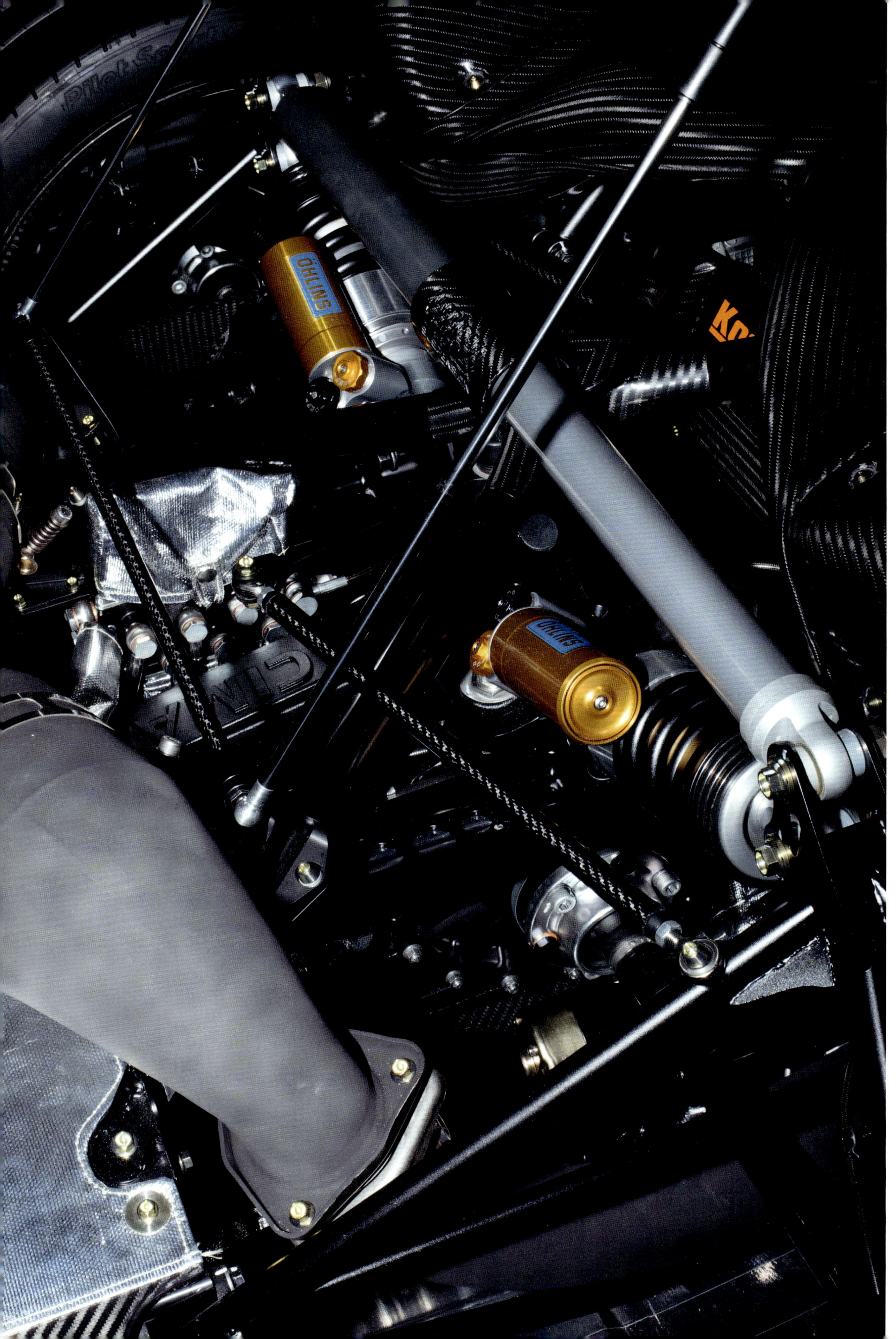
ÖHLINS
ÖHLINS

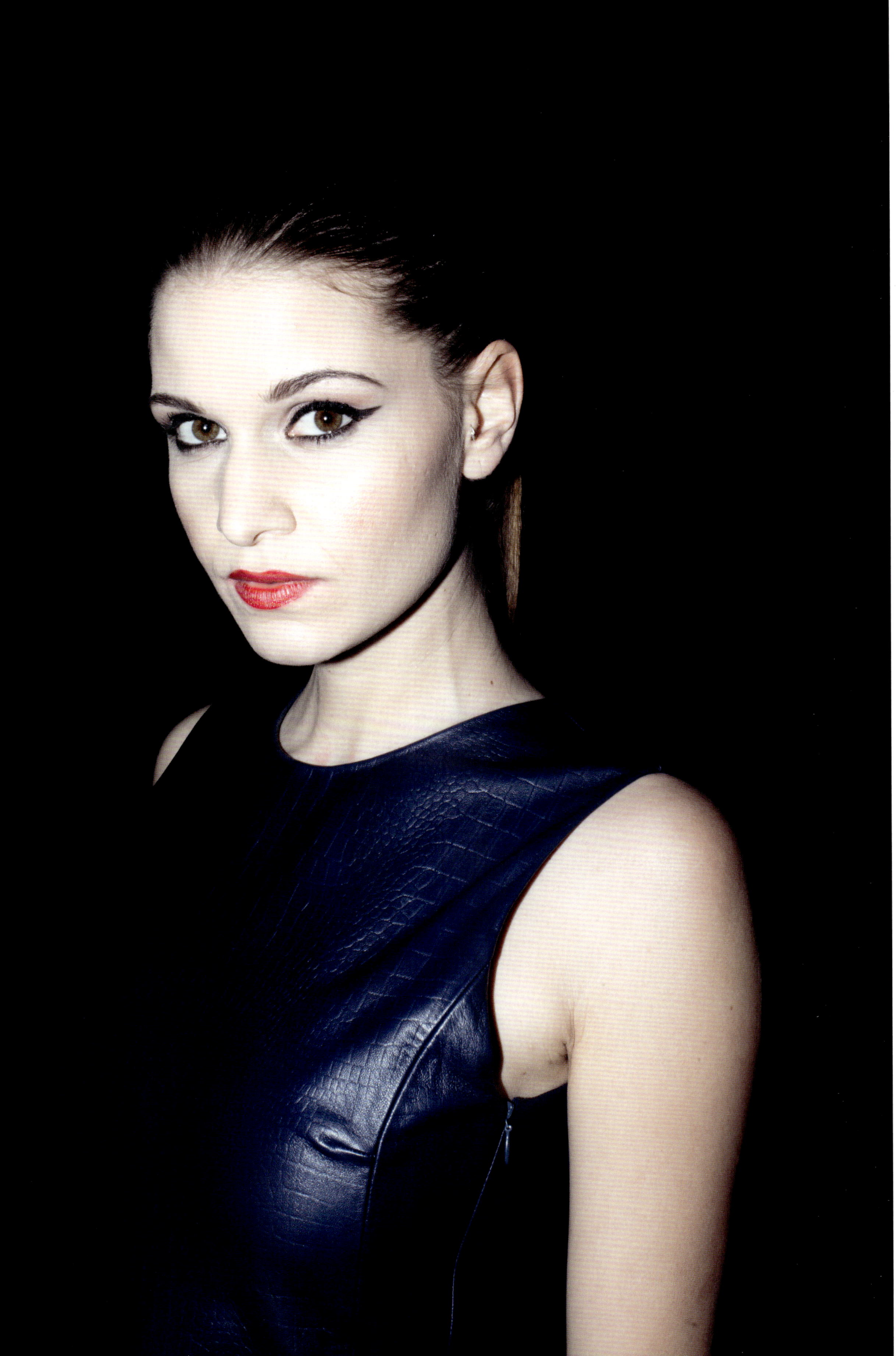

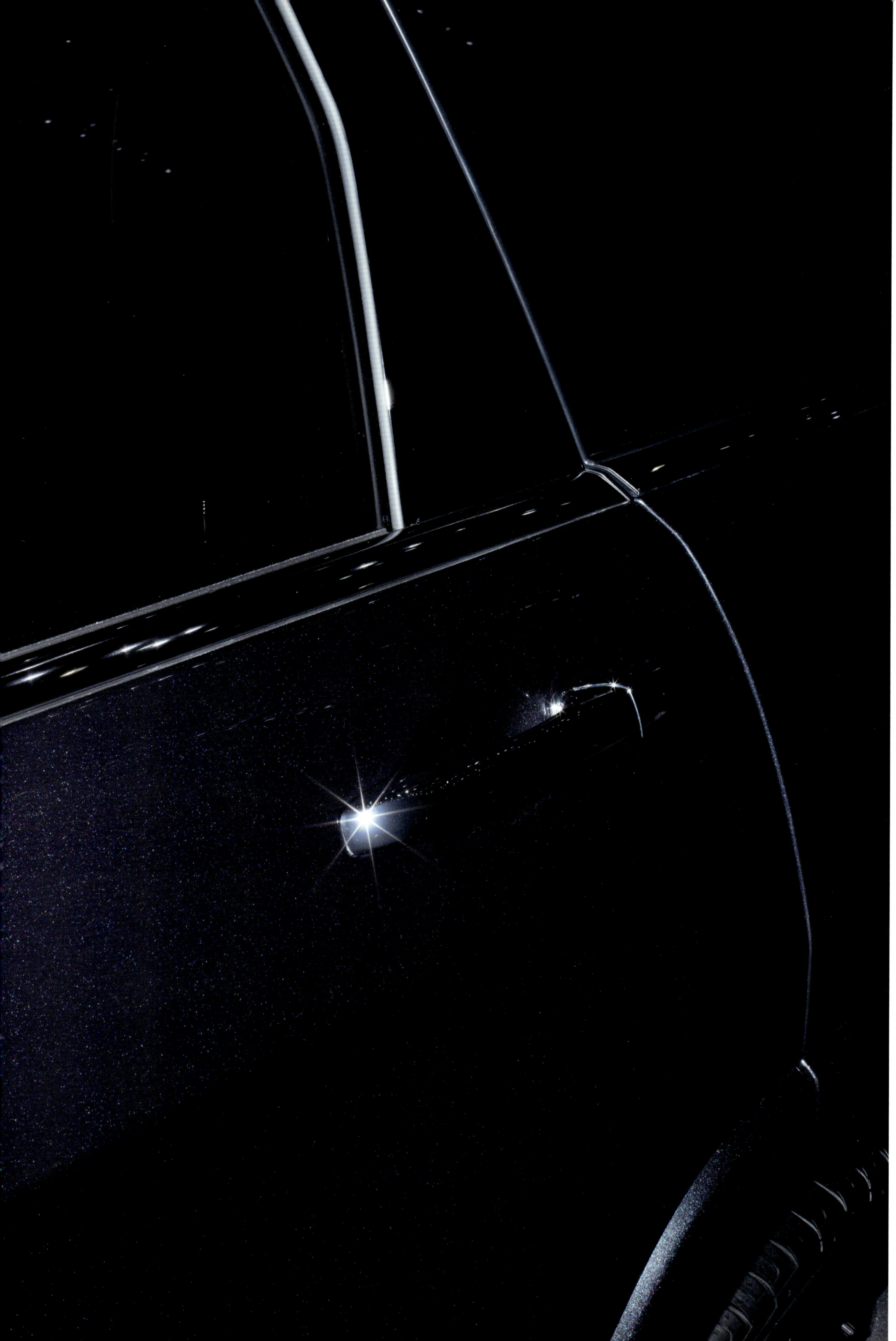

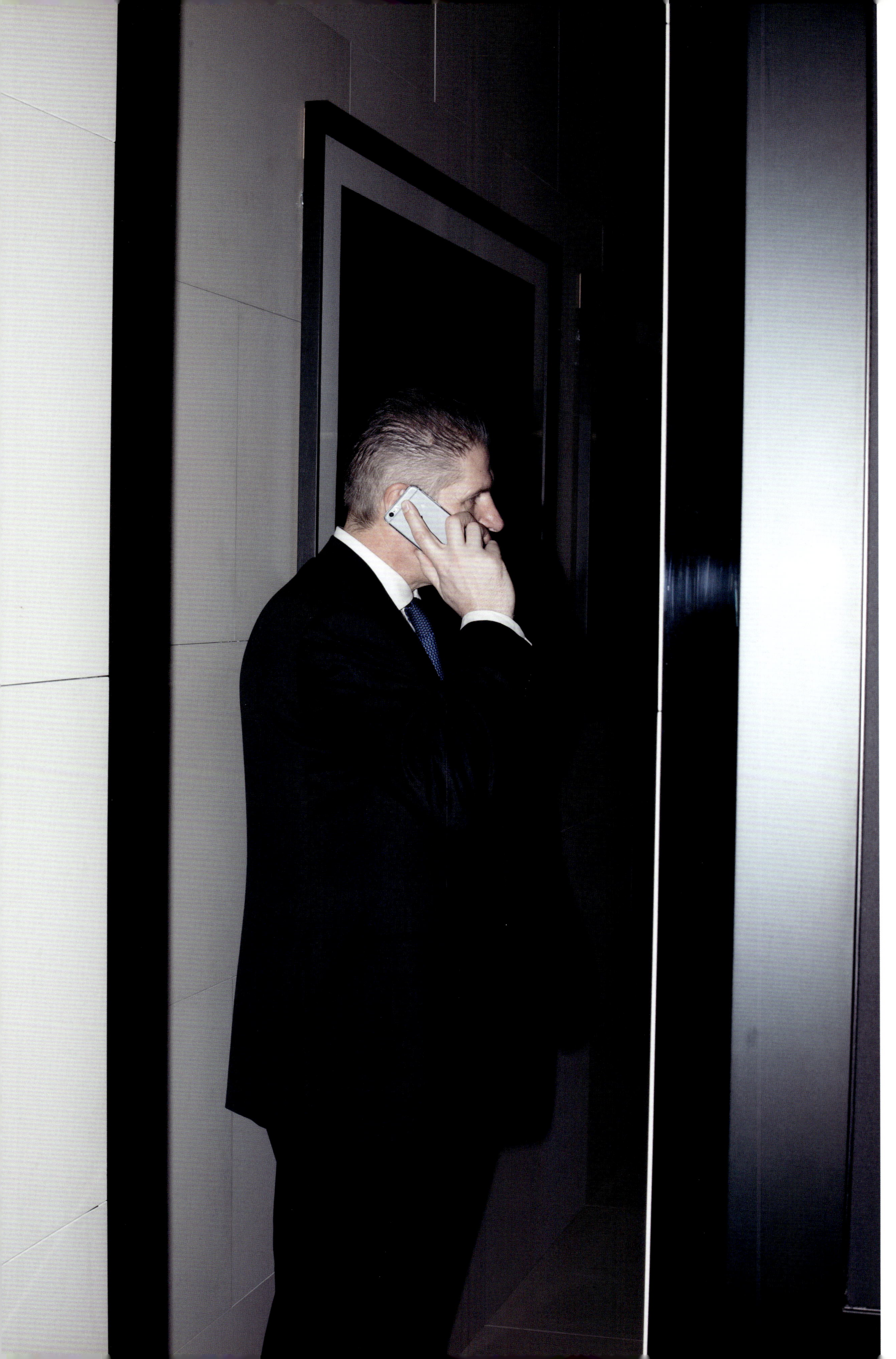

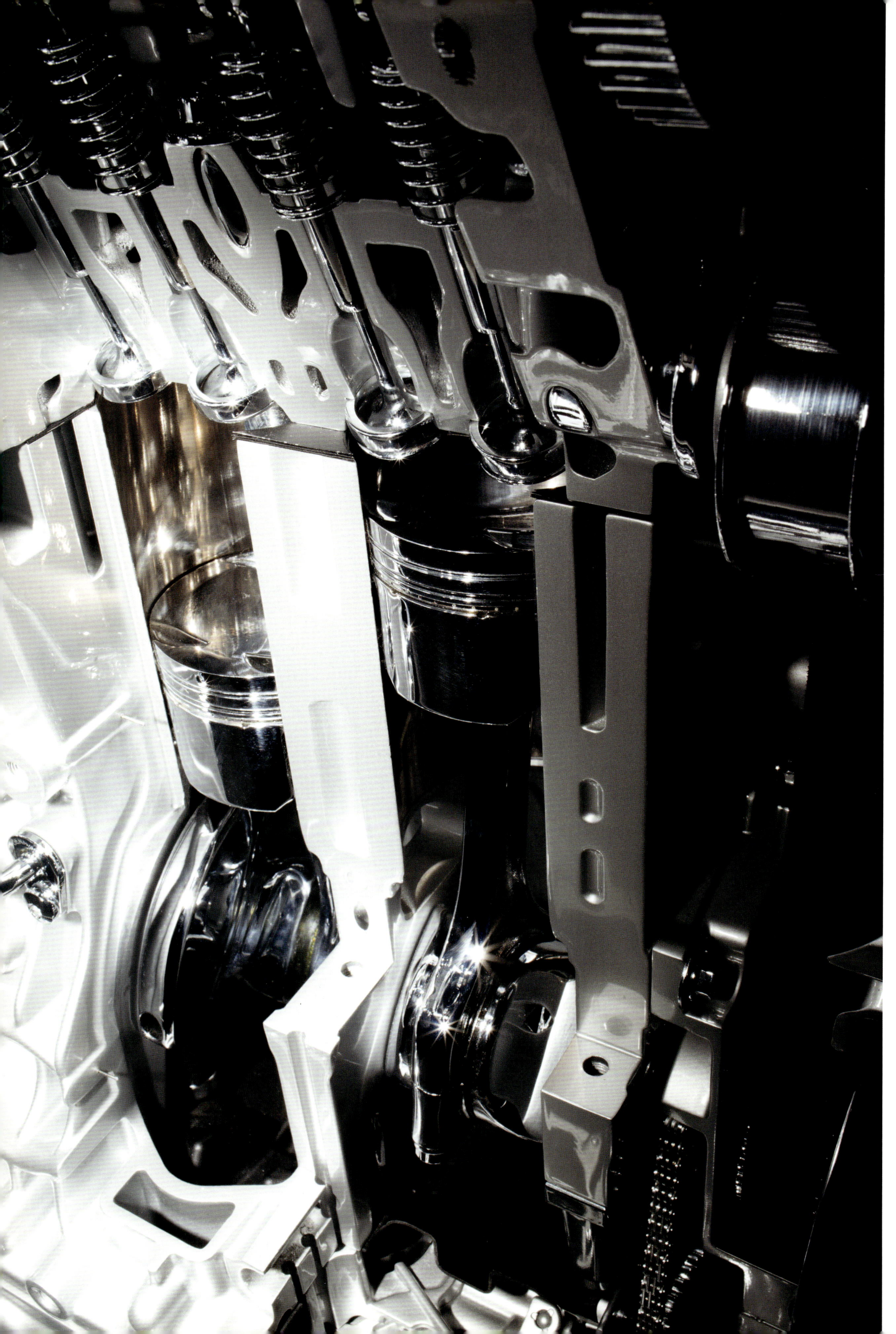

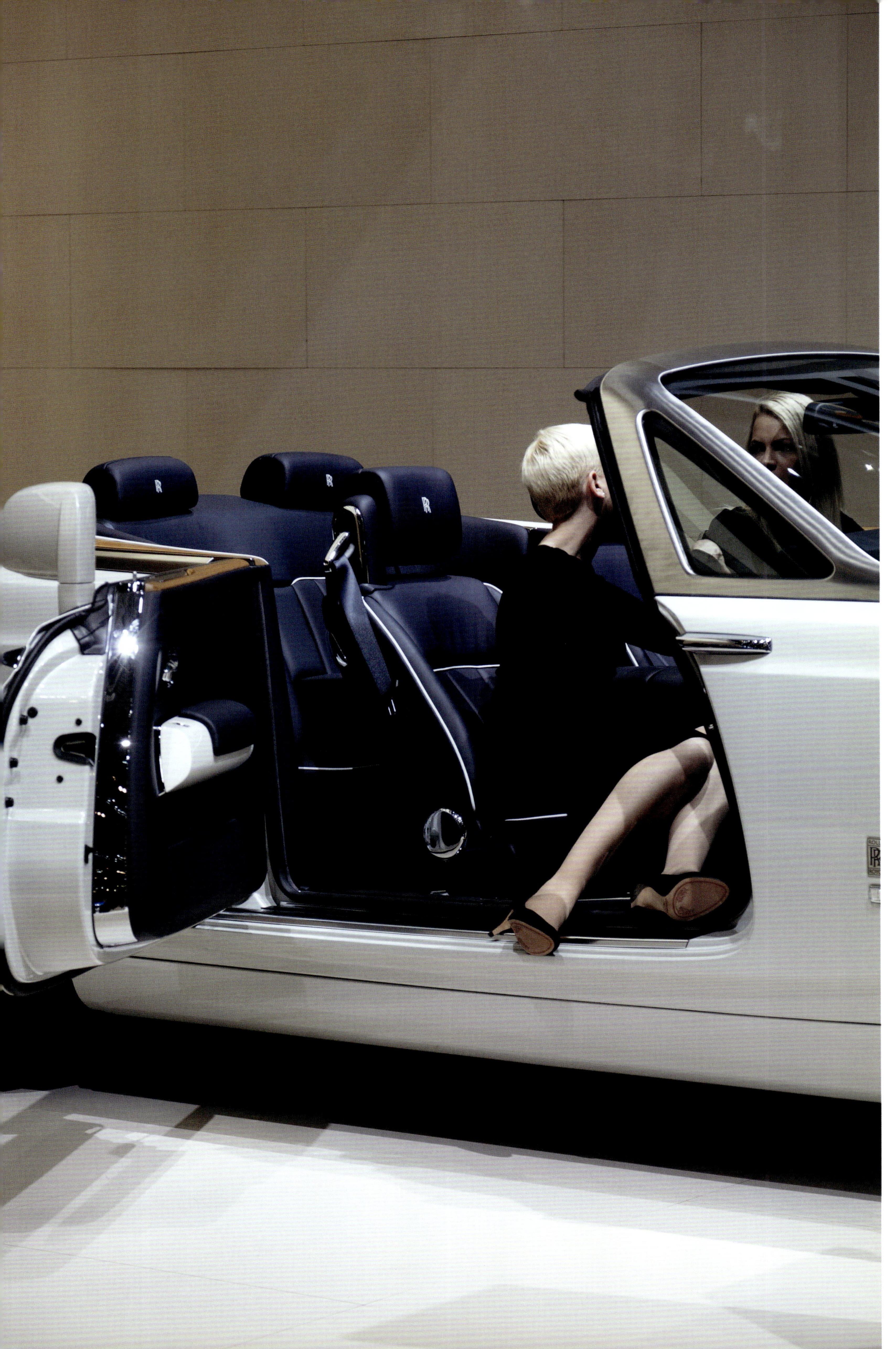

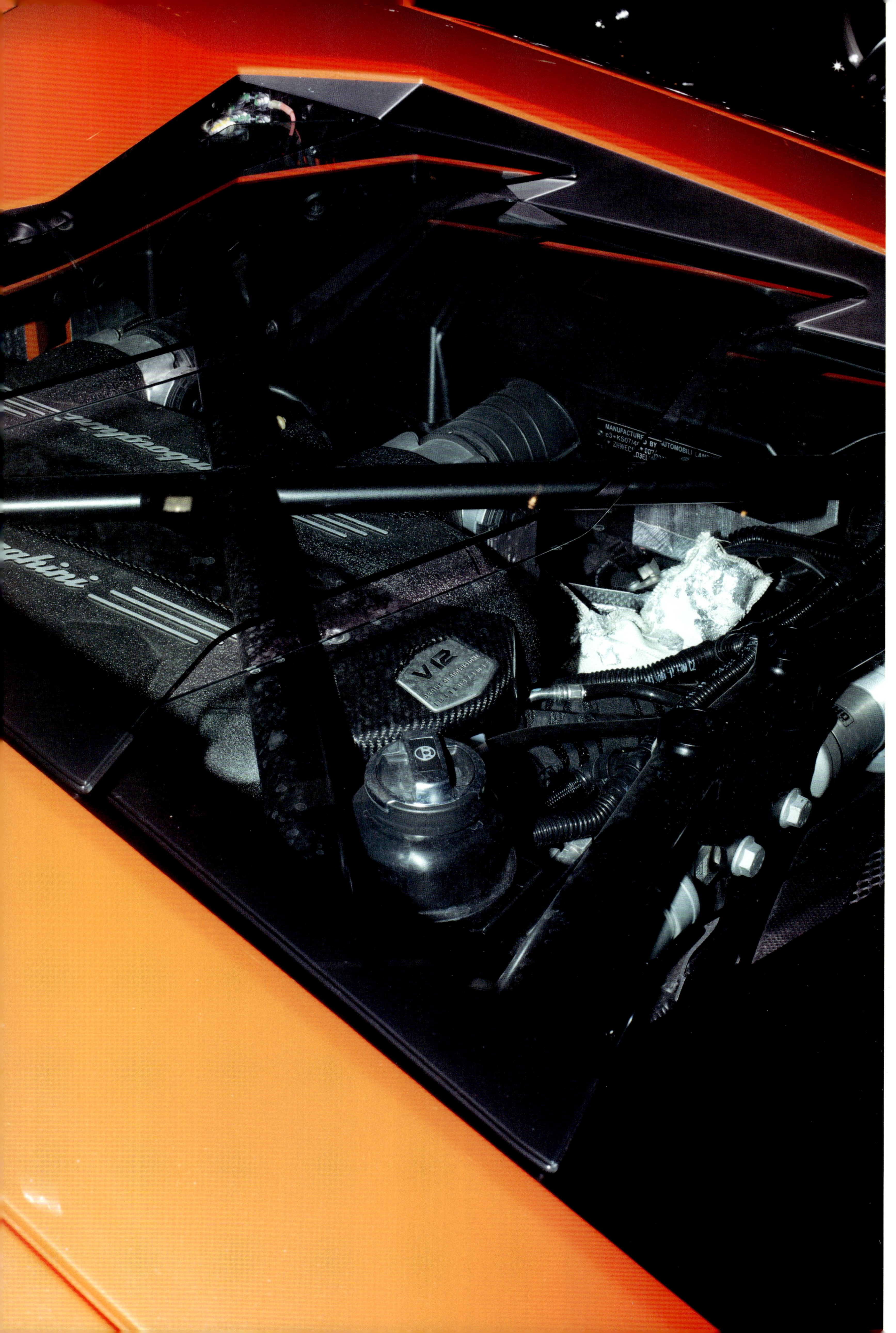

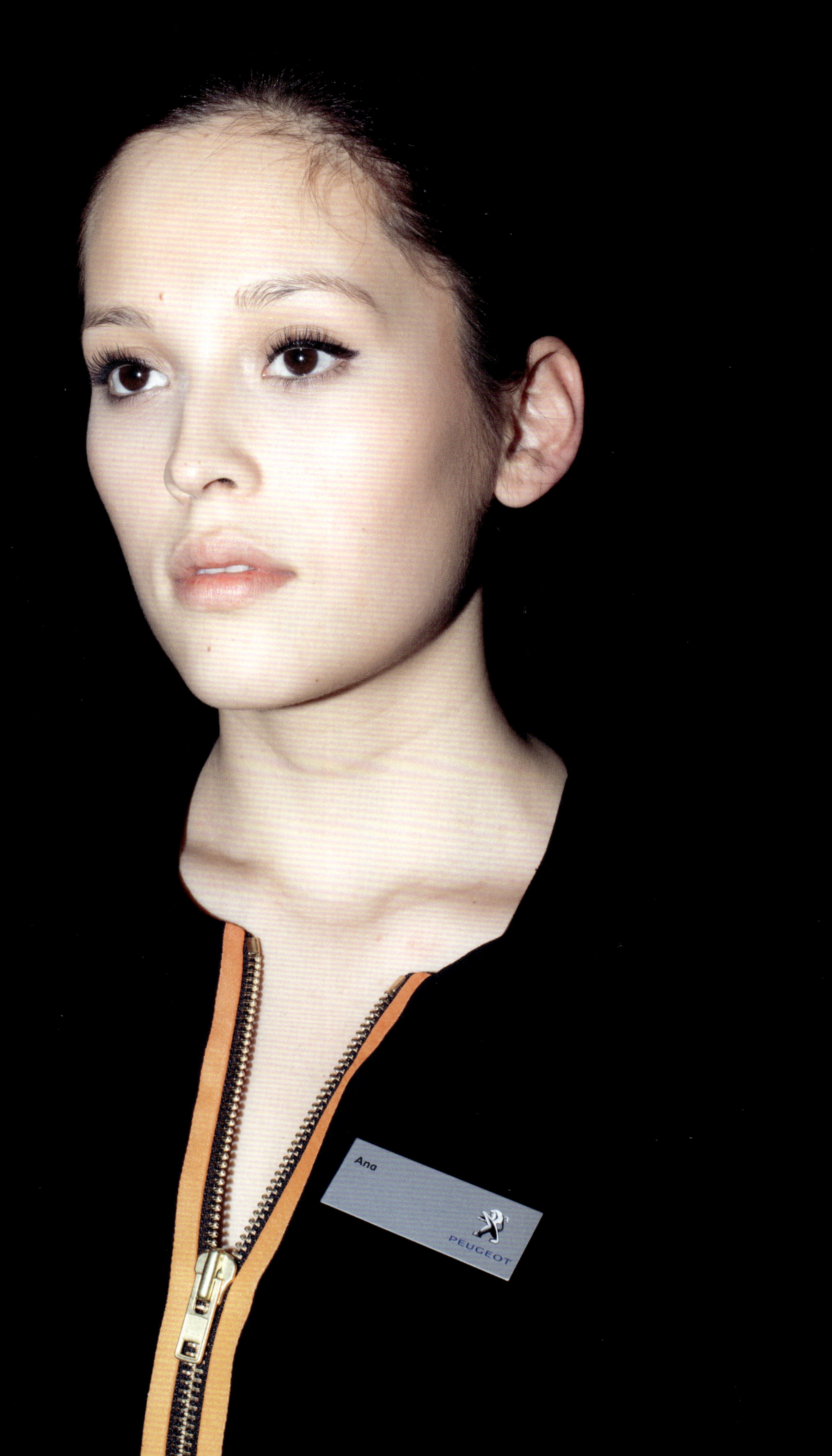
Ana
PEUGEOT

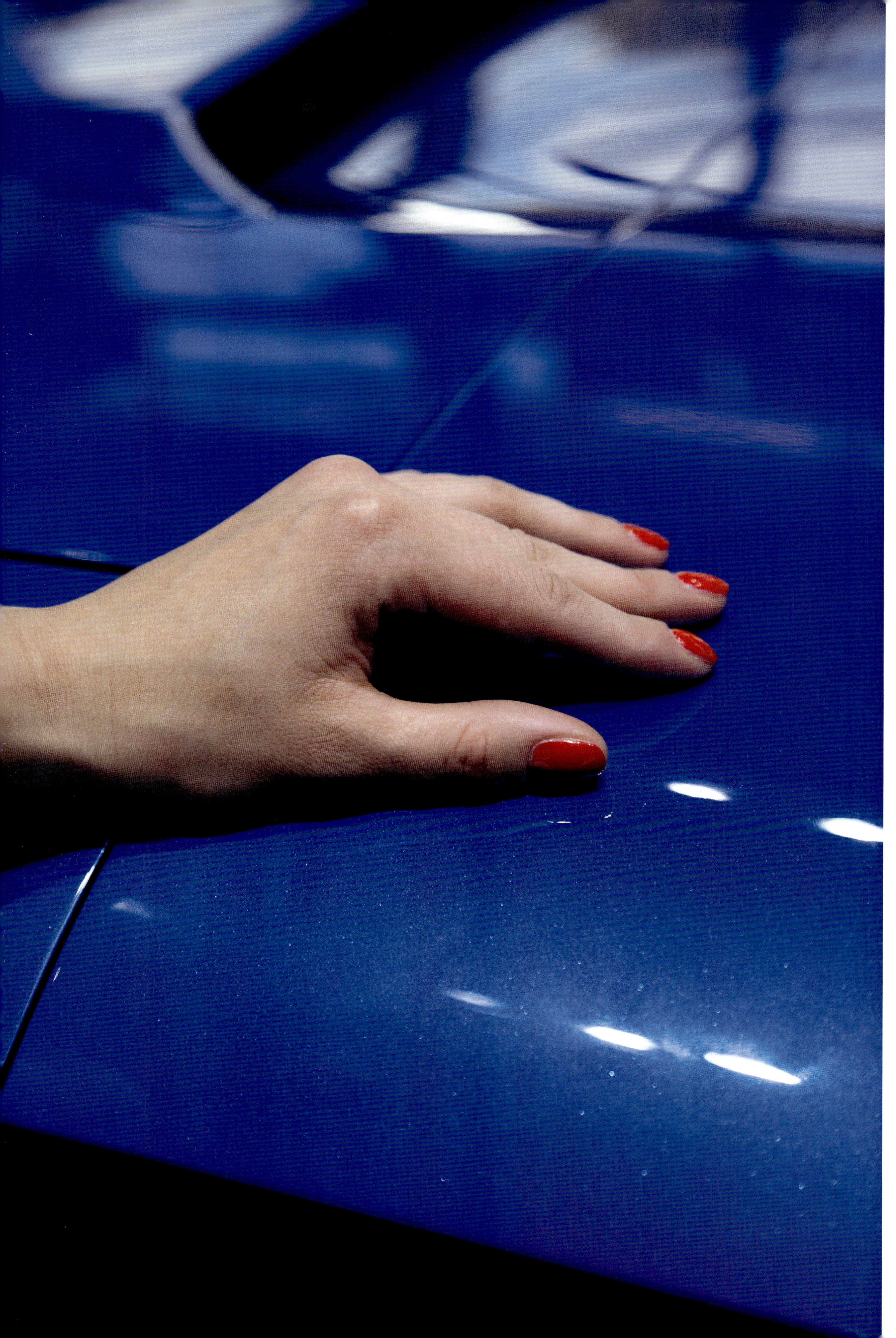

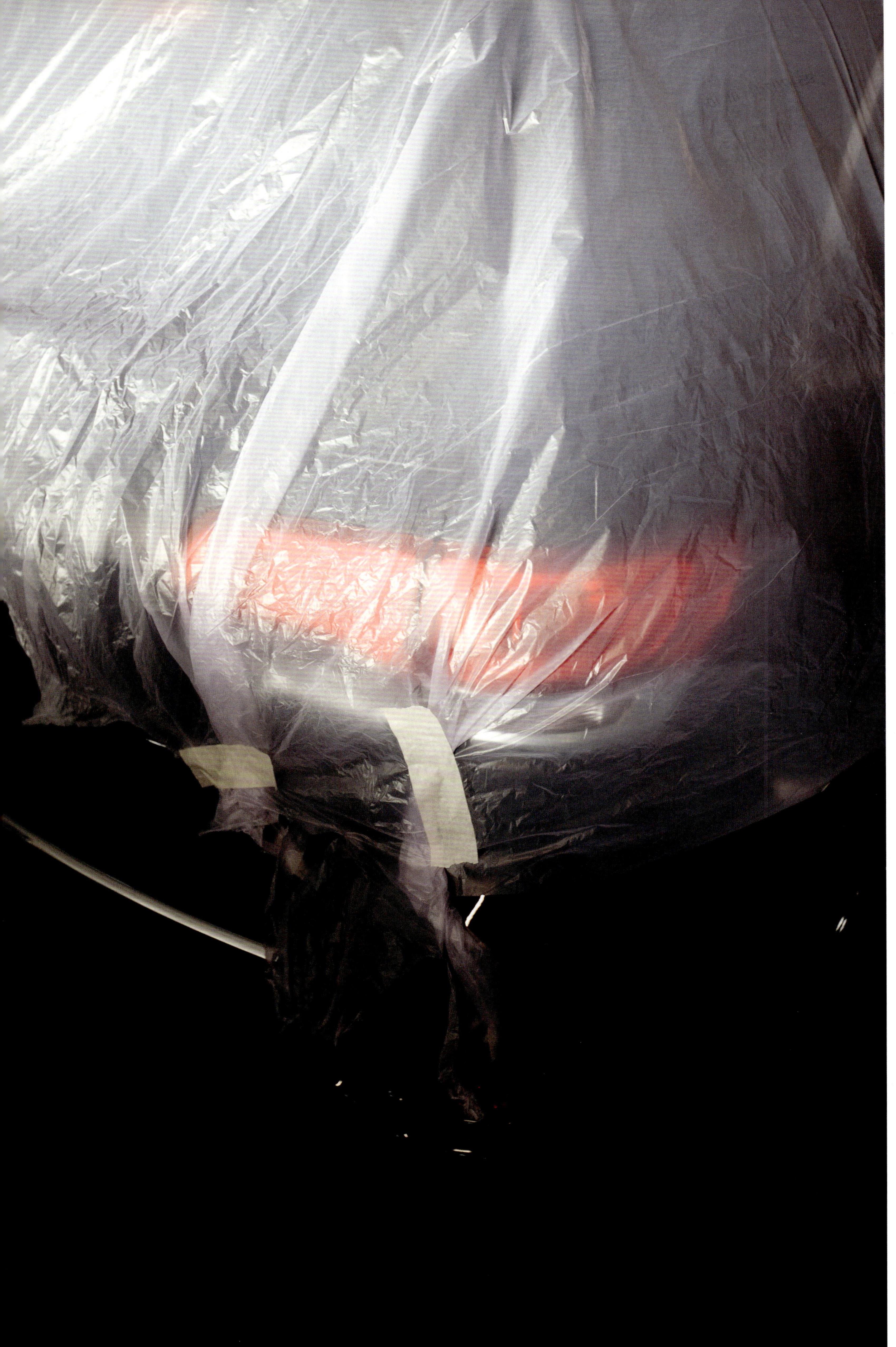

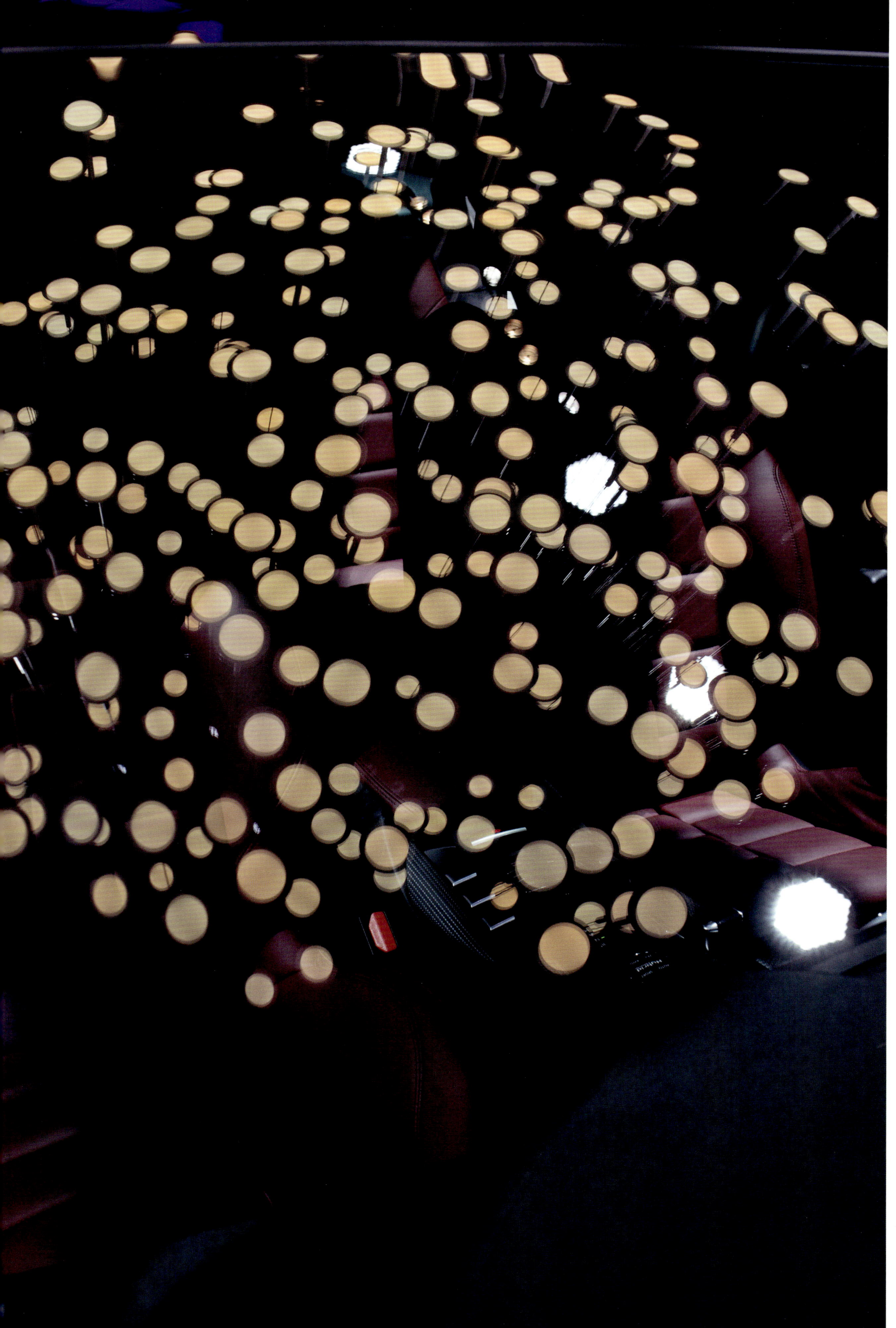

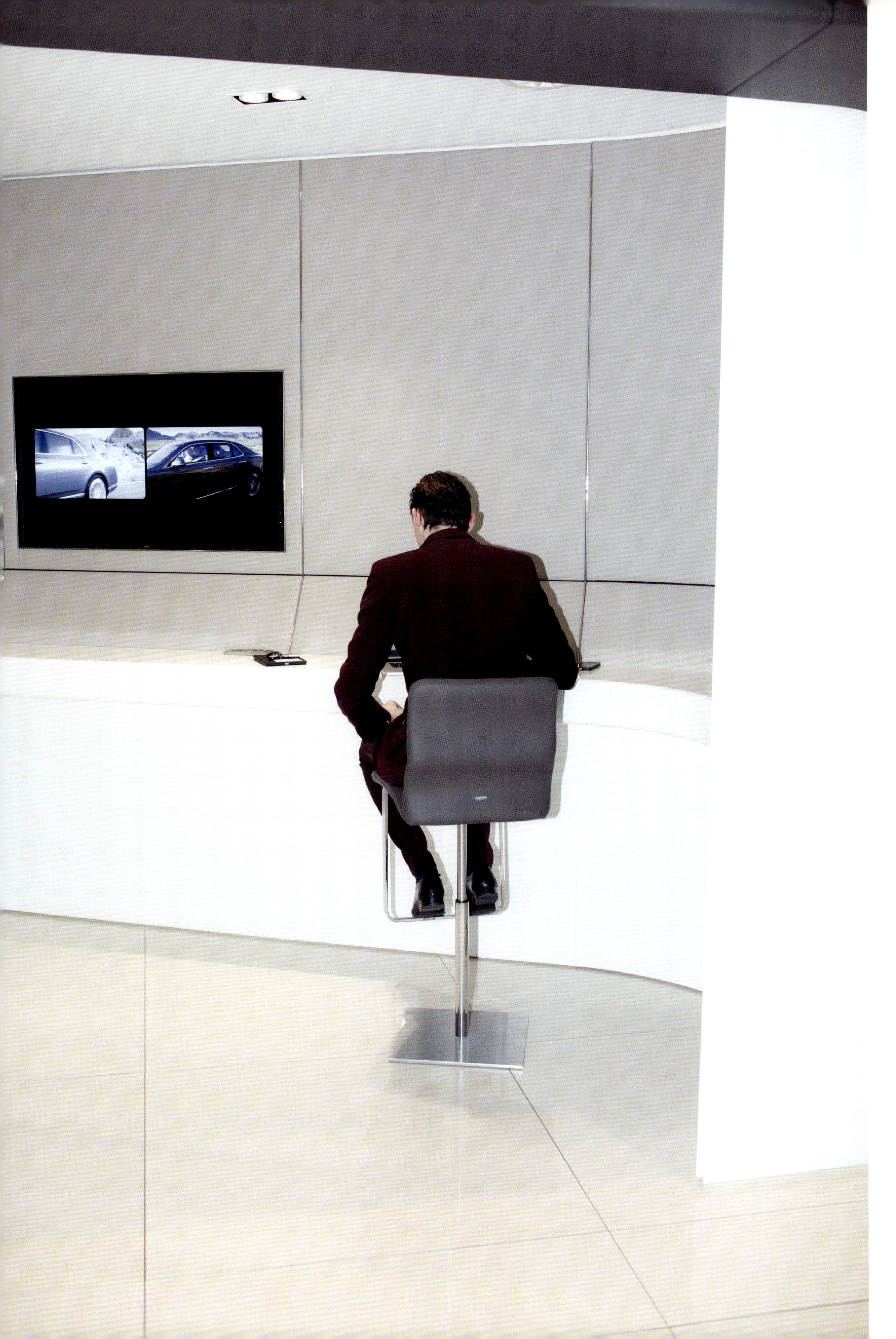

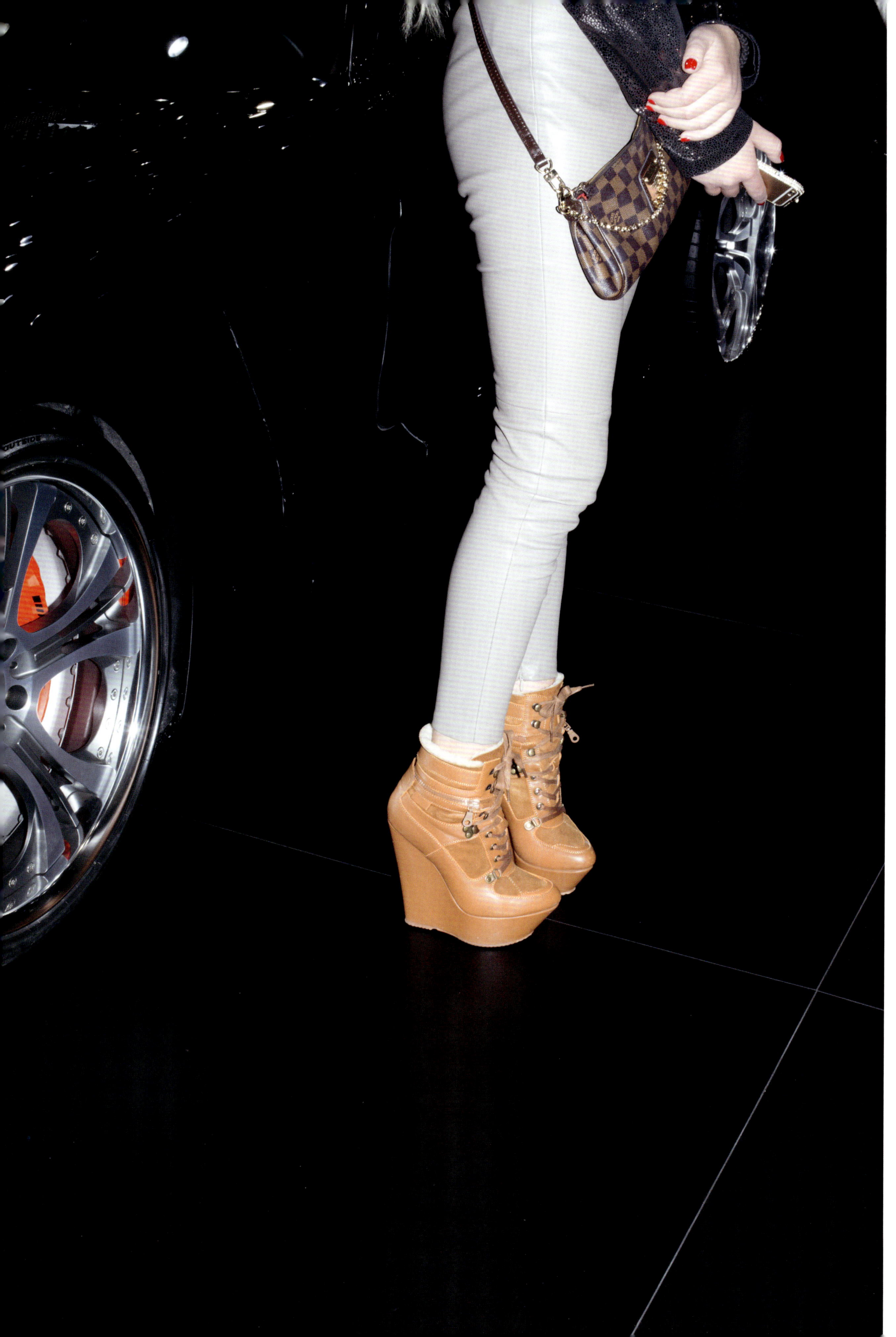

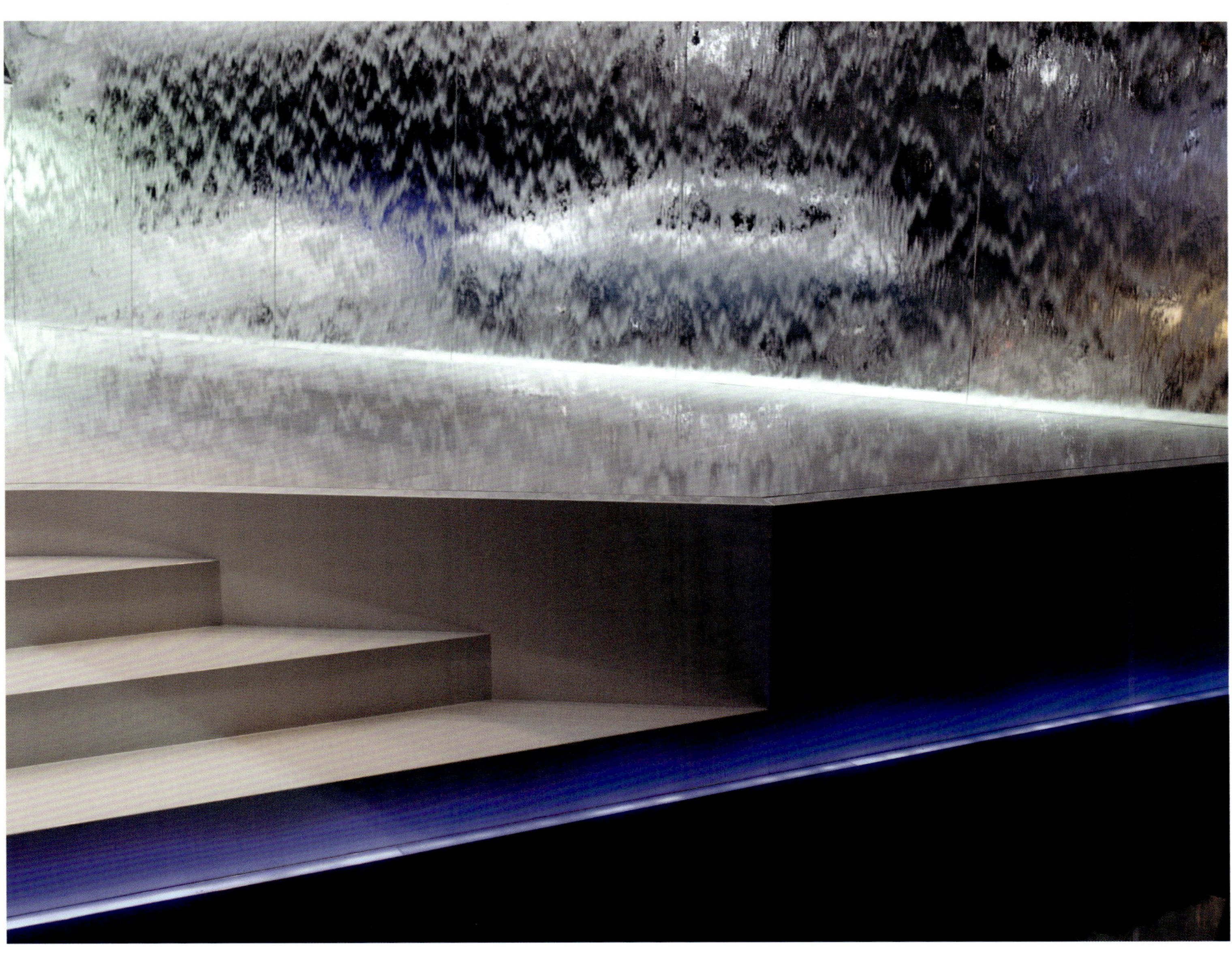

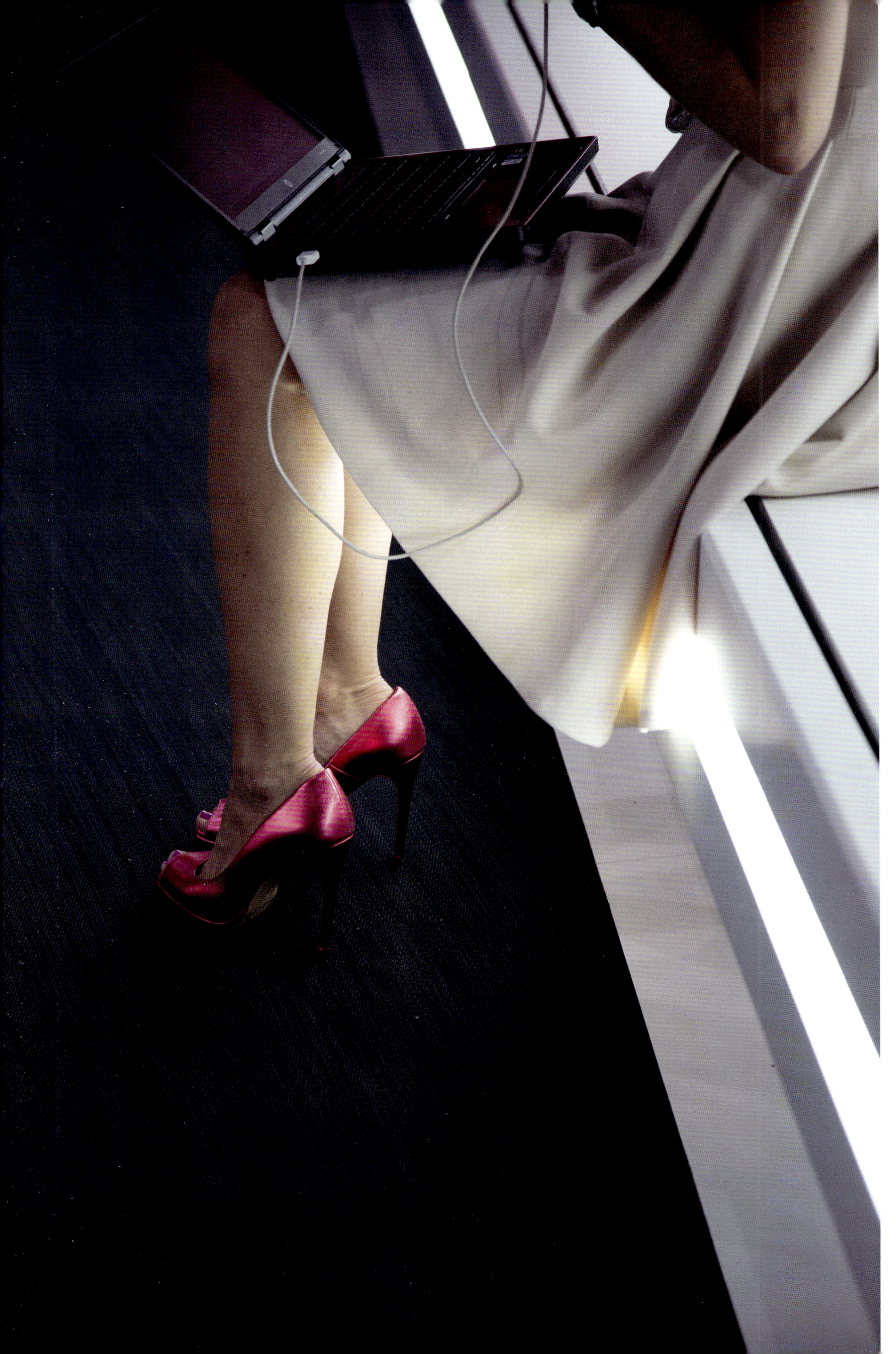

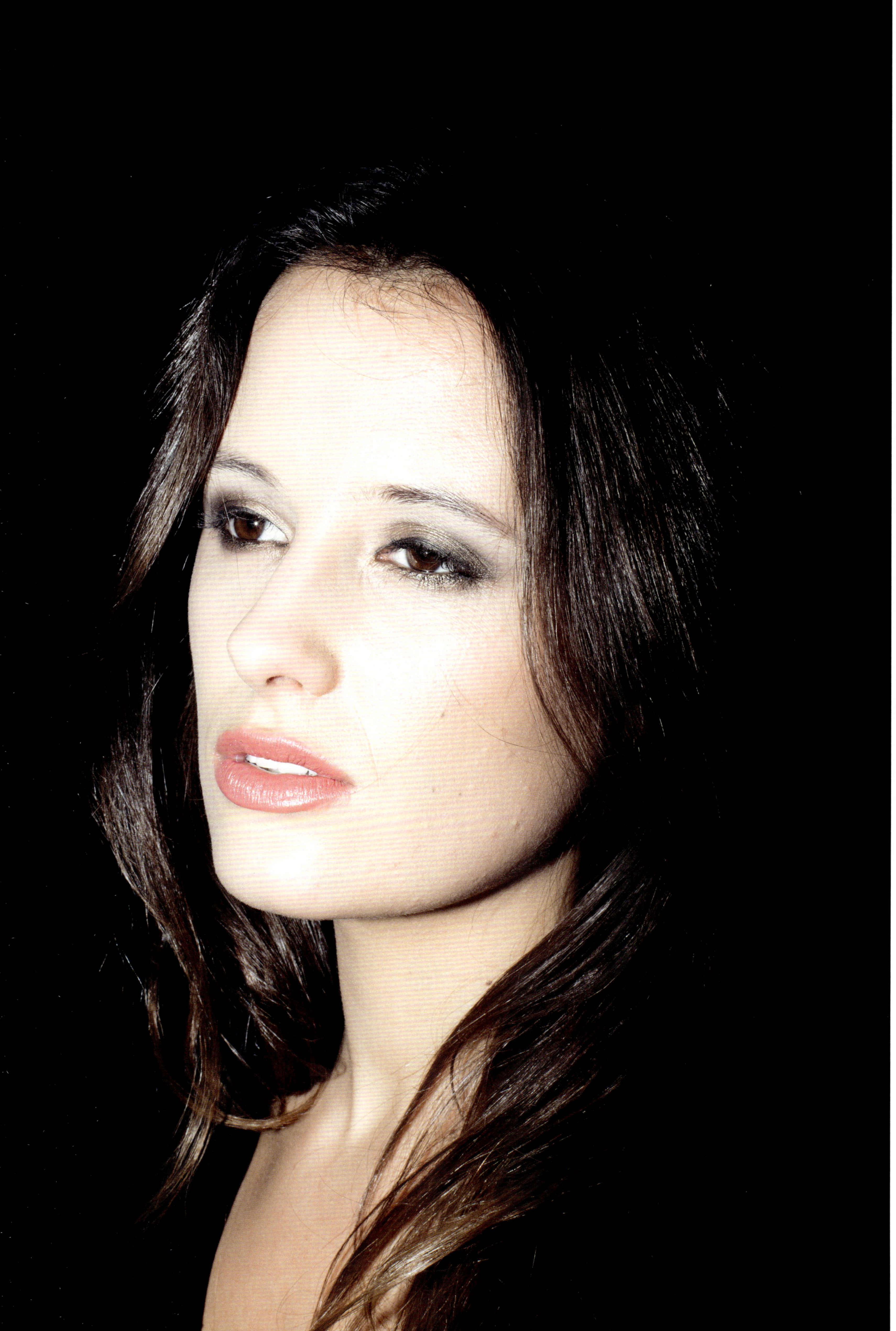

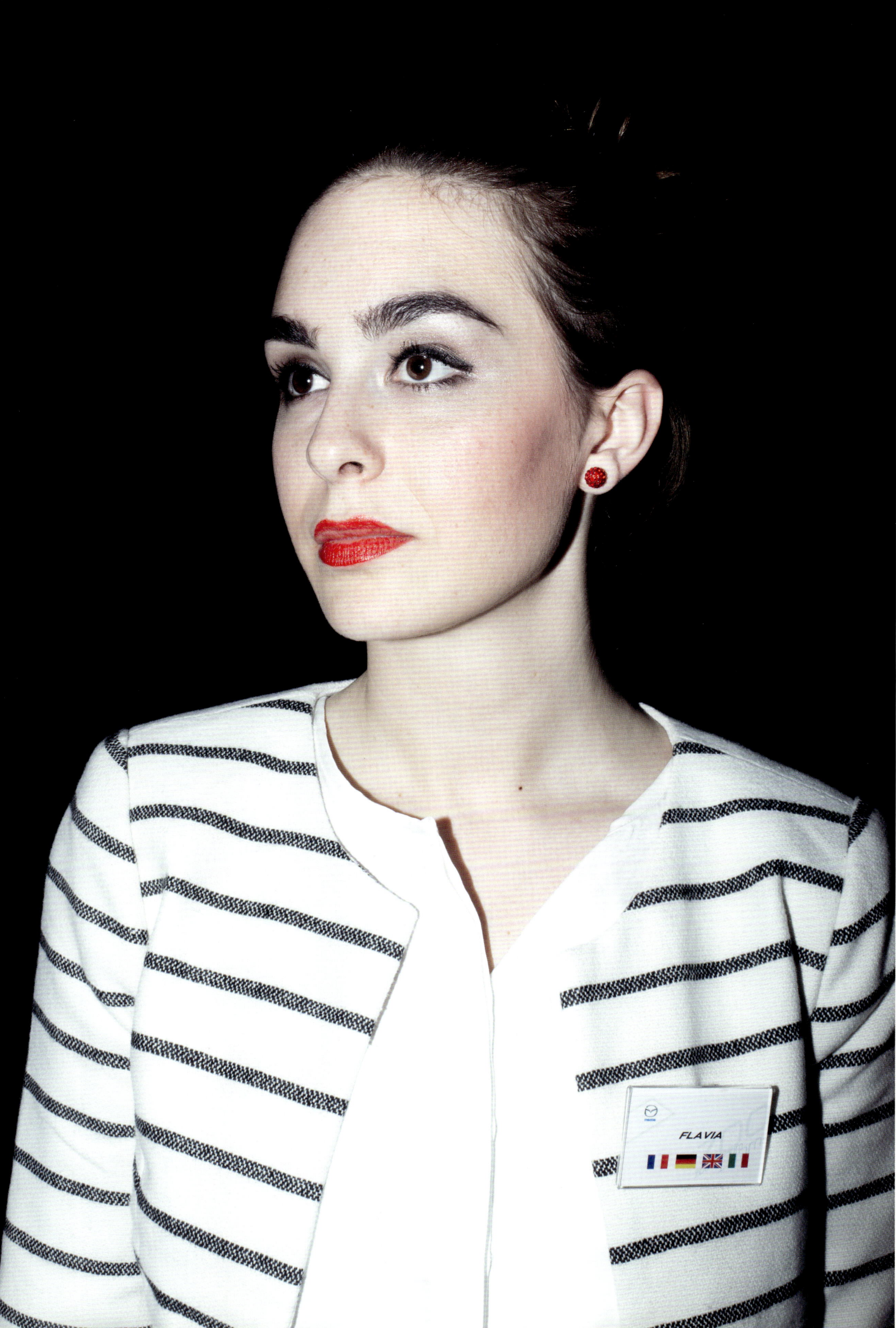

FLAVIA

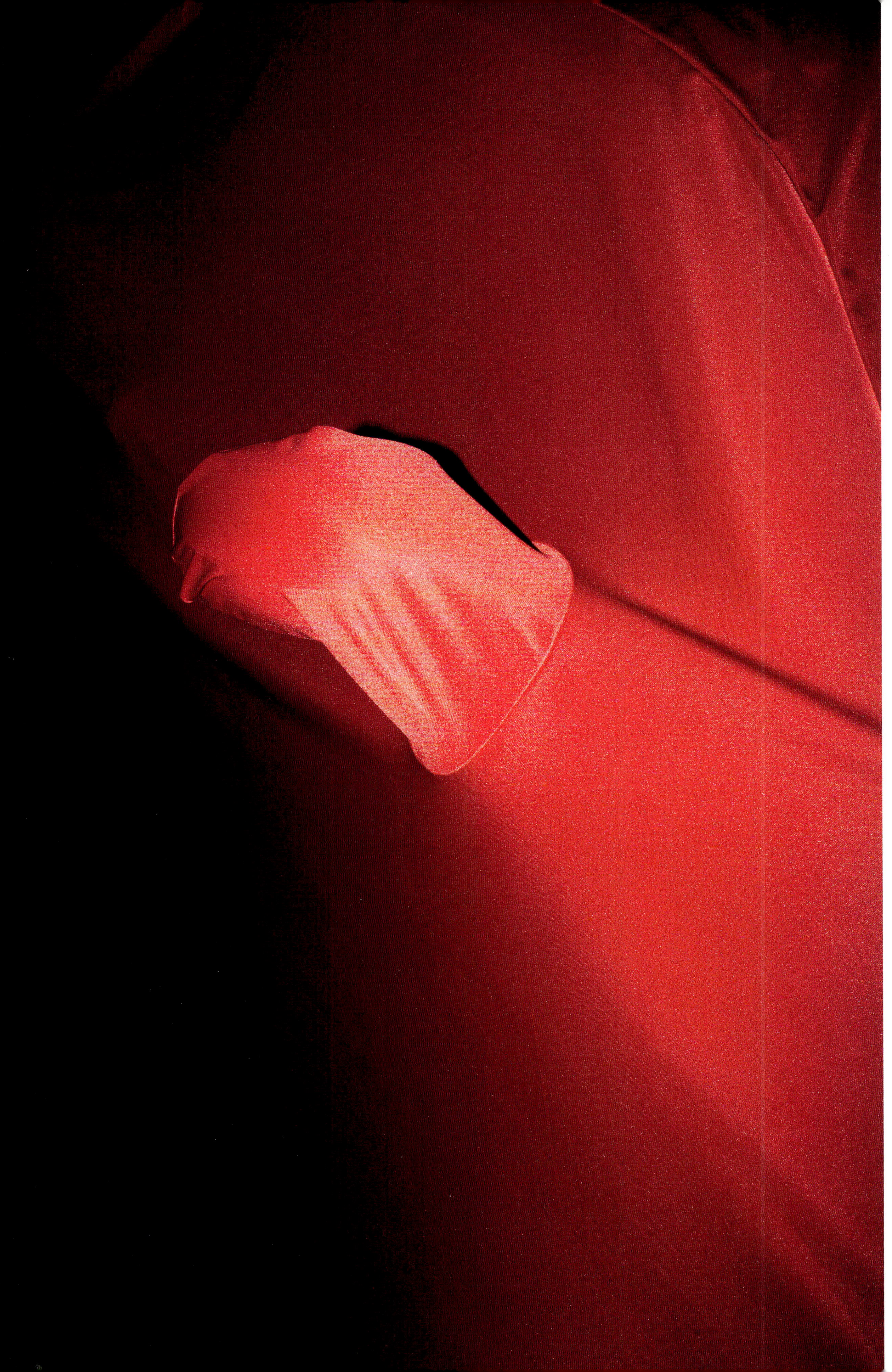

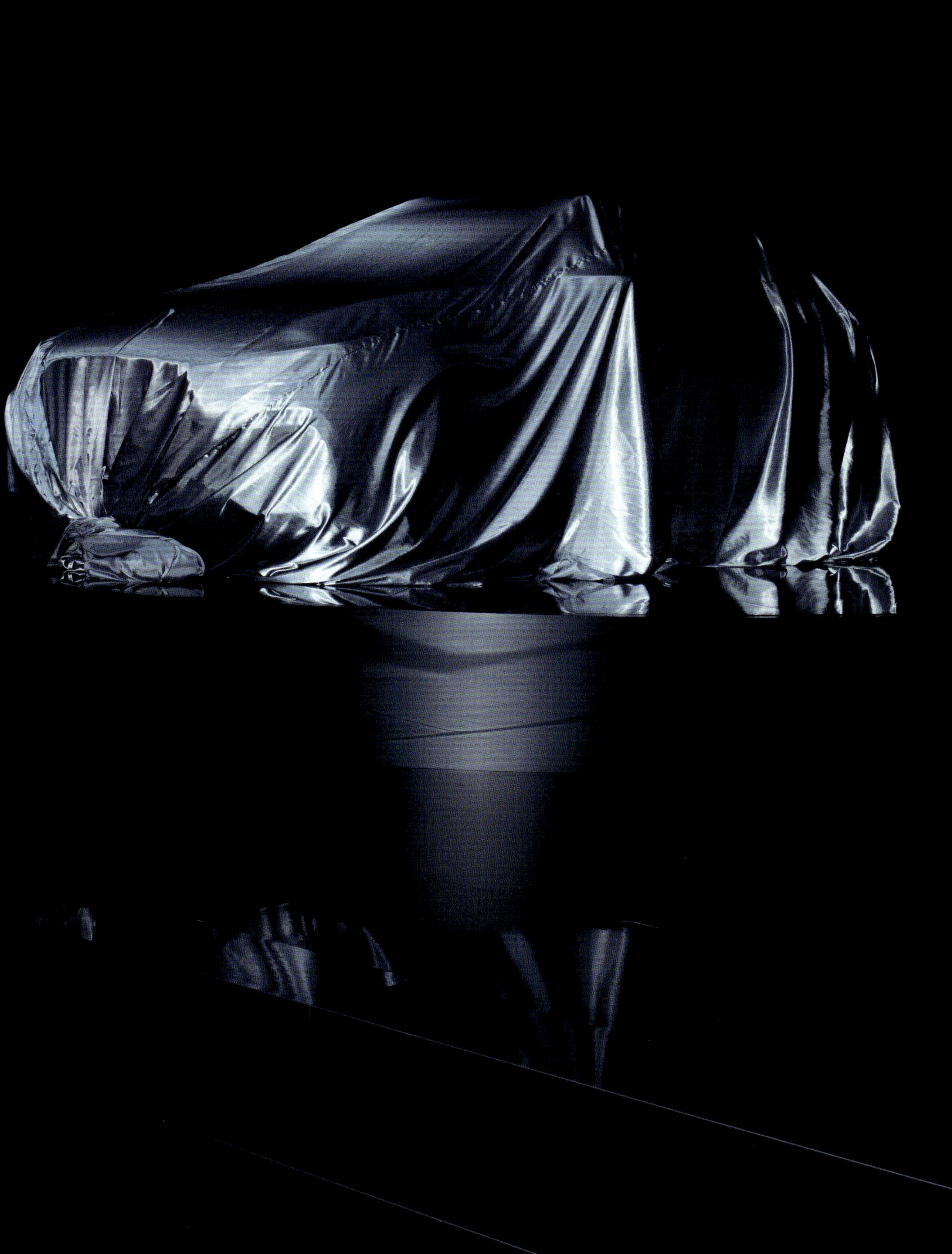

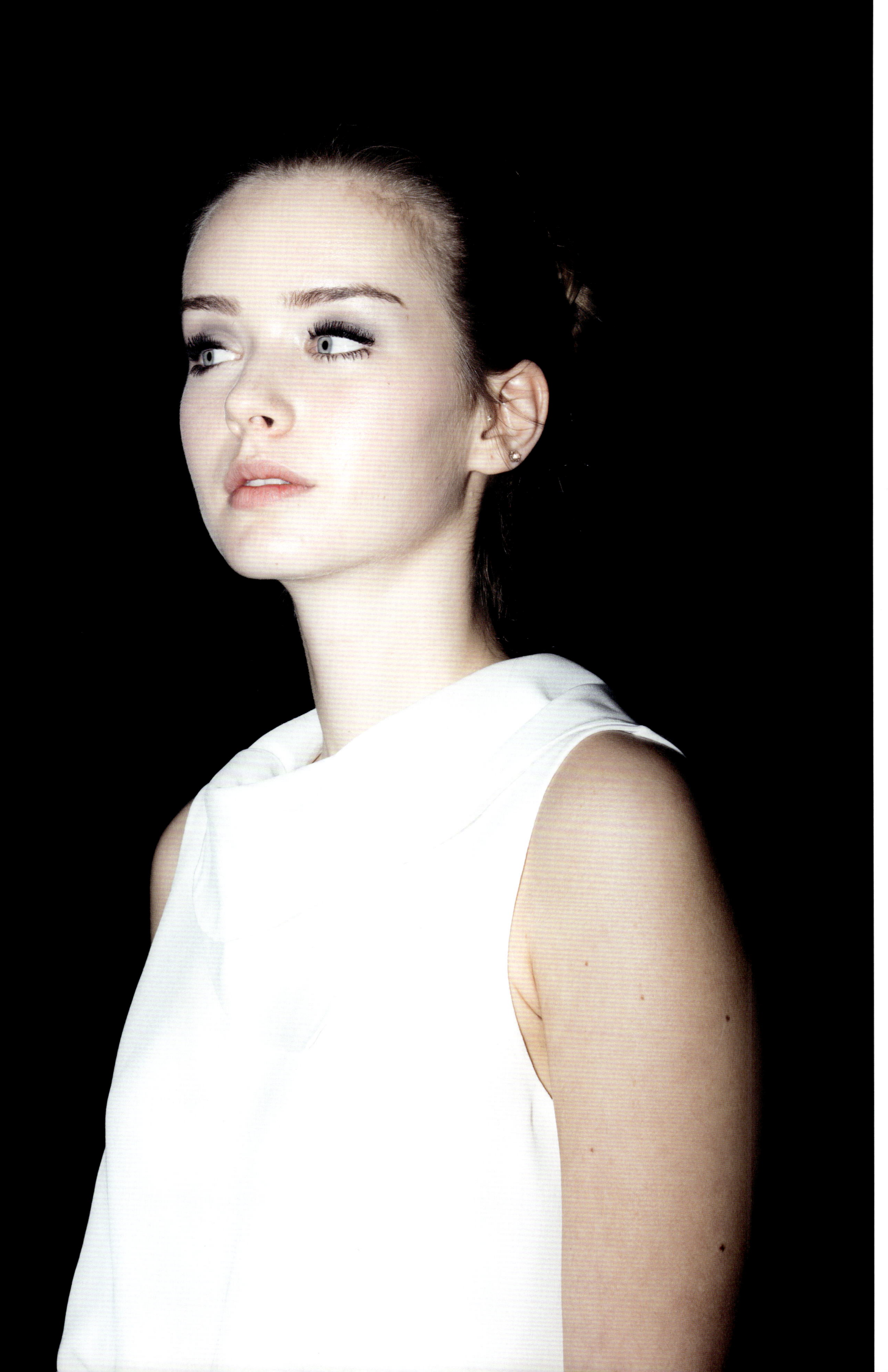

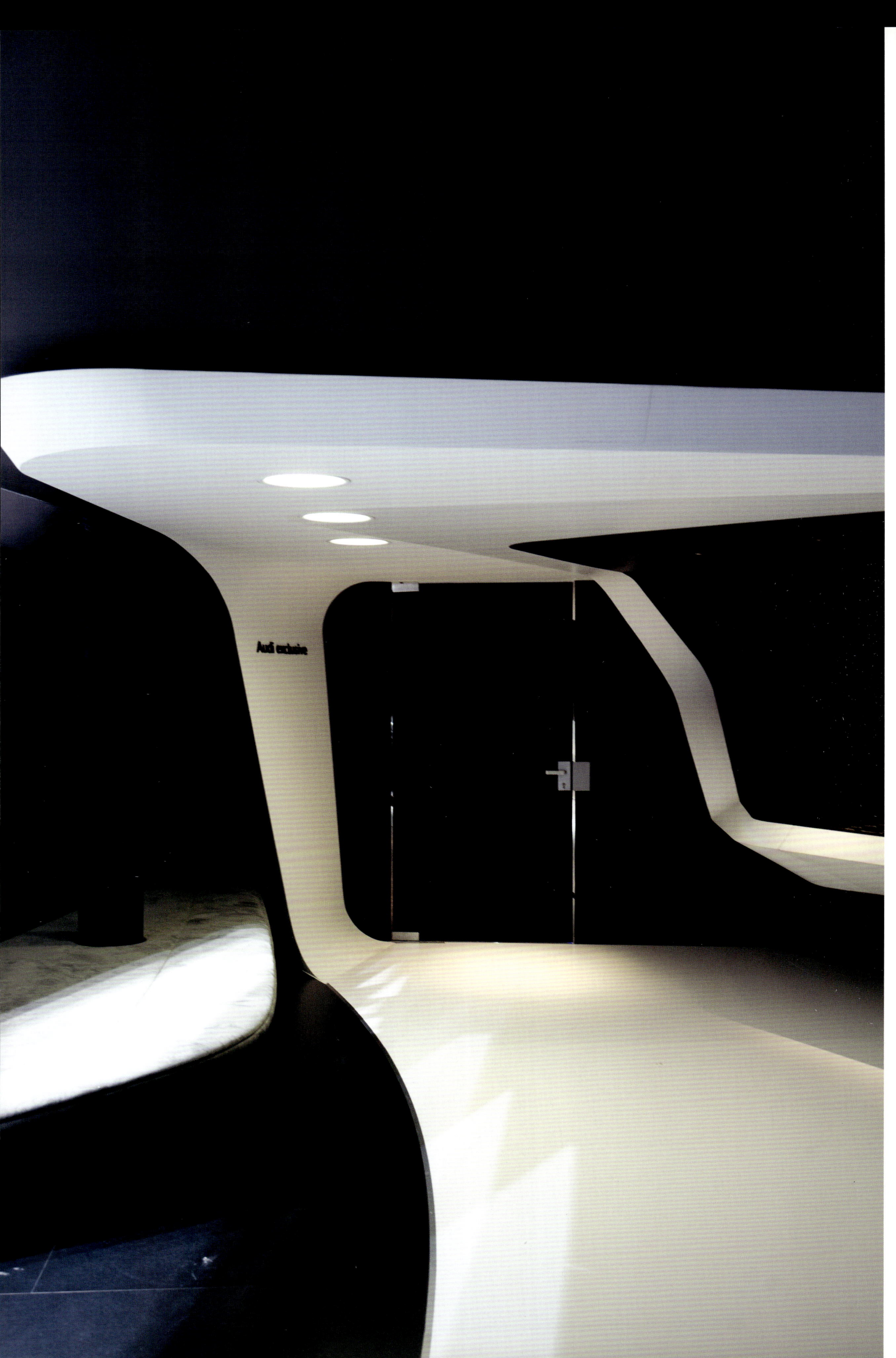

Audi exclusive

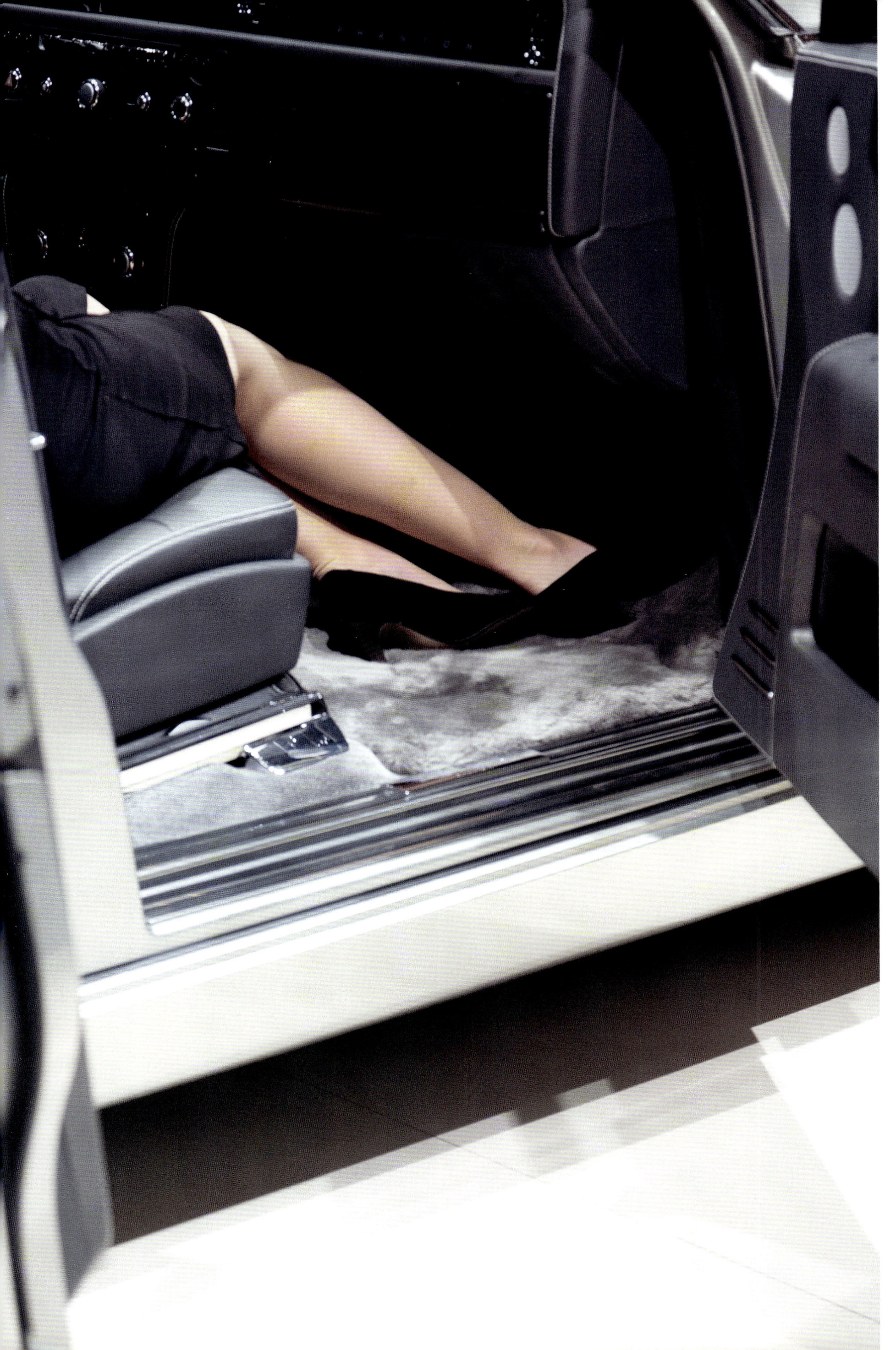

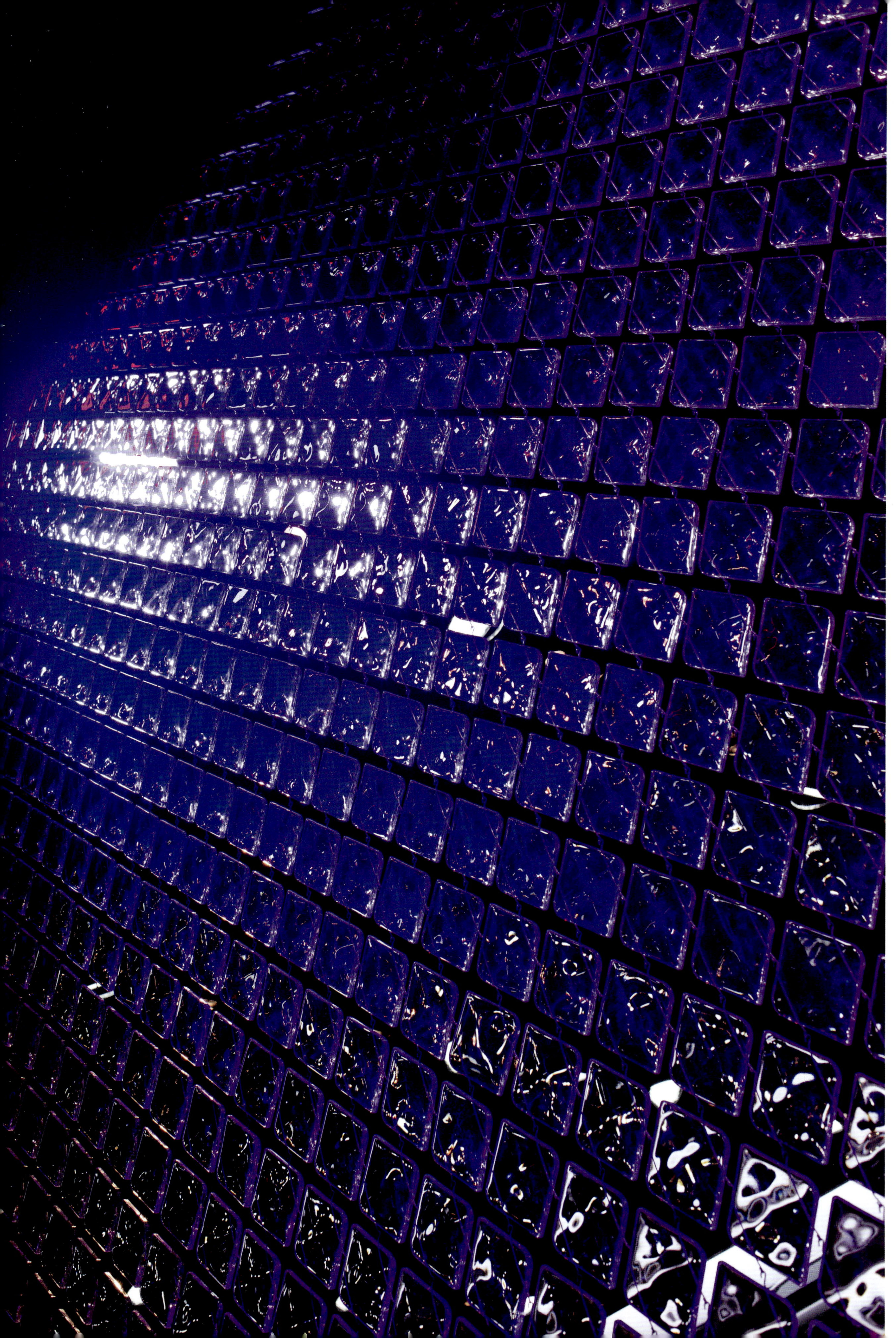

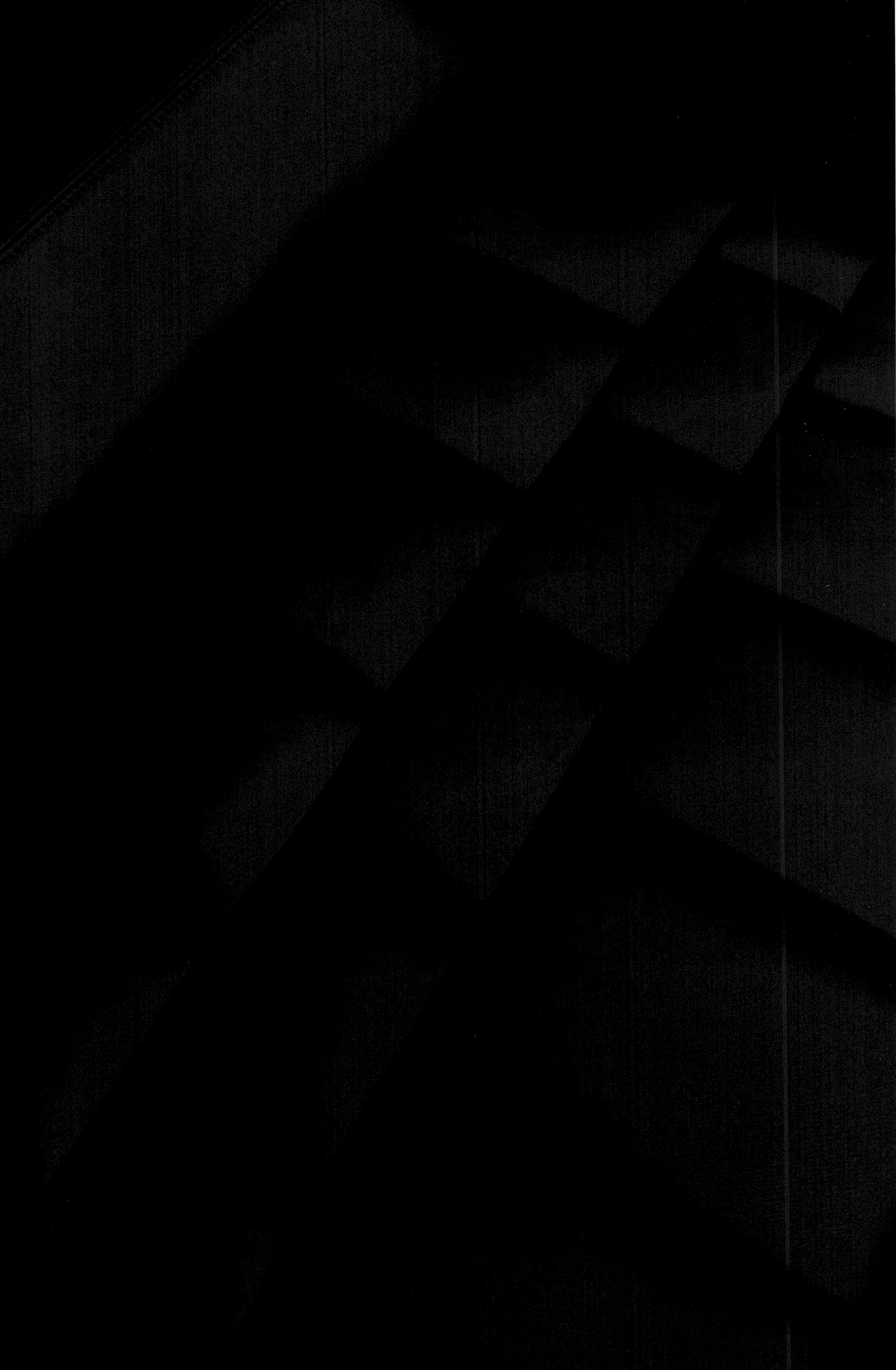

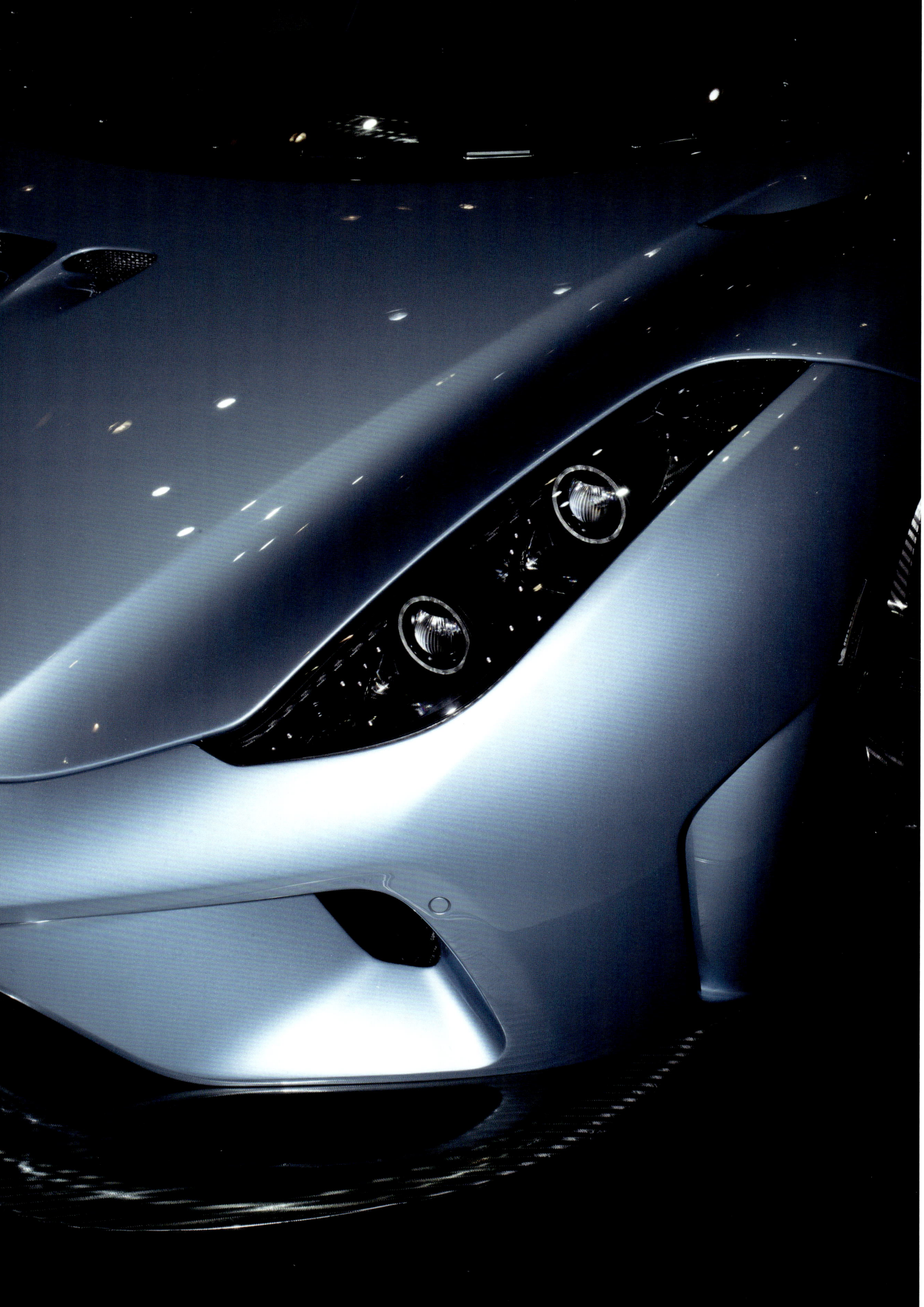

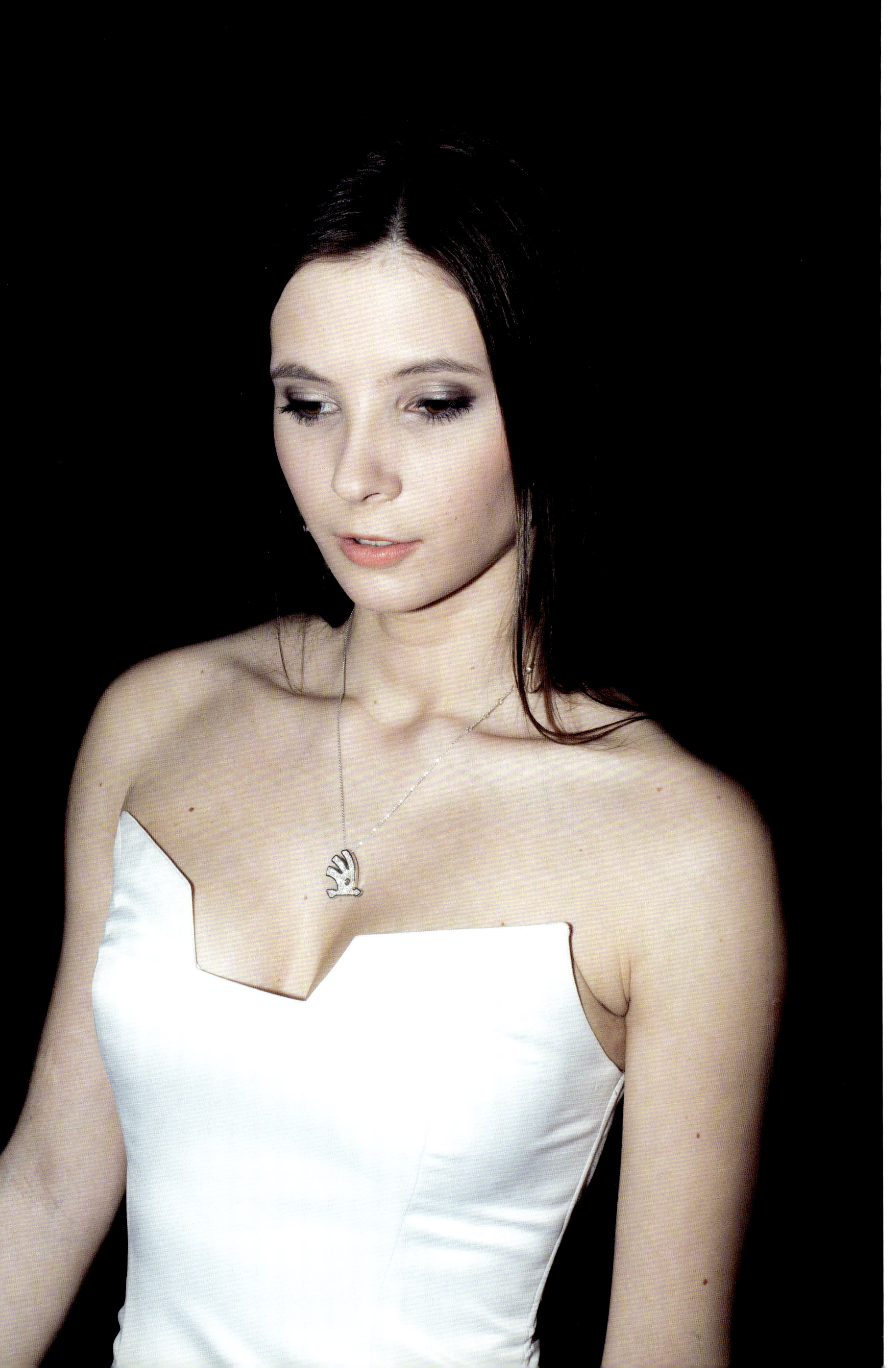

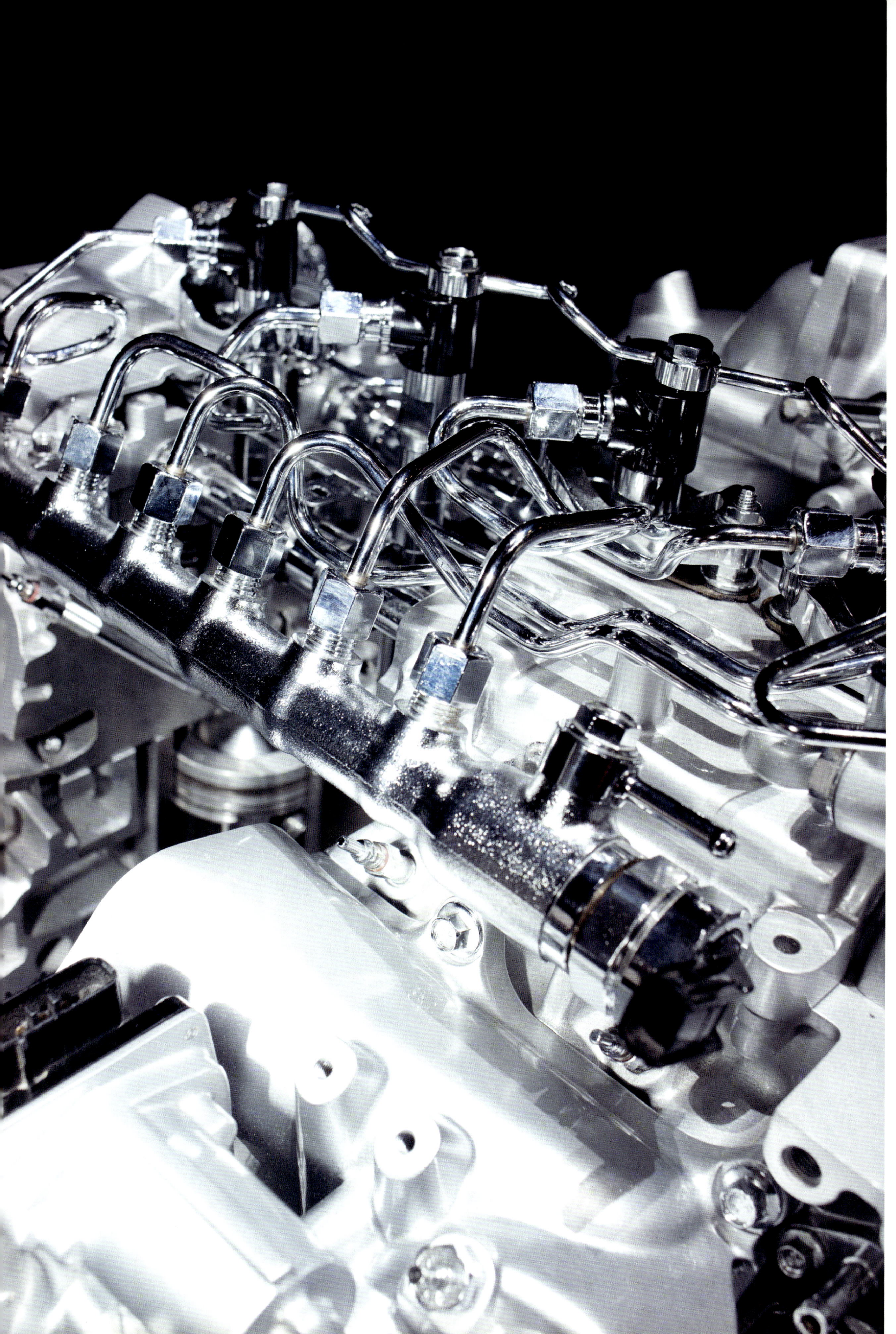

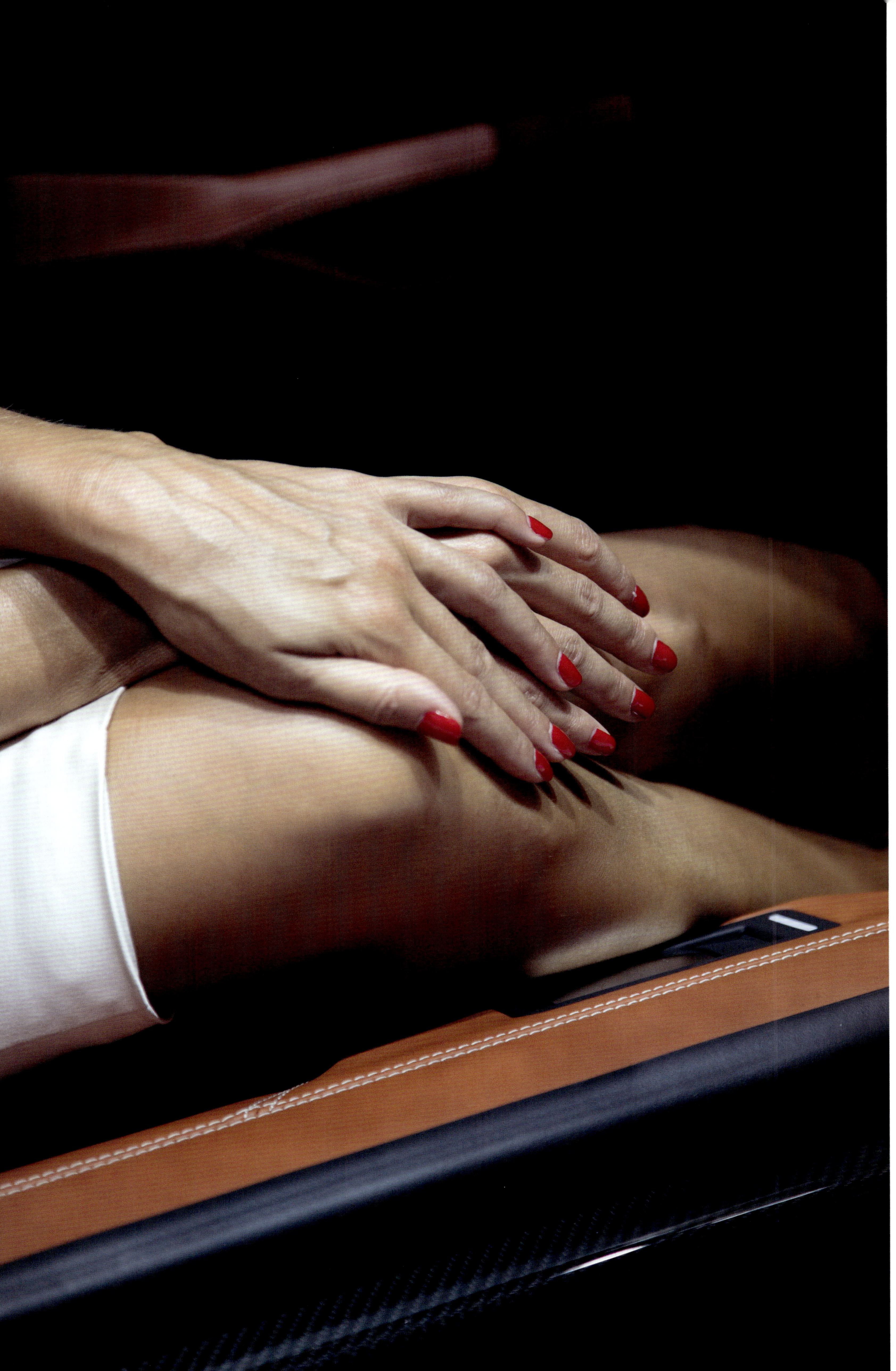

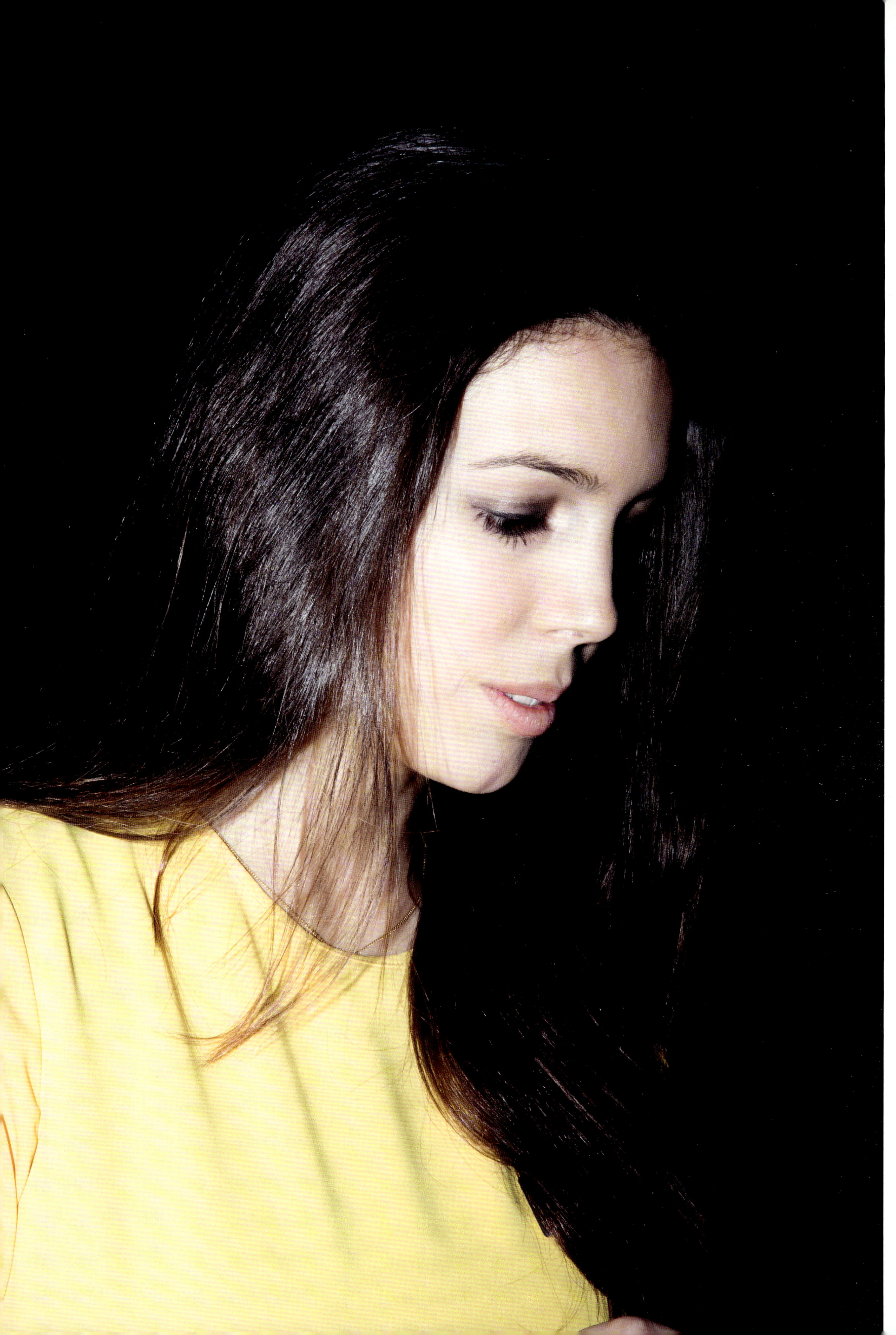

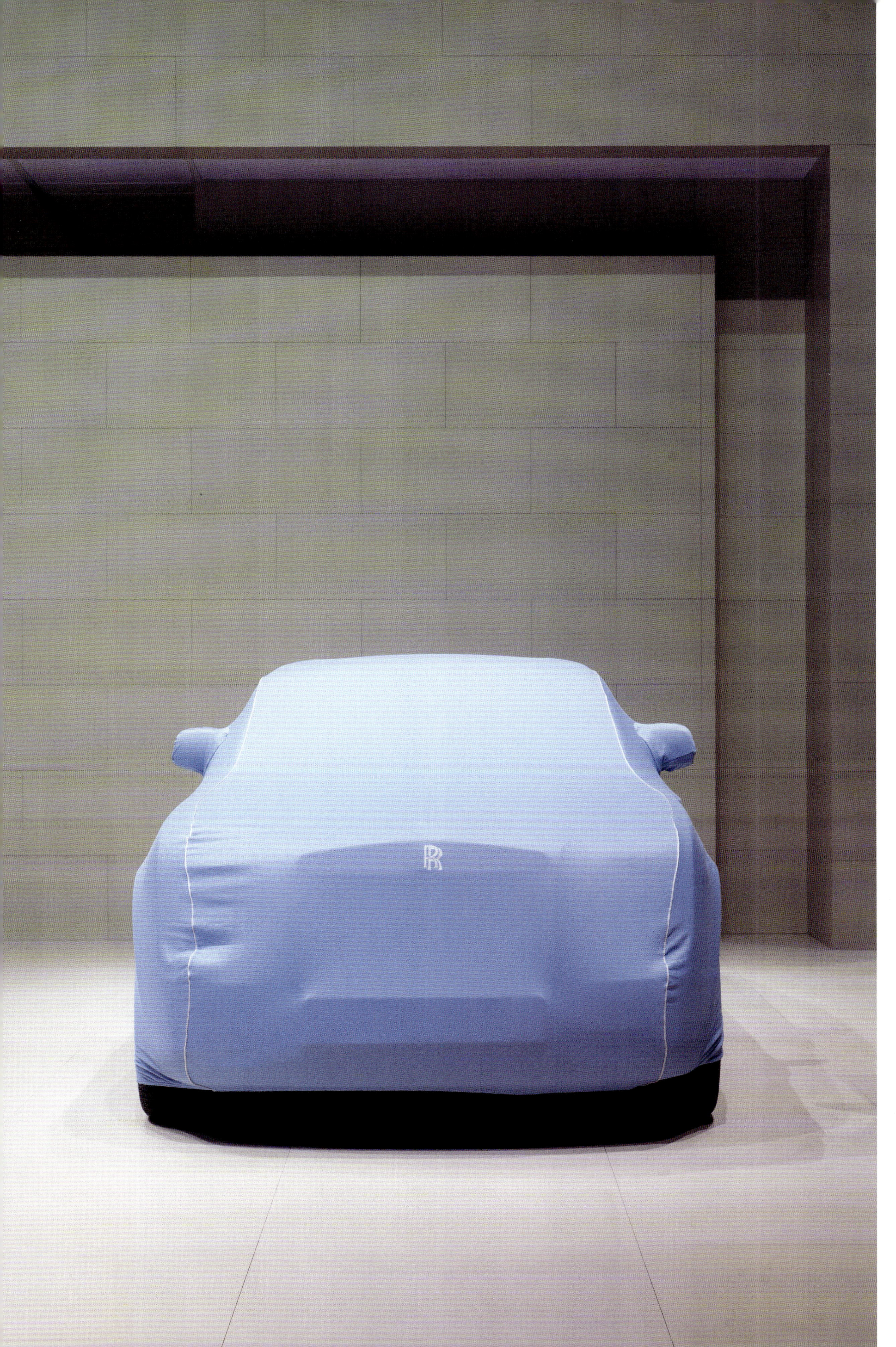

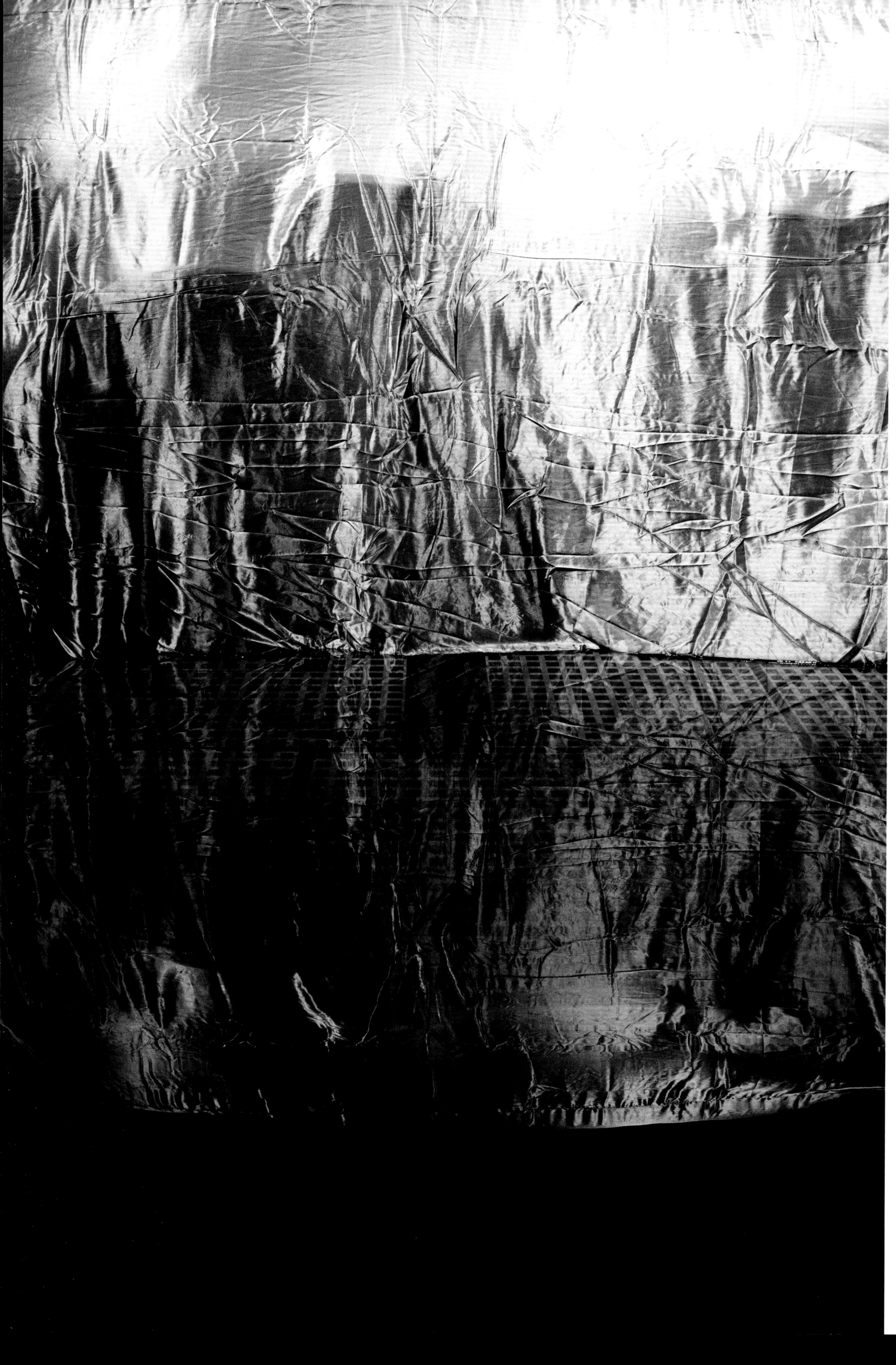

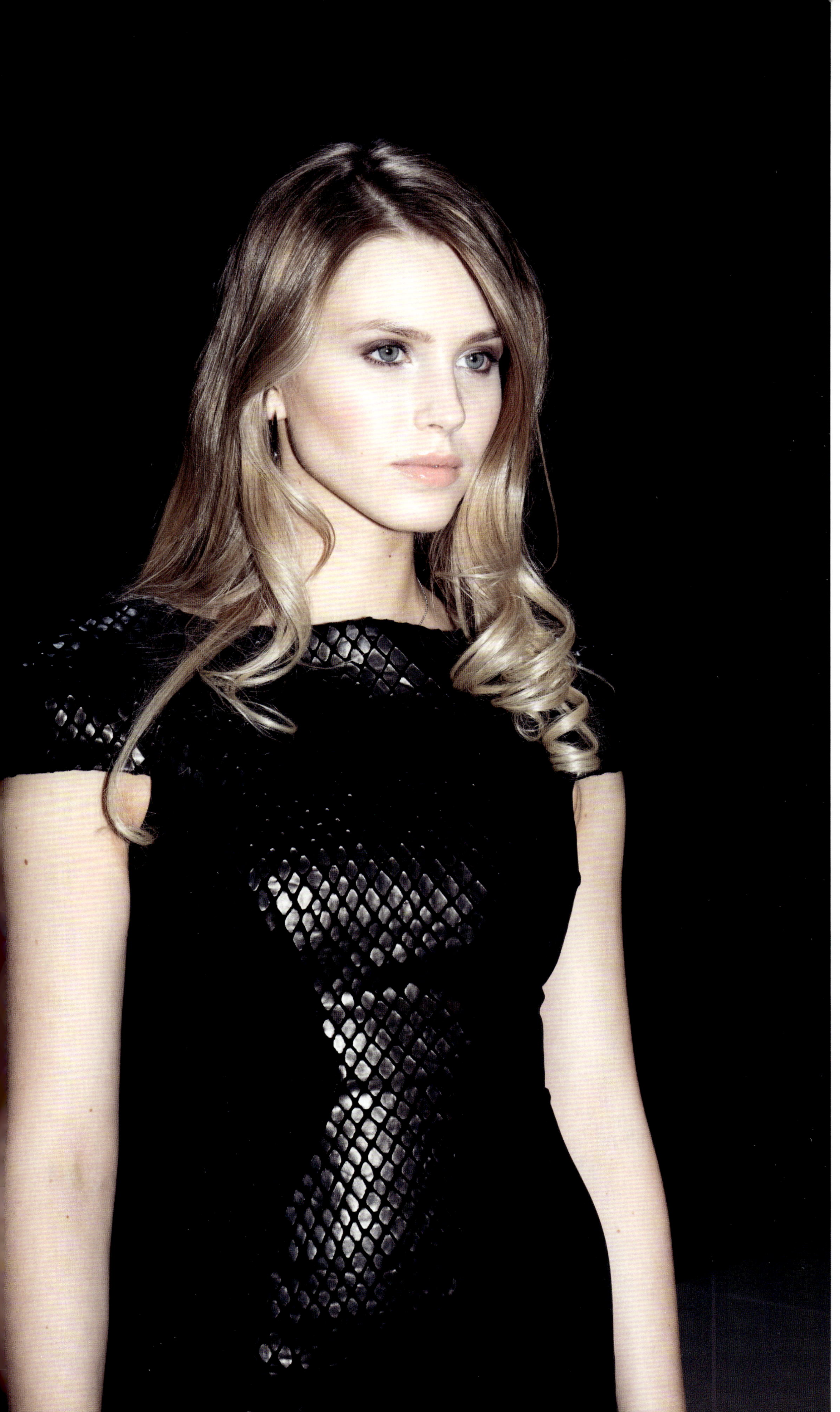

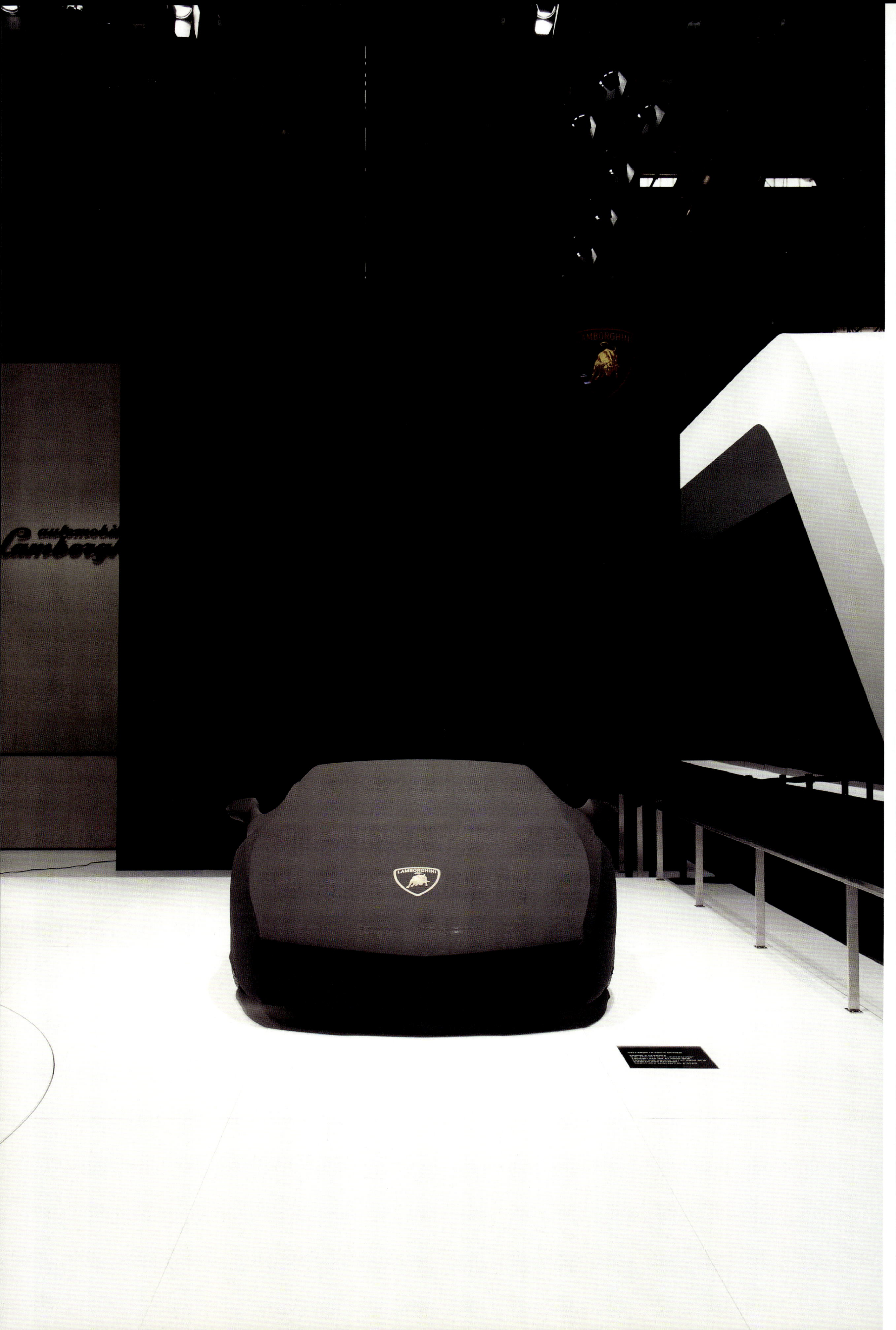

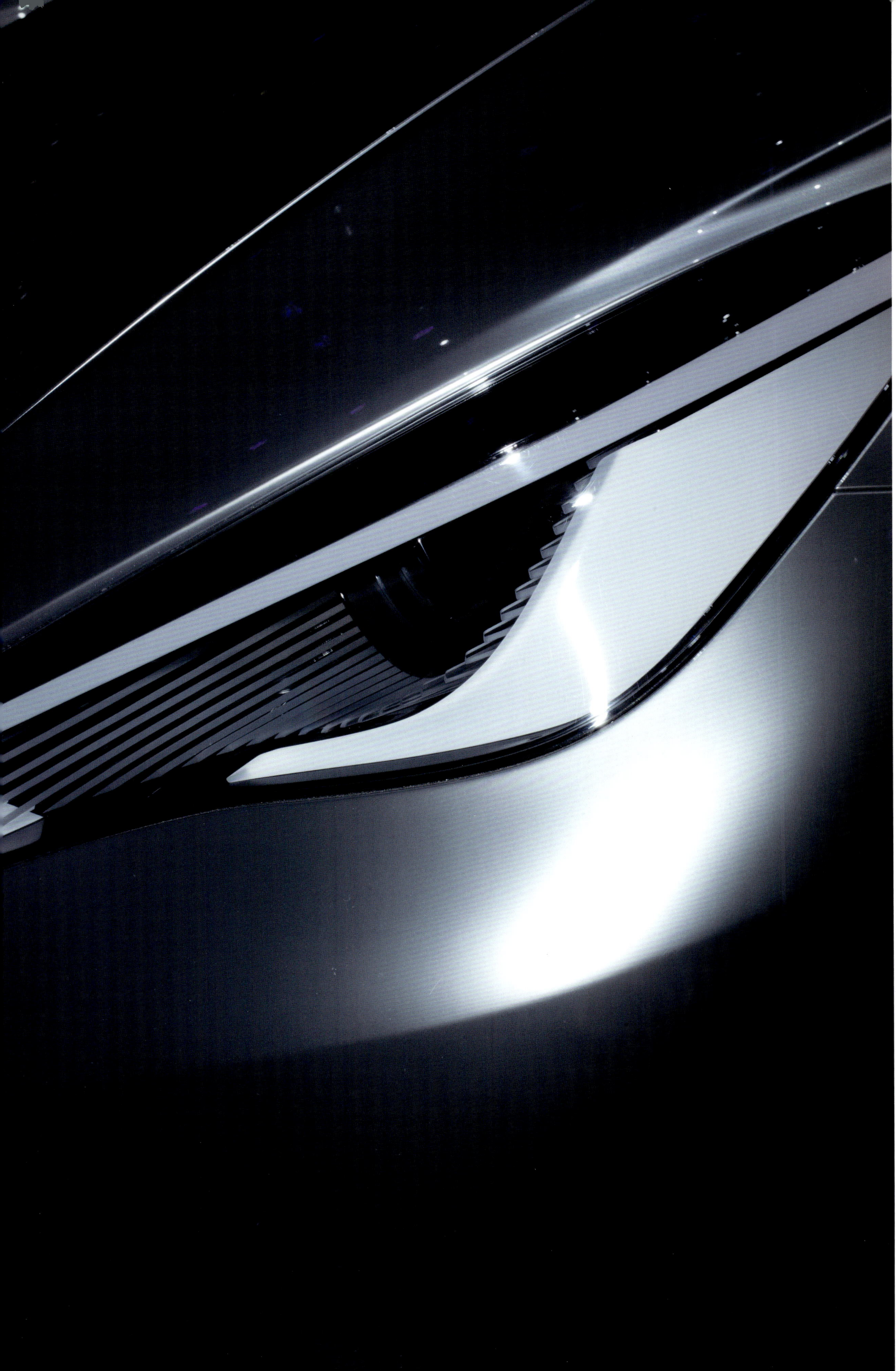

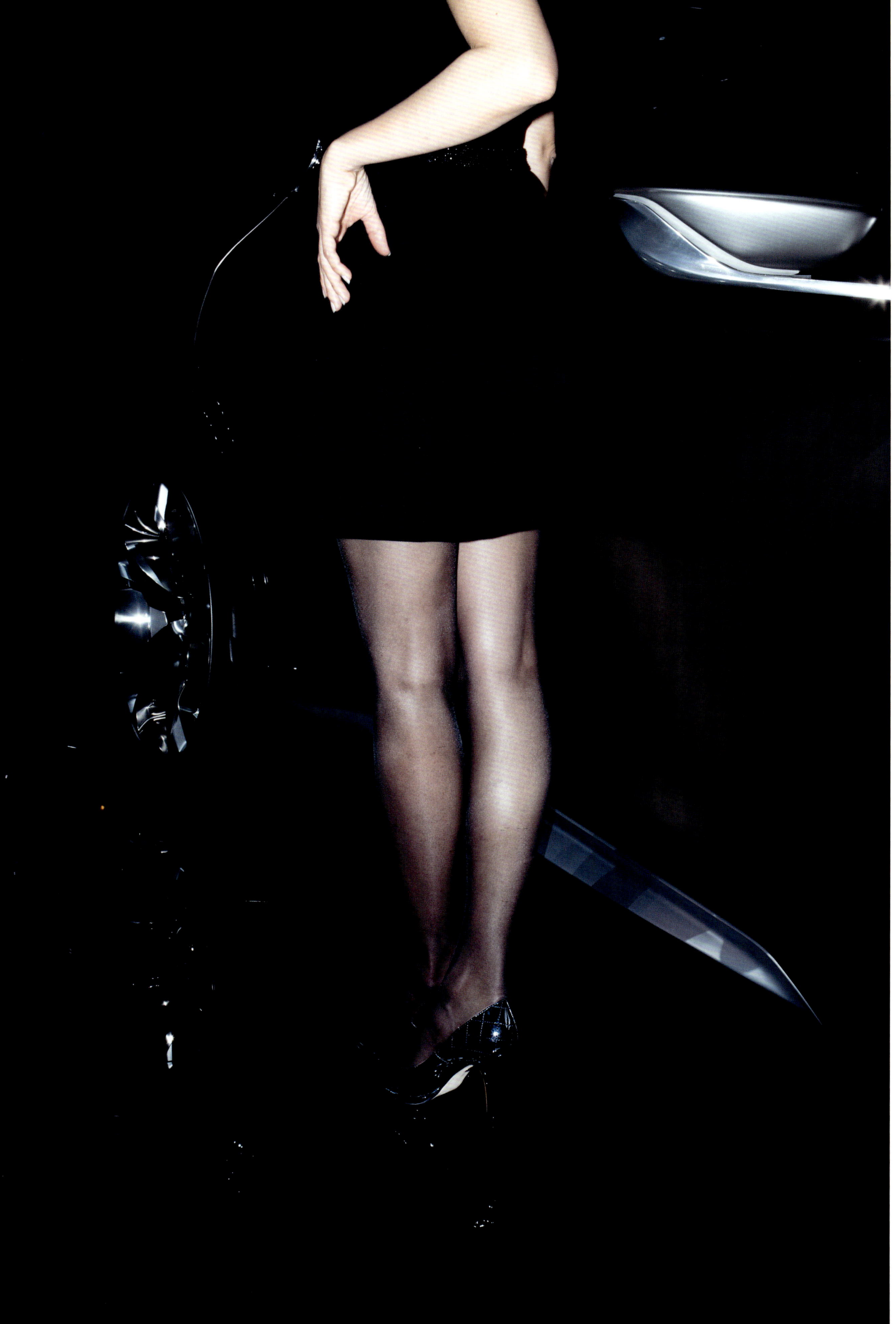

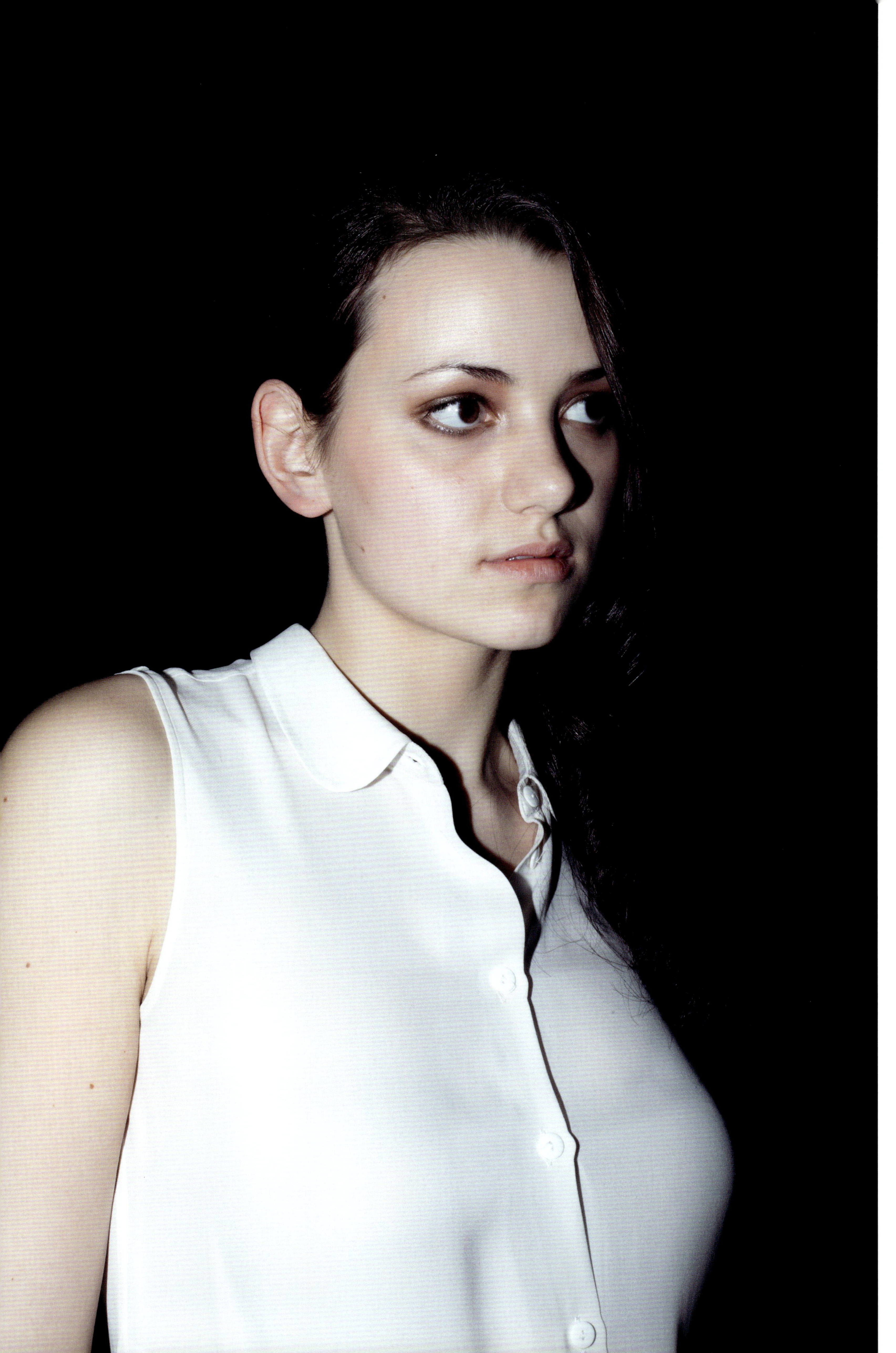

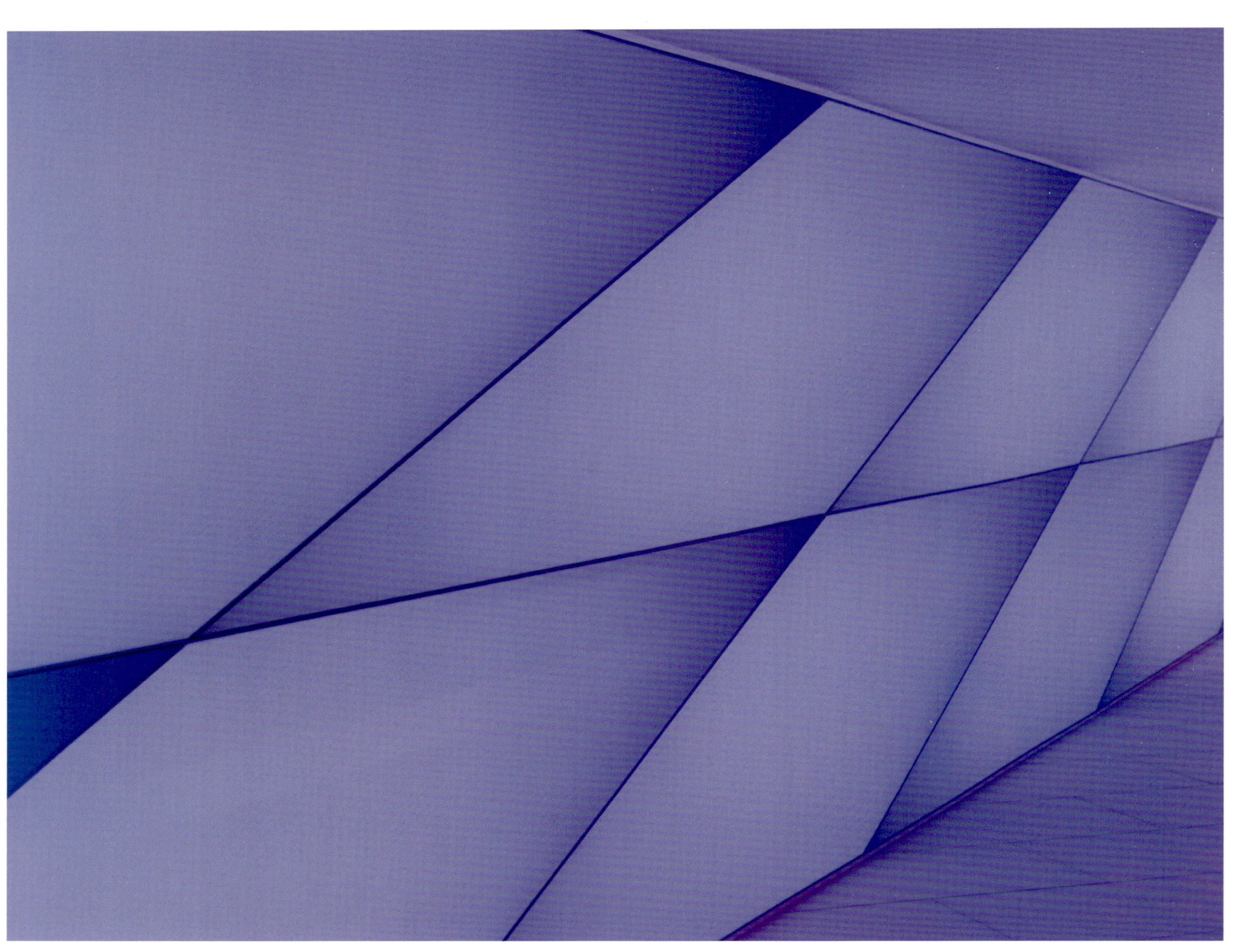

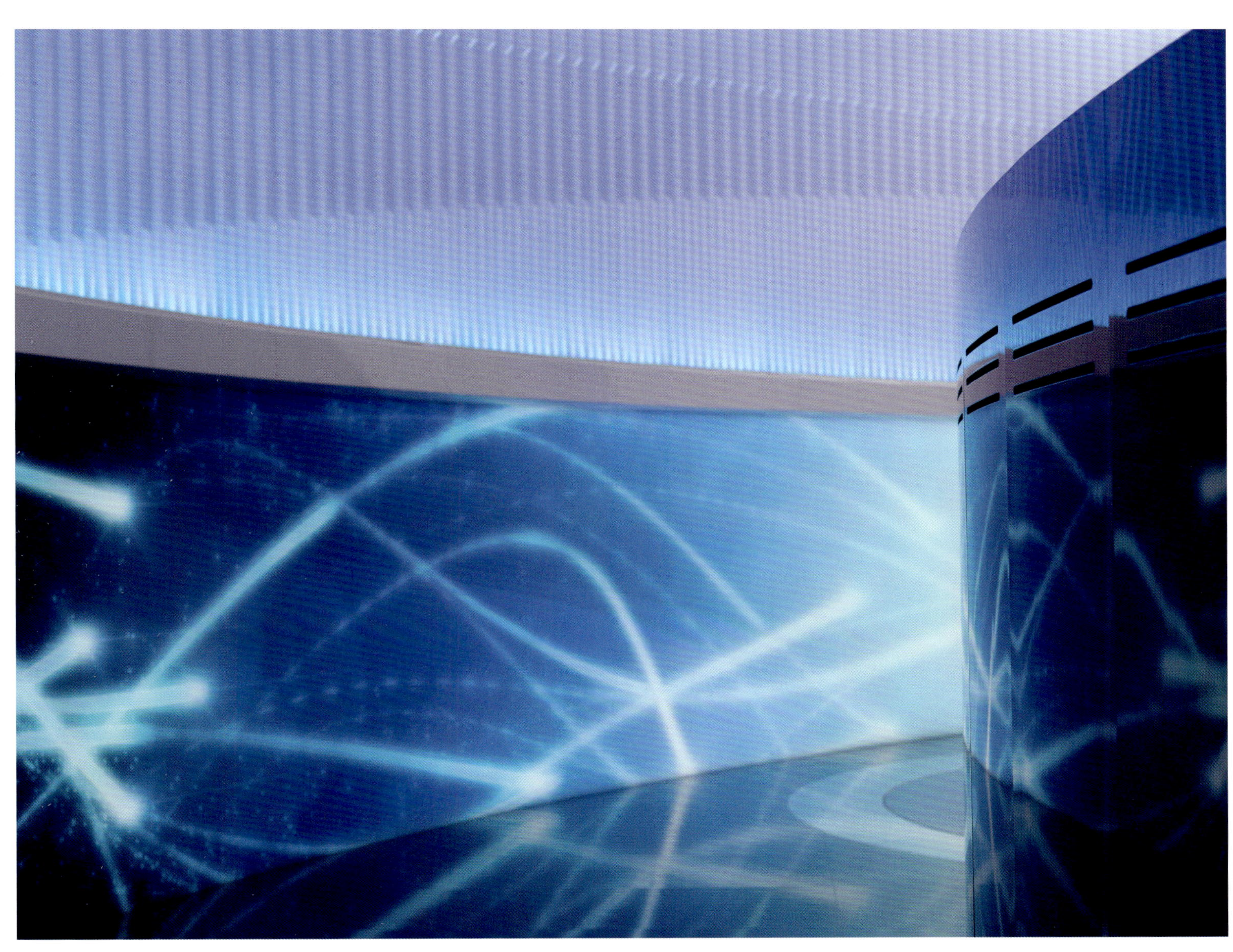

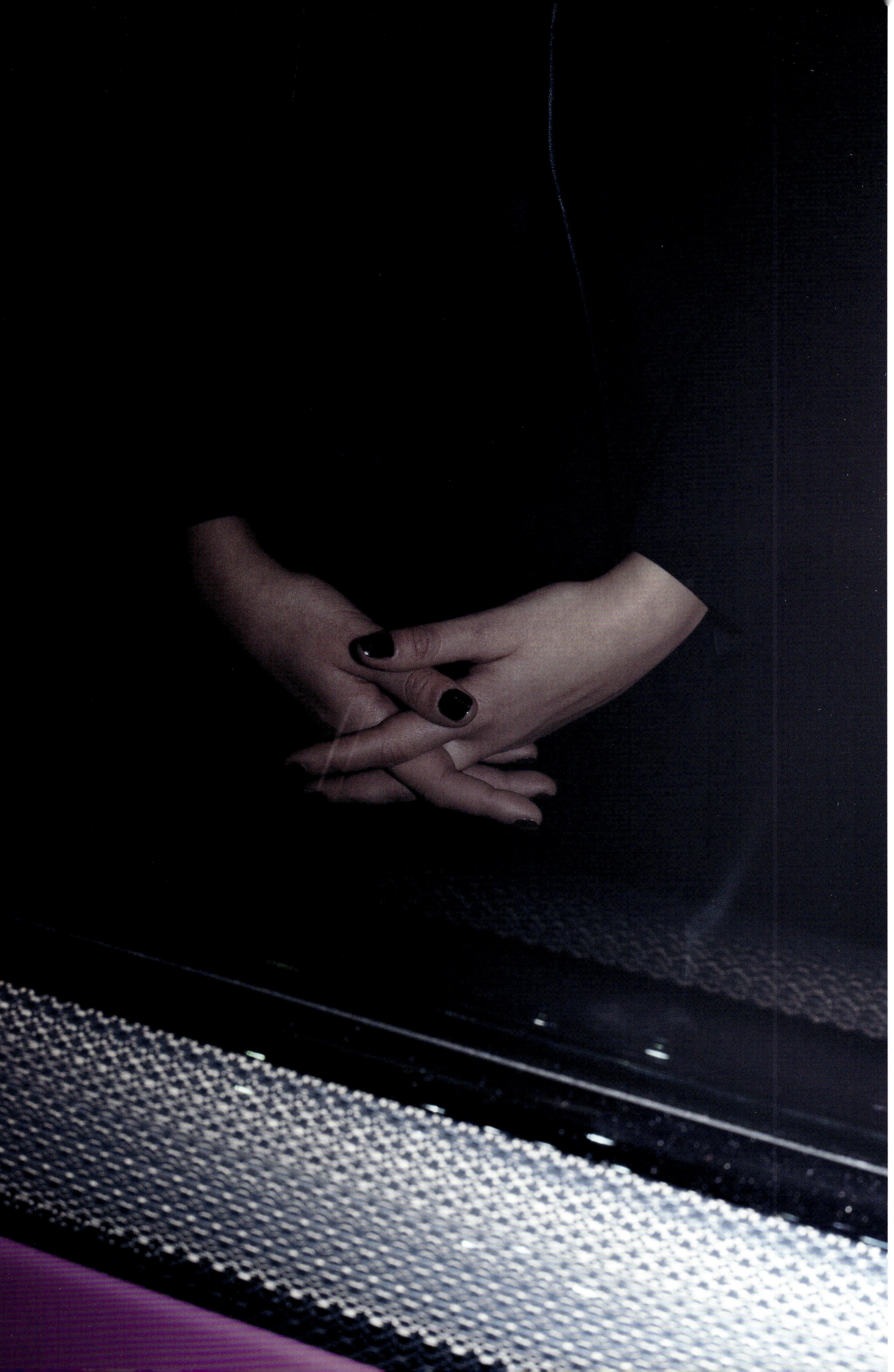

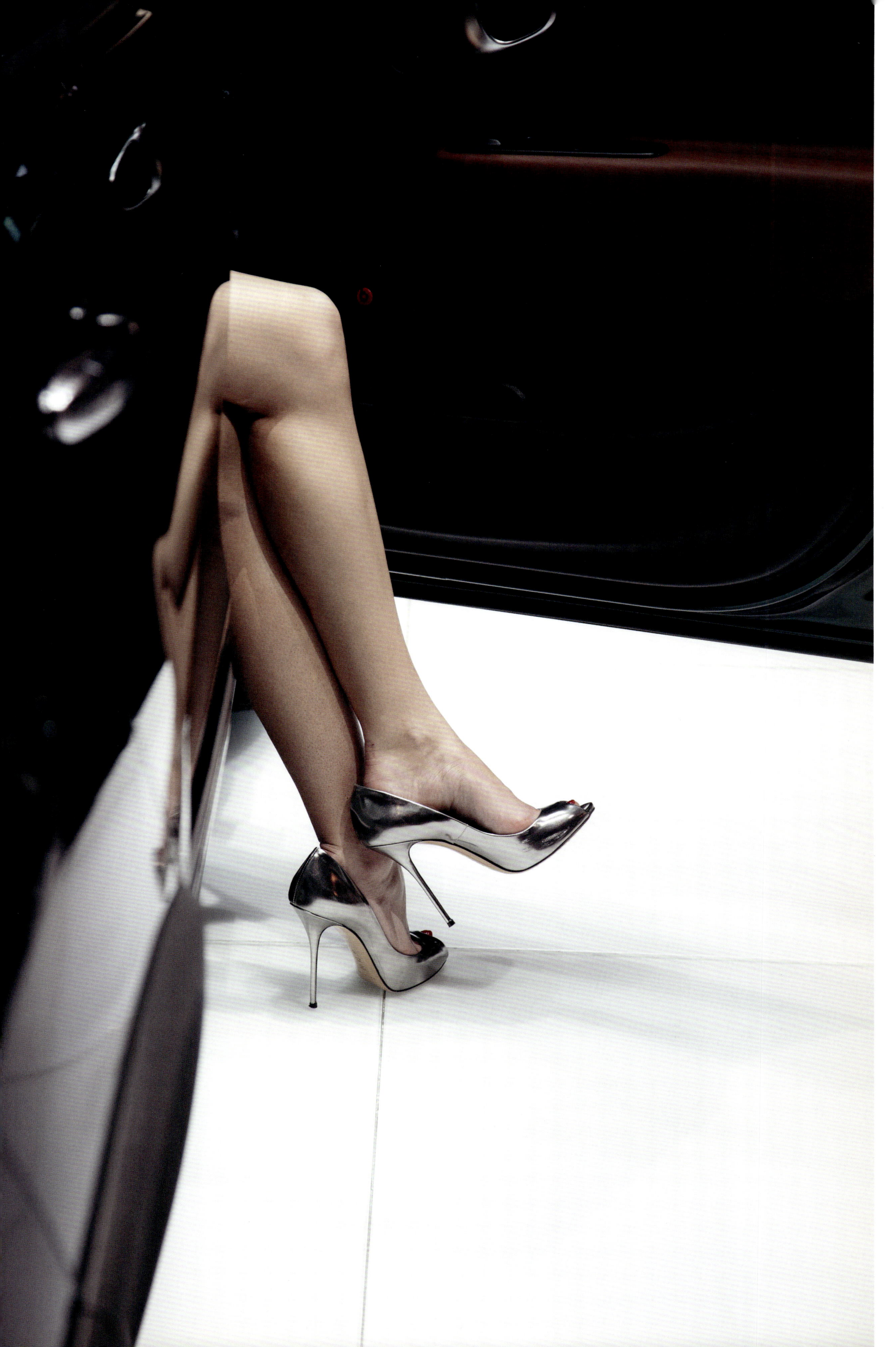

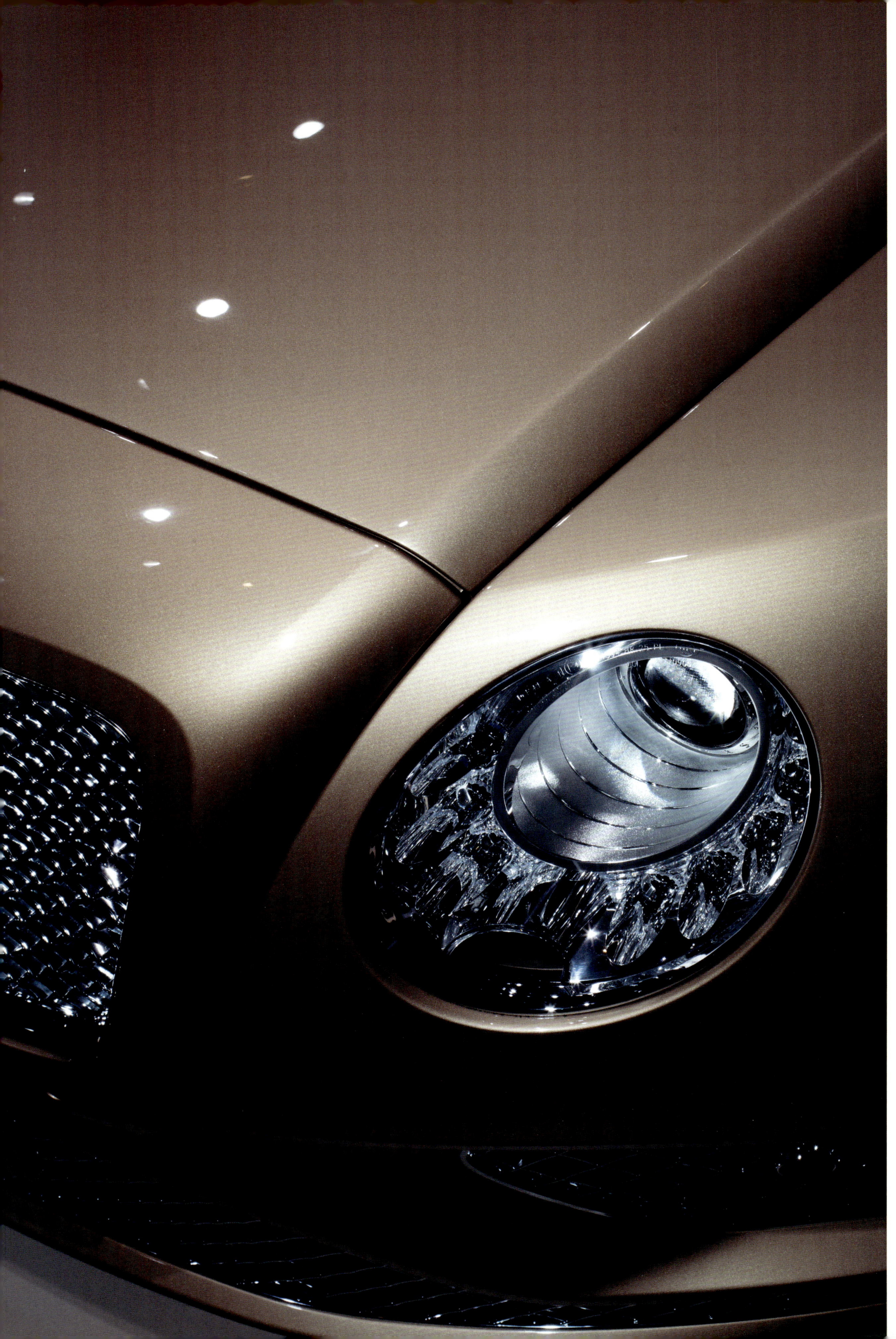

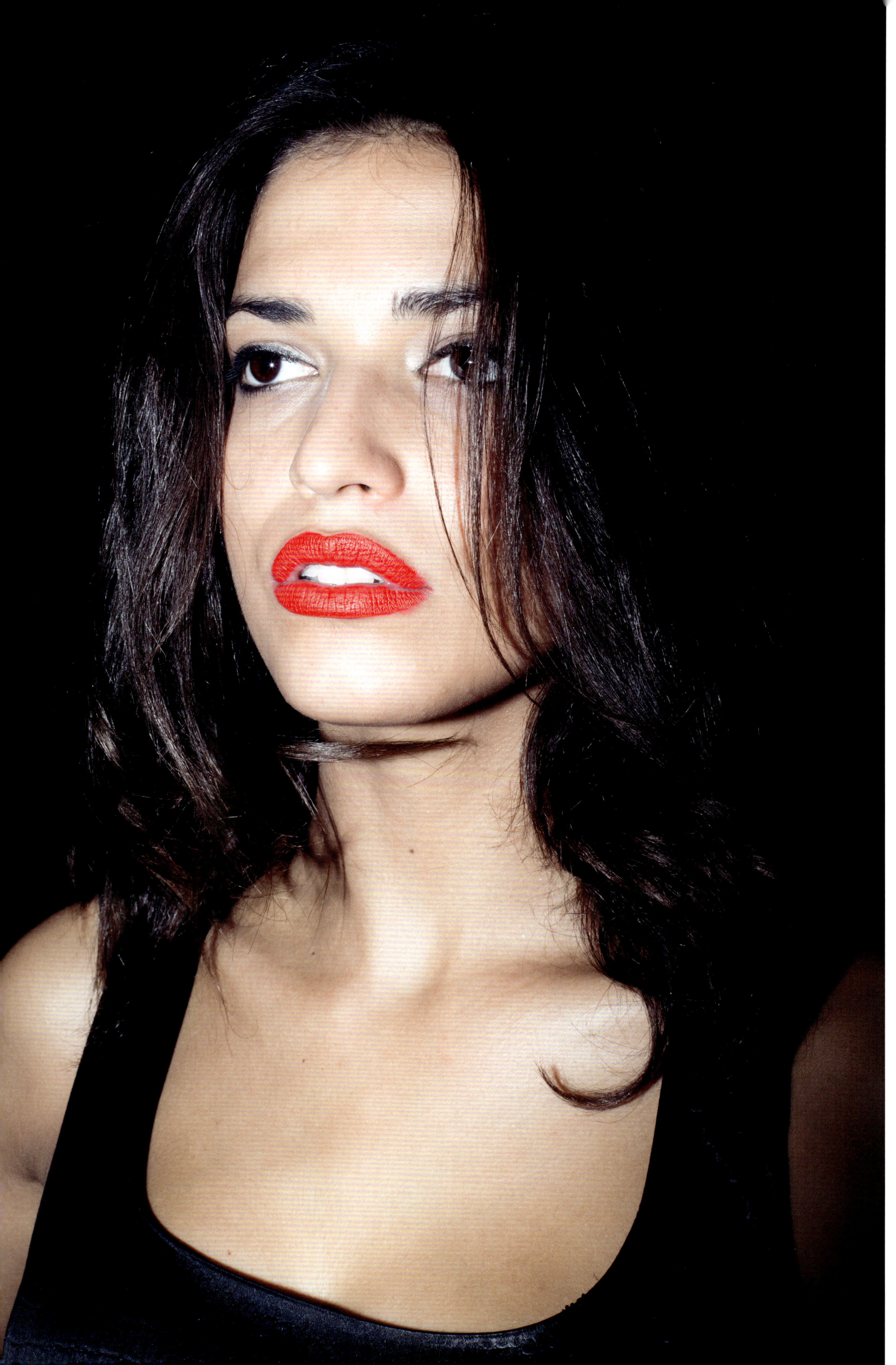

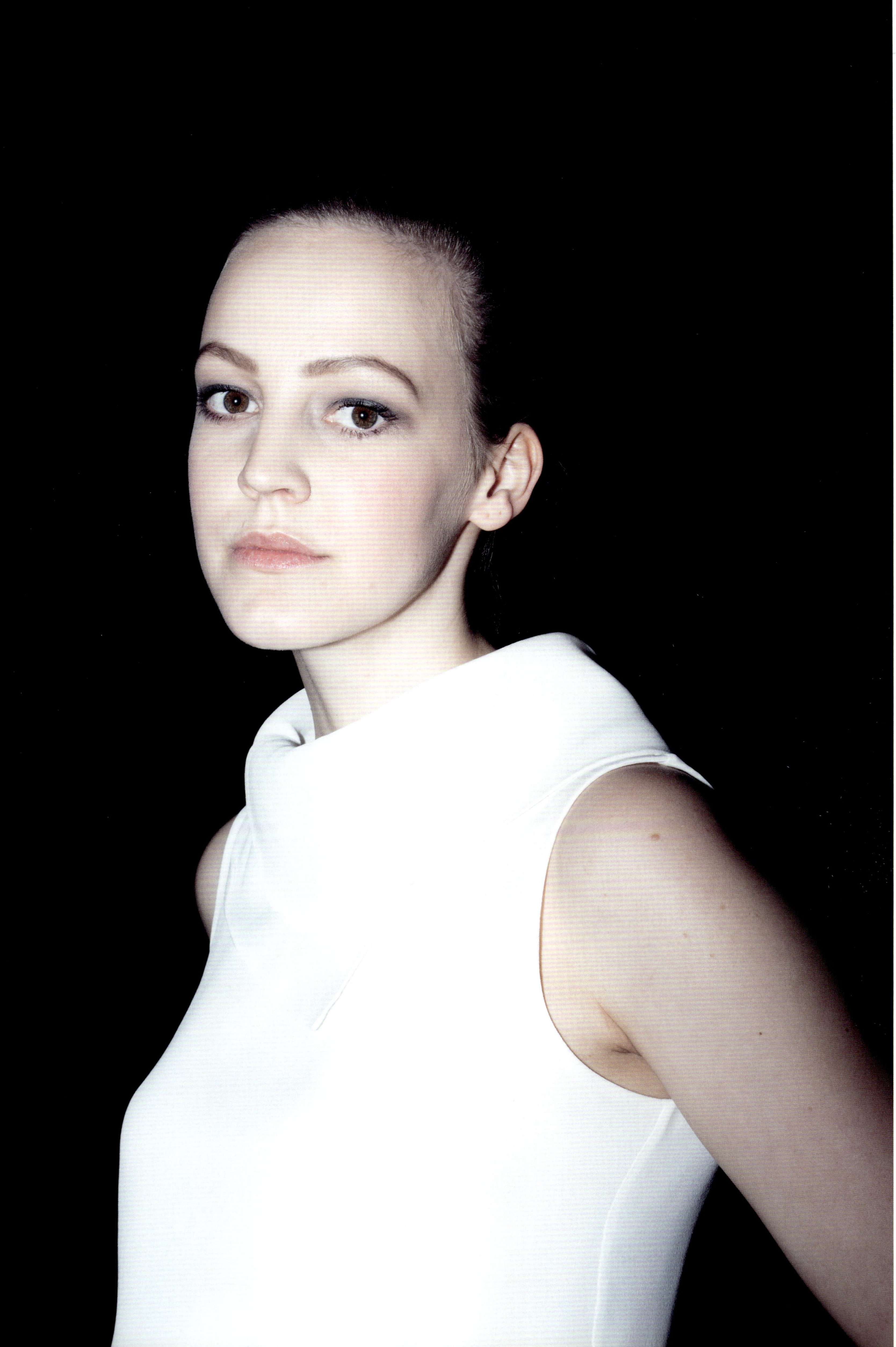

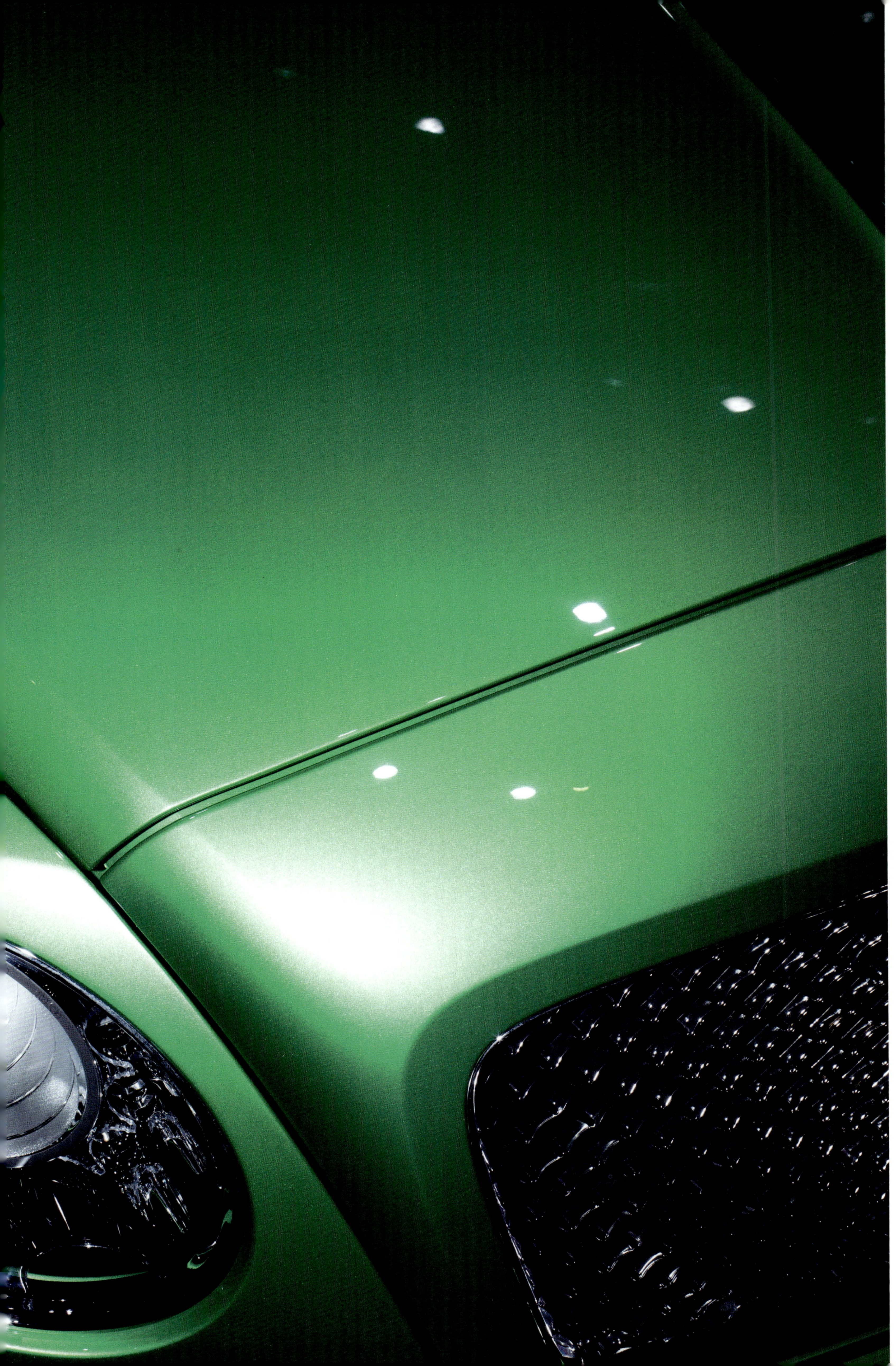

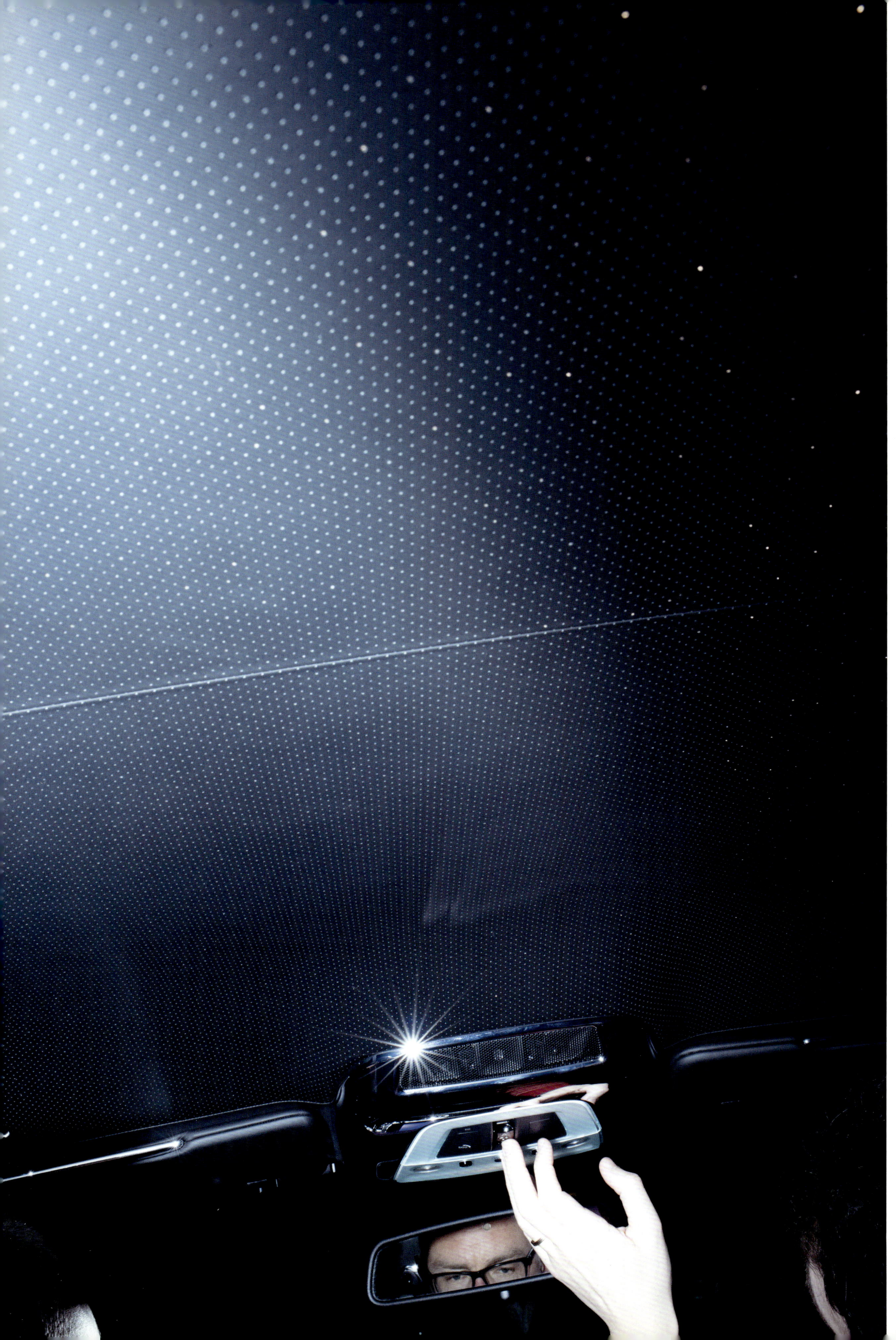

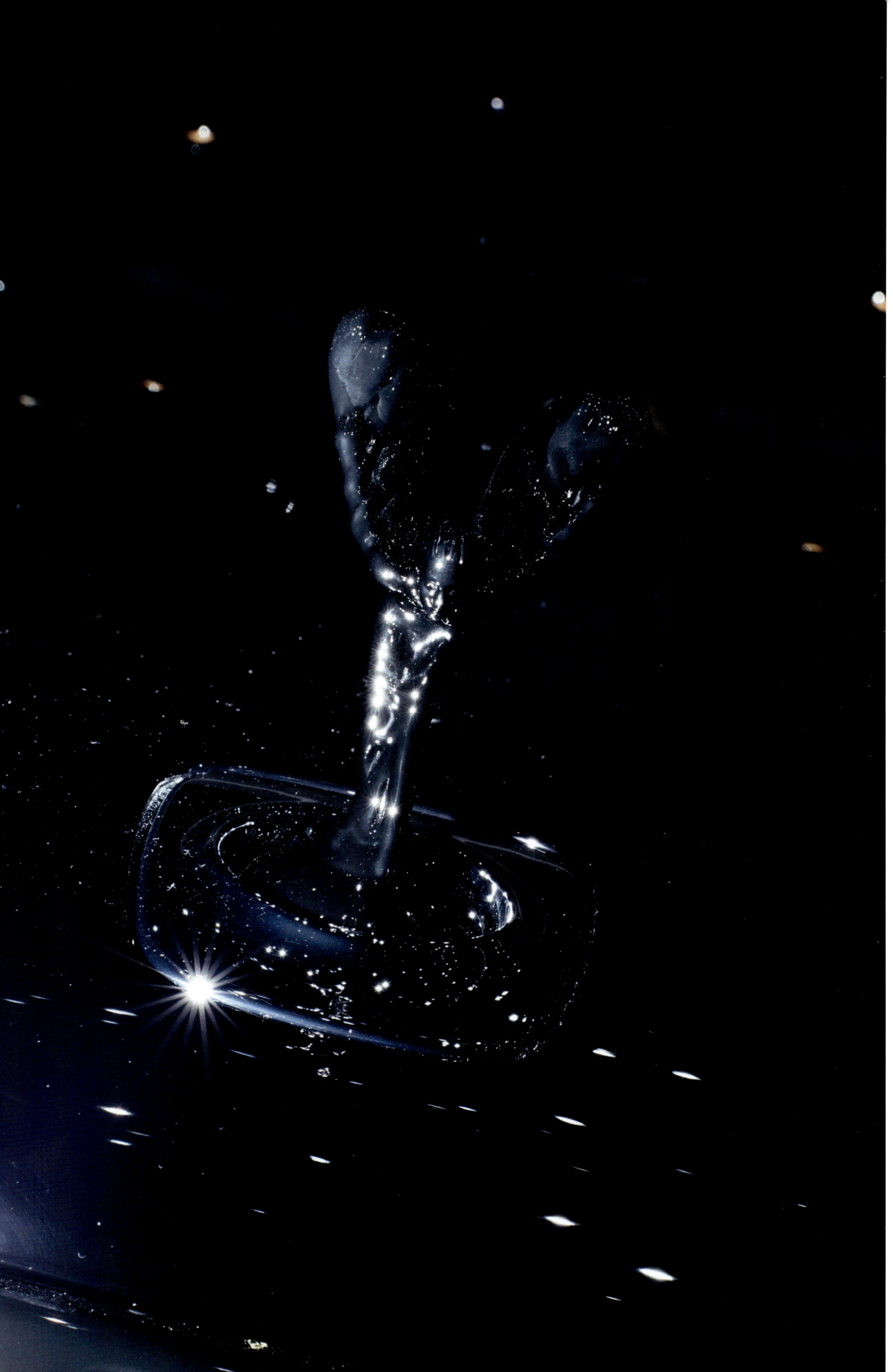

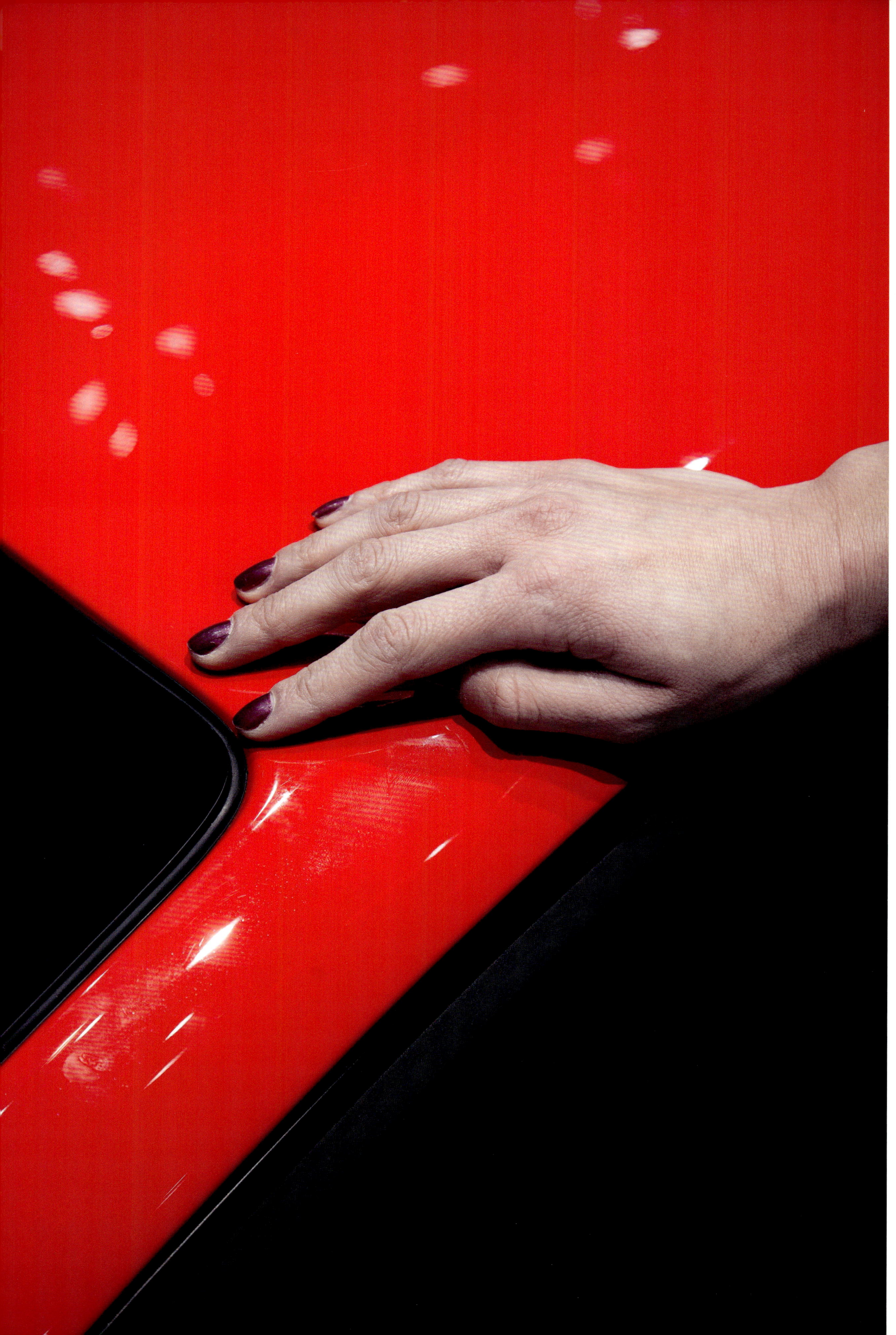

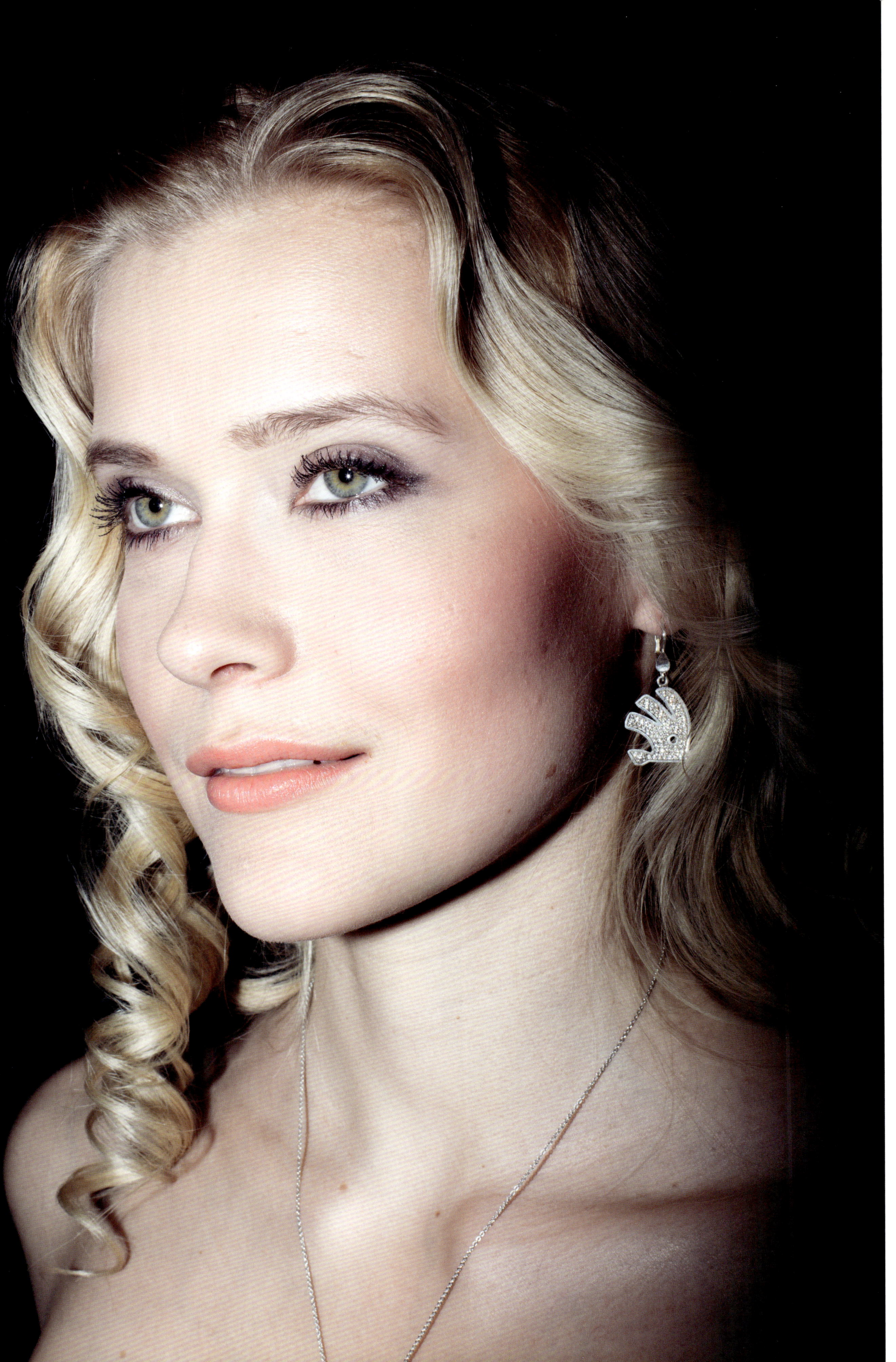

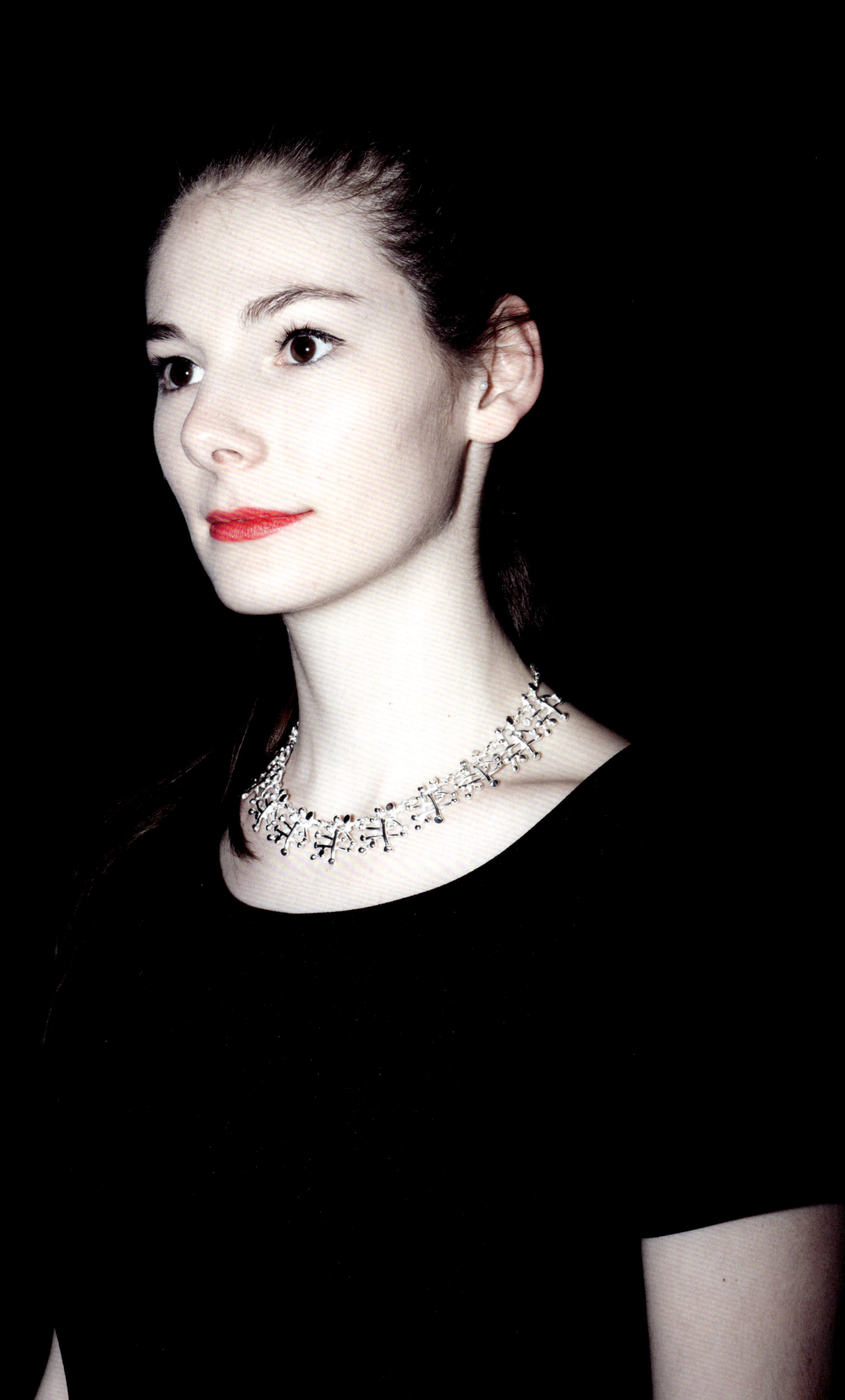

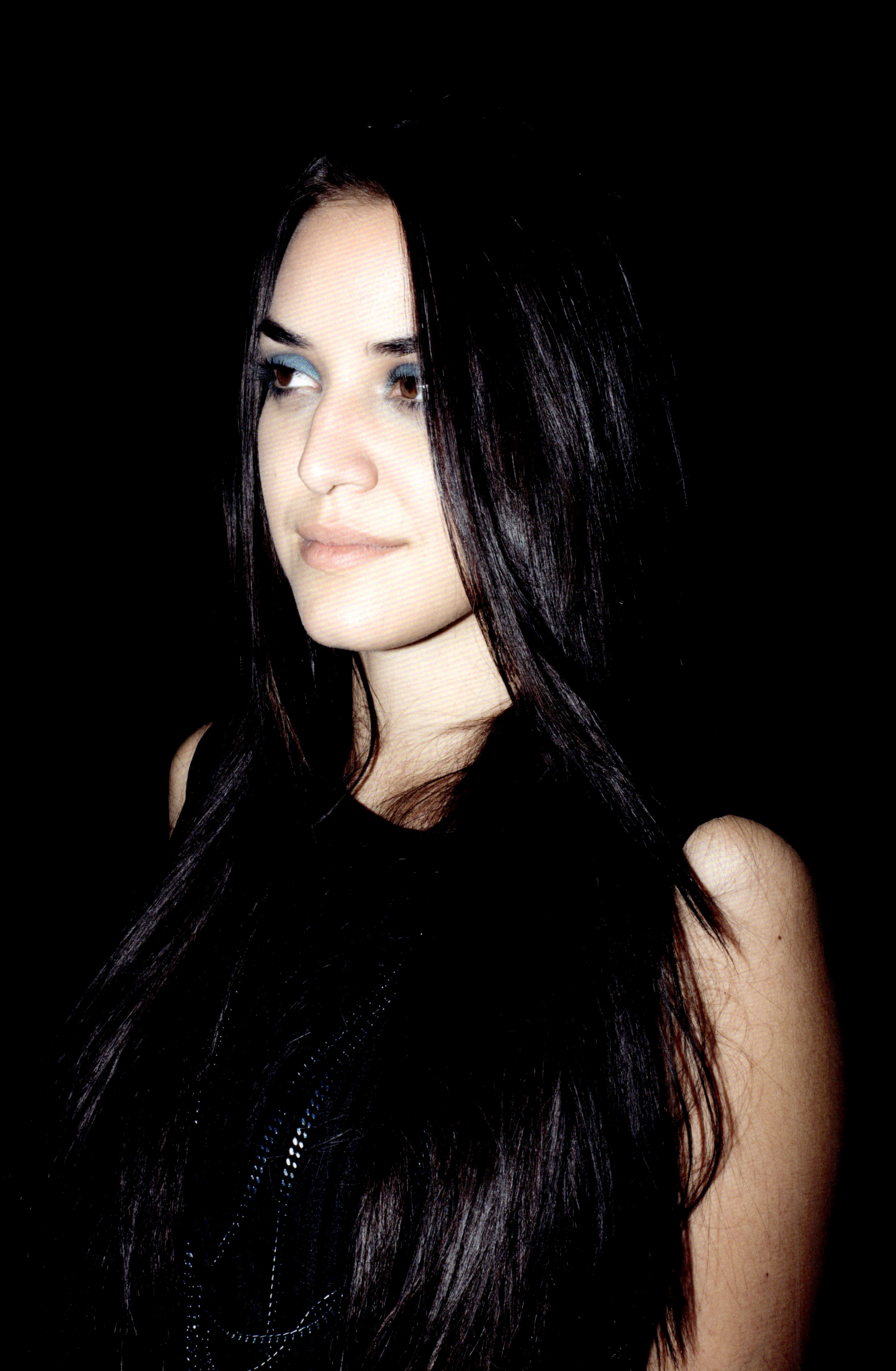

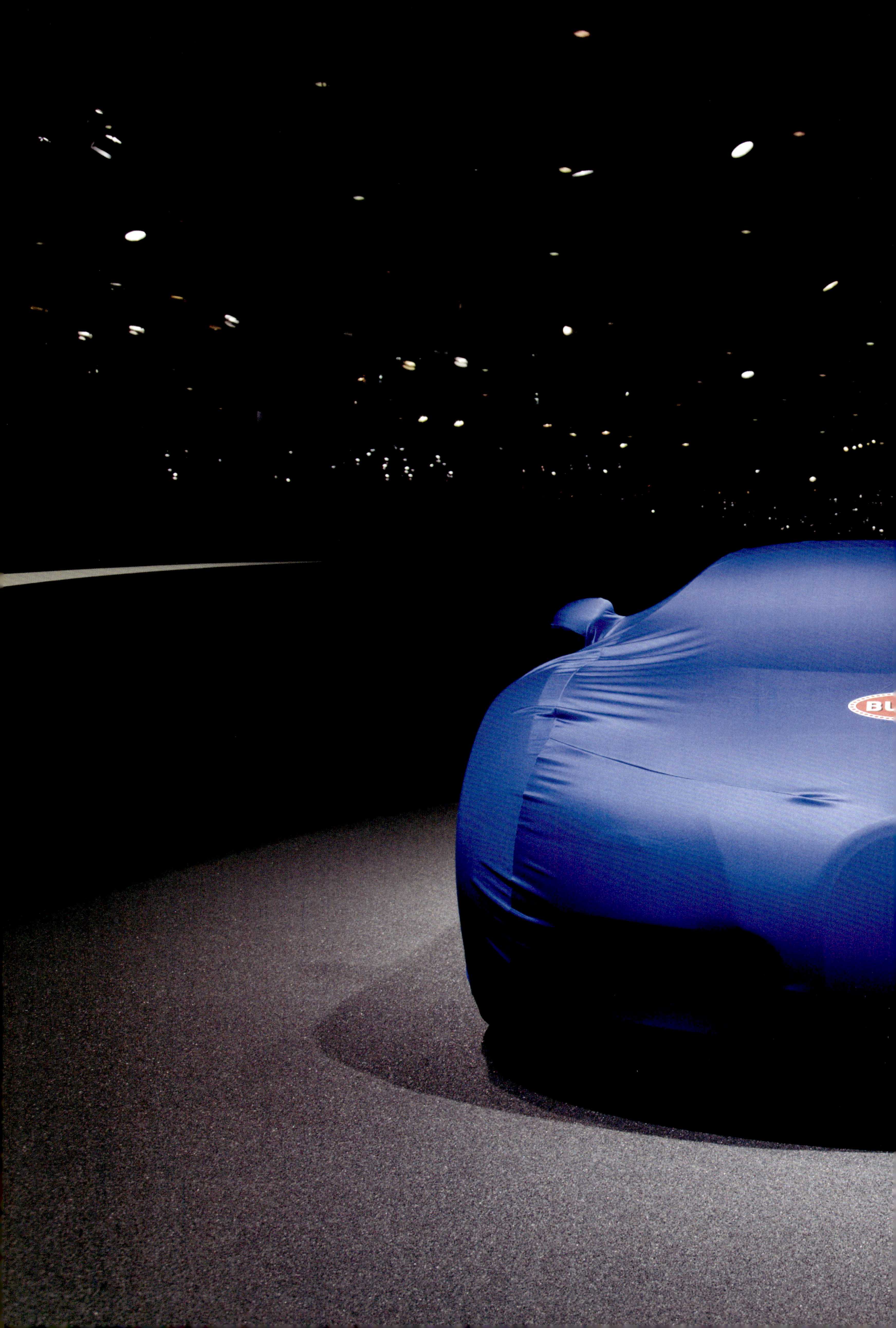

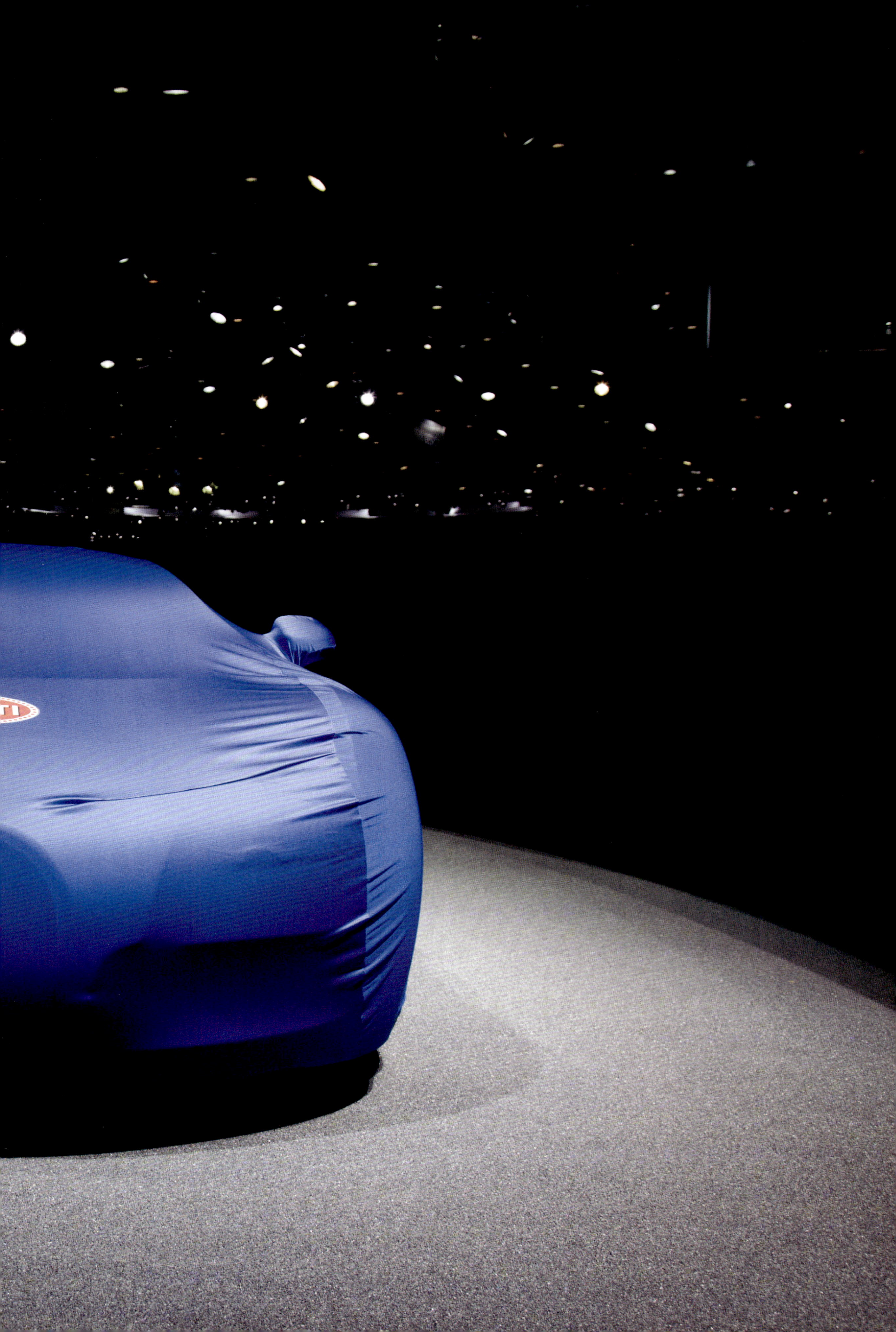

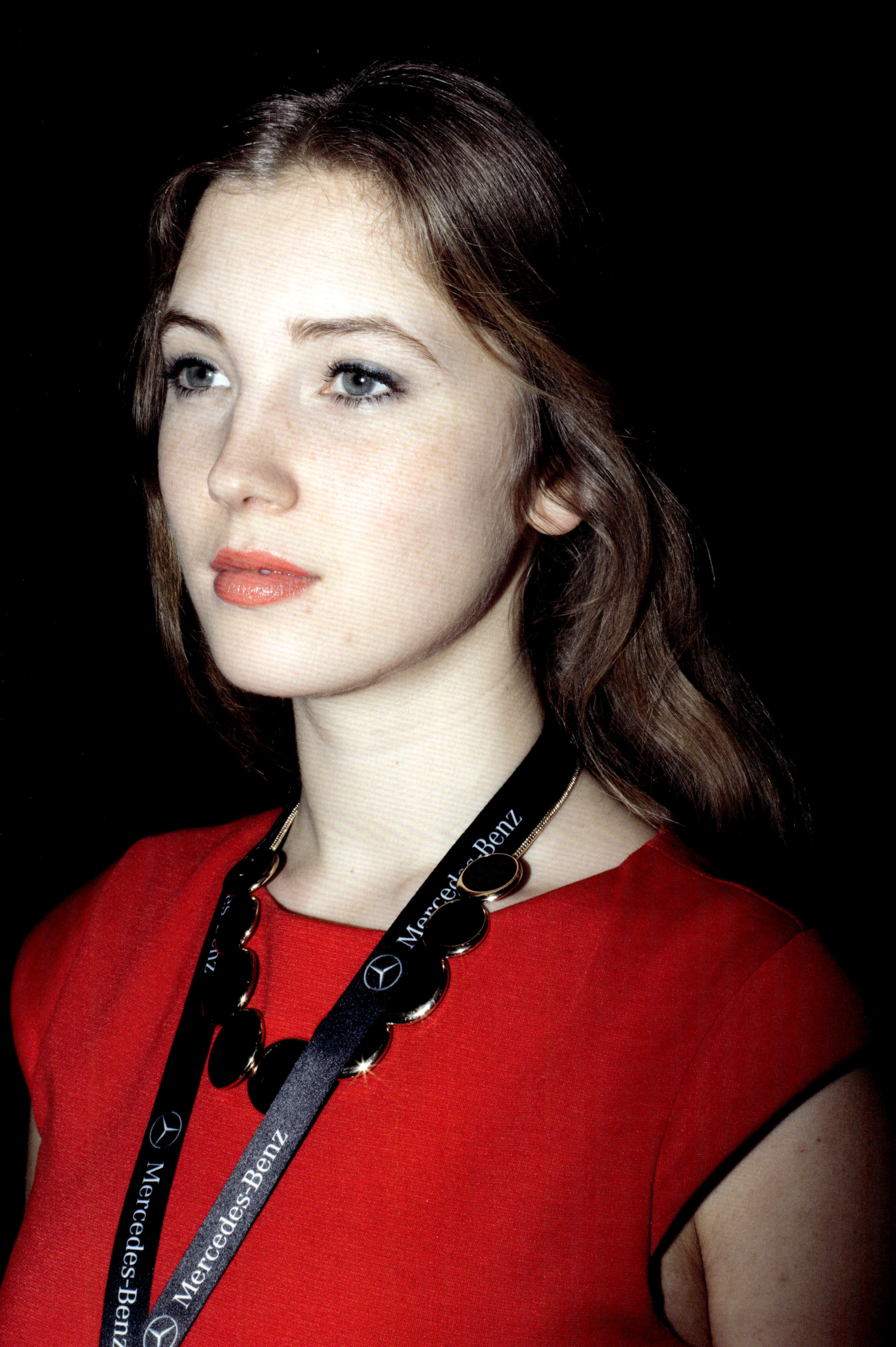
Mercedes-Benz
Mercedes-Benz
Mercedes-Benz
Mercedes-Benz

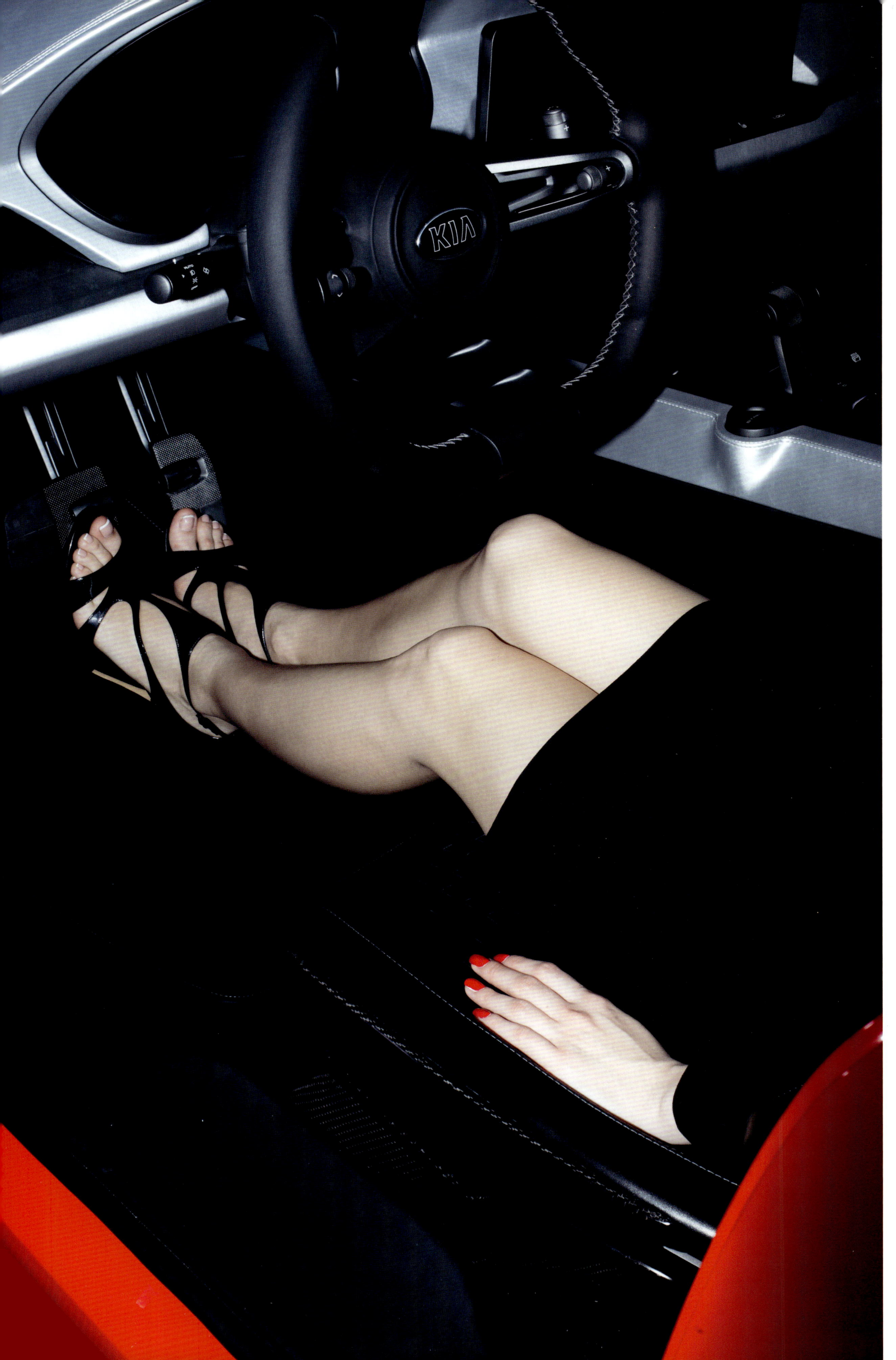

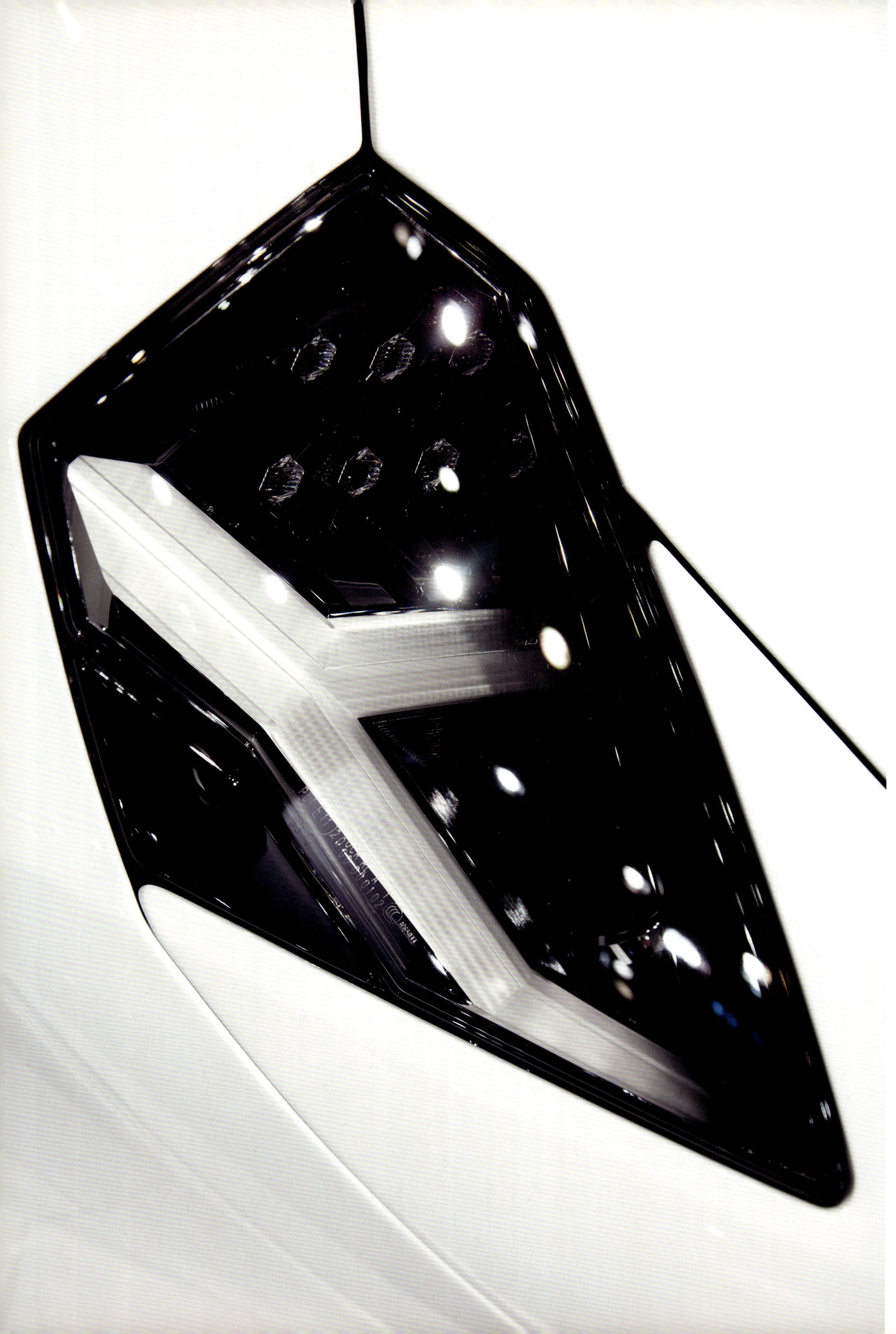

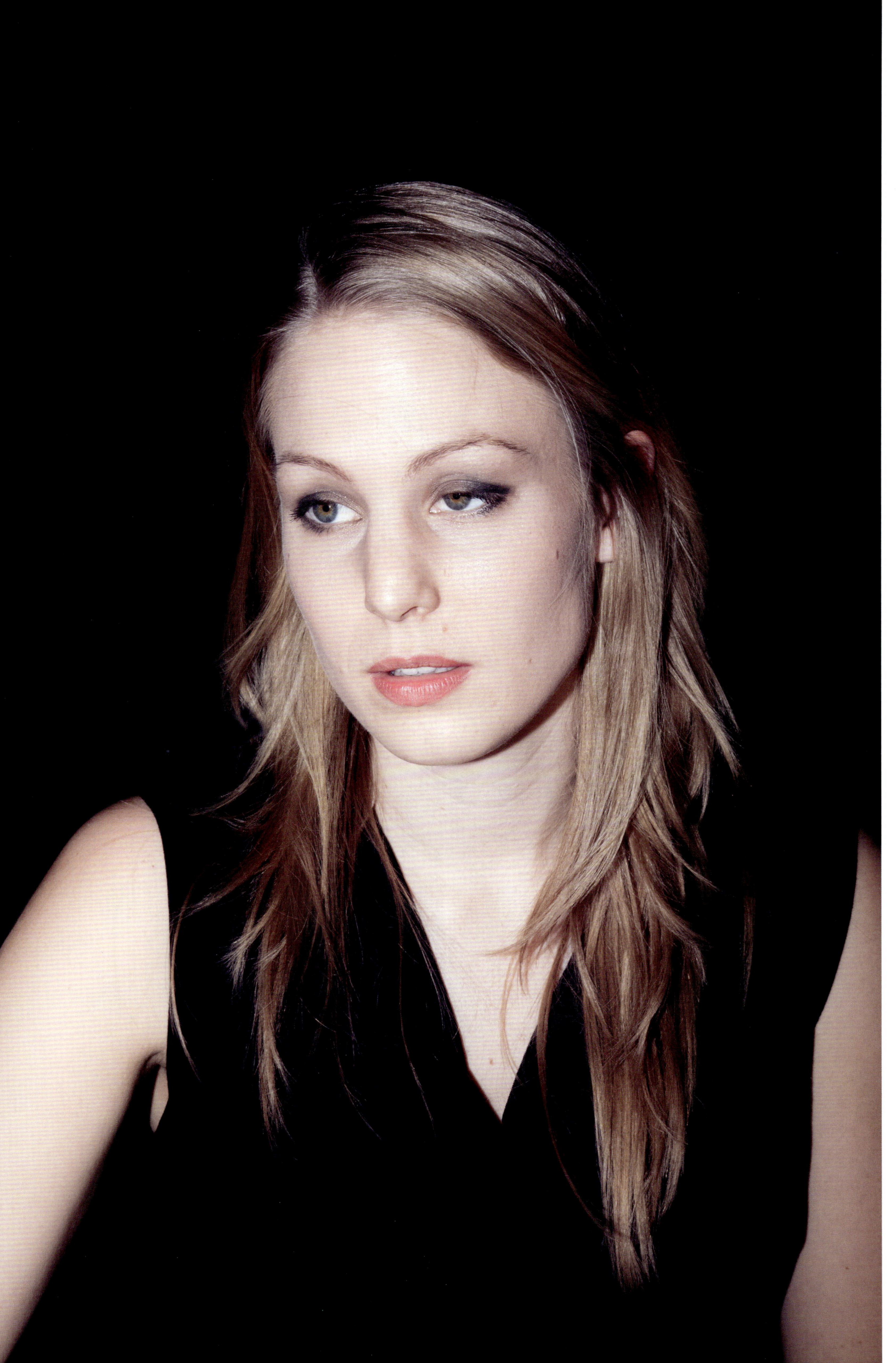

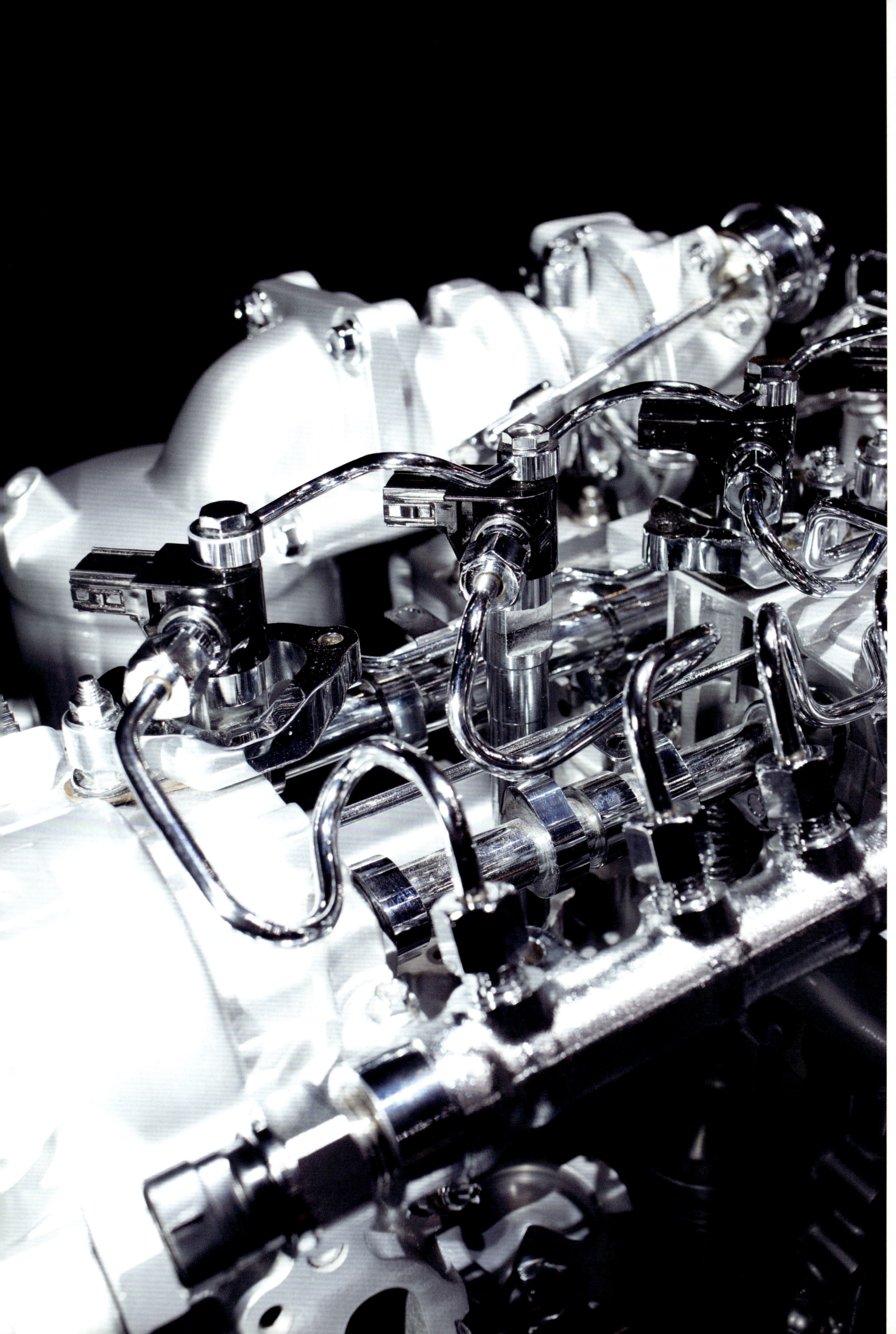

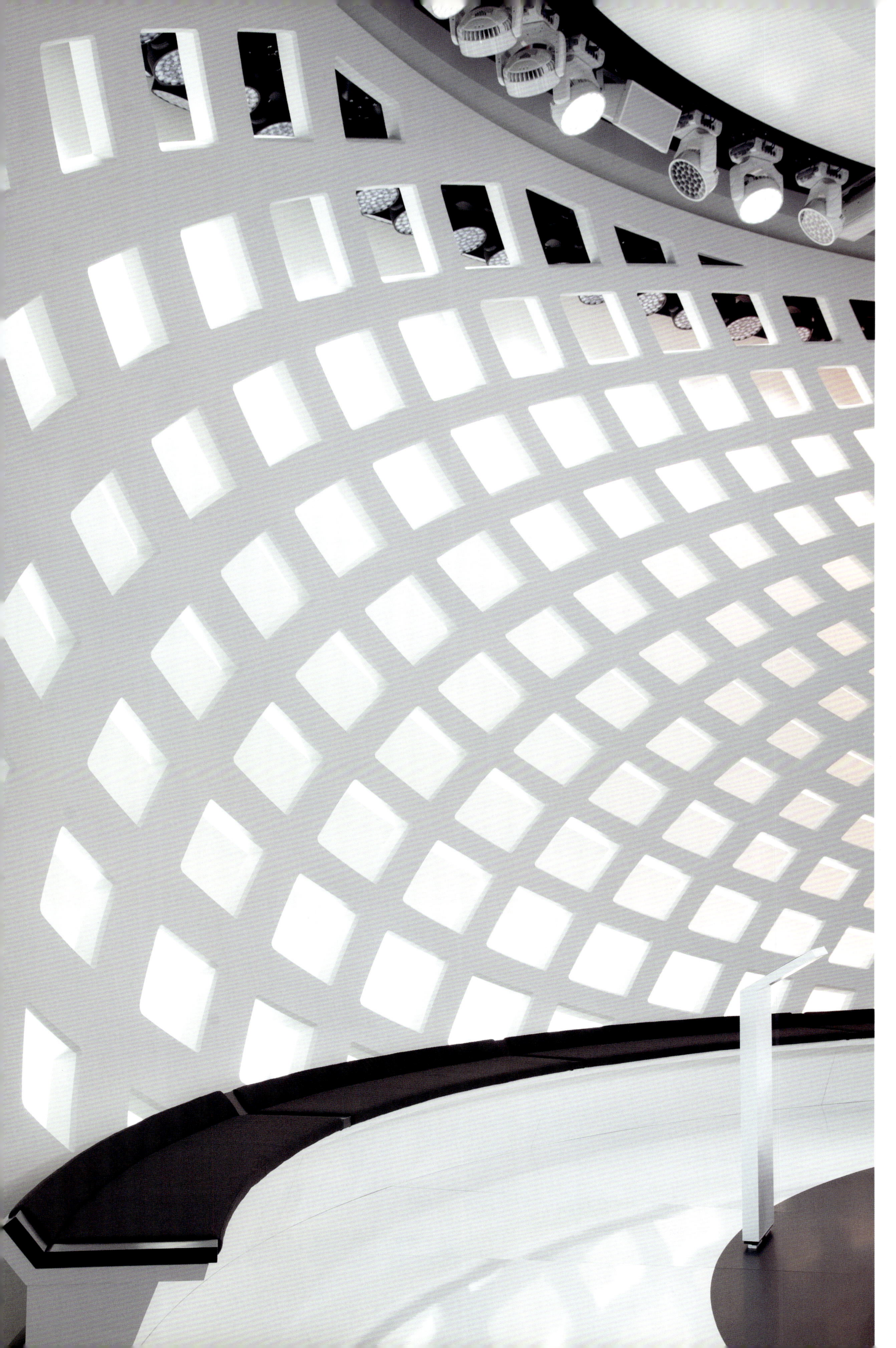

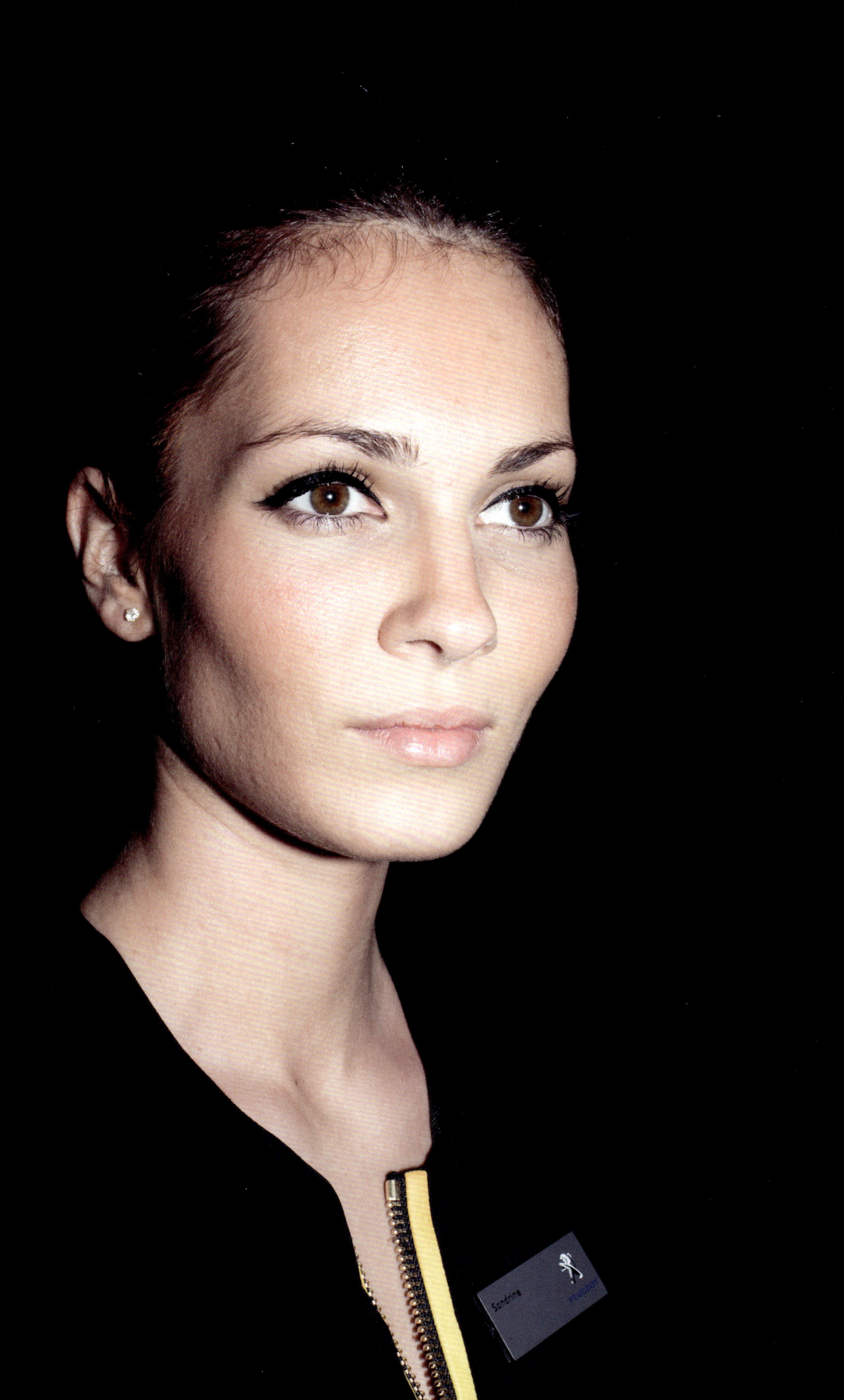
Sandrine
PEUGEOT

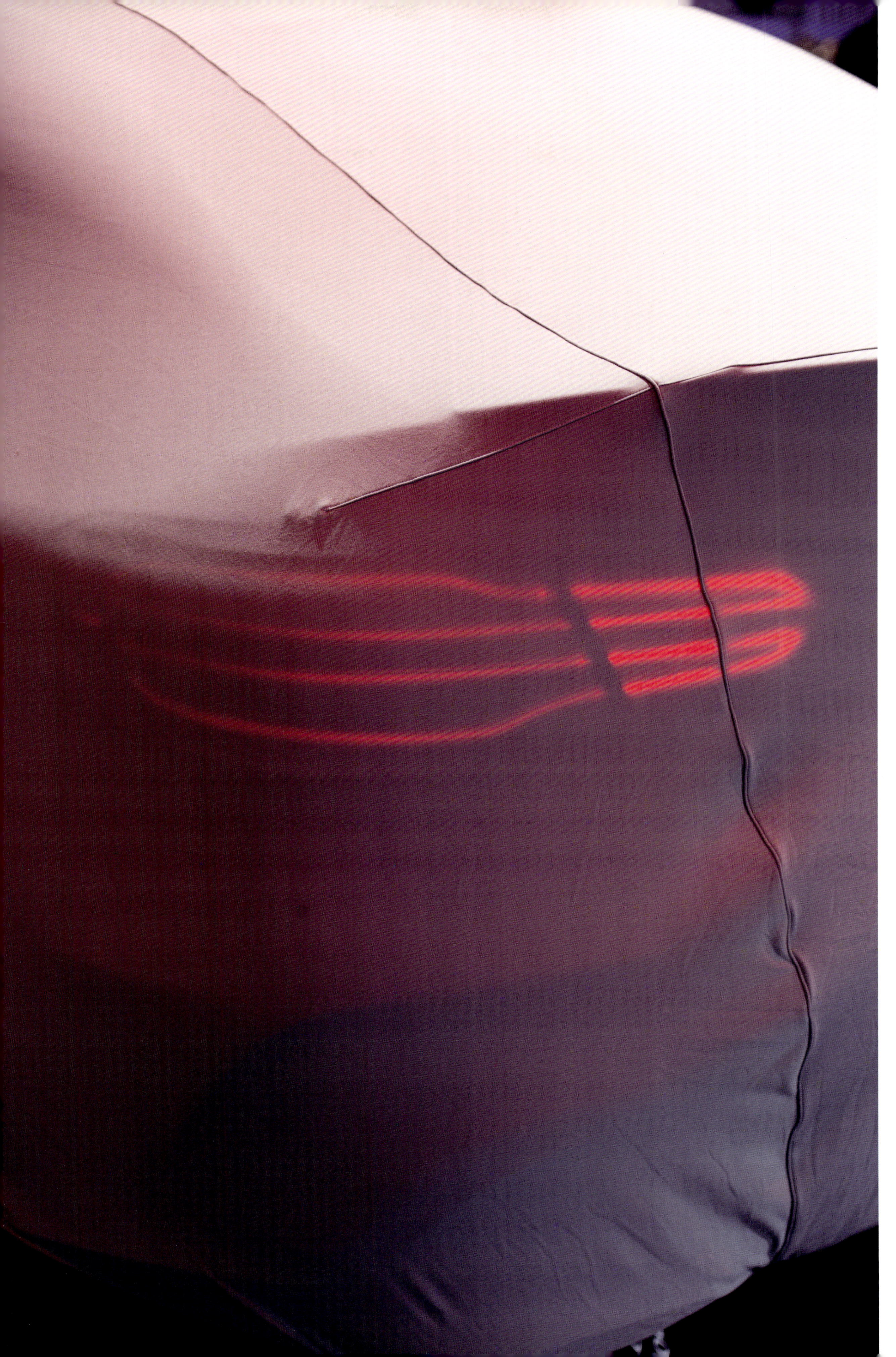

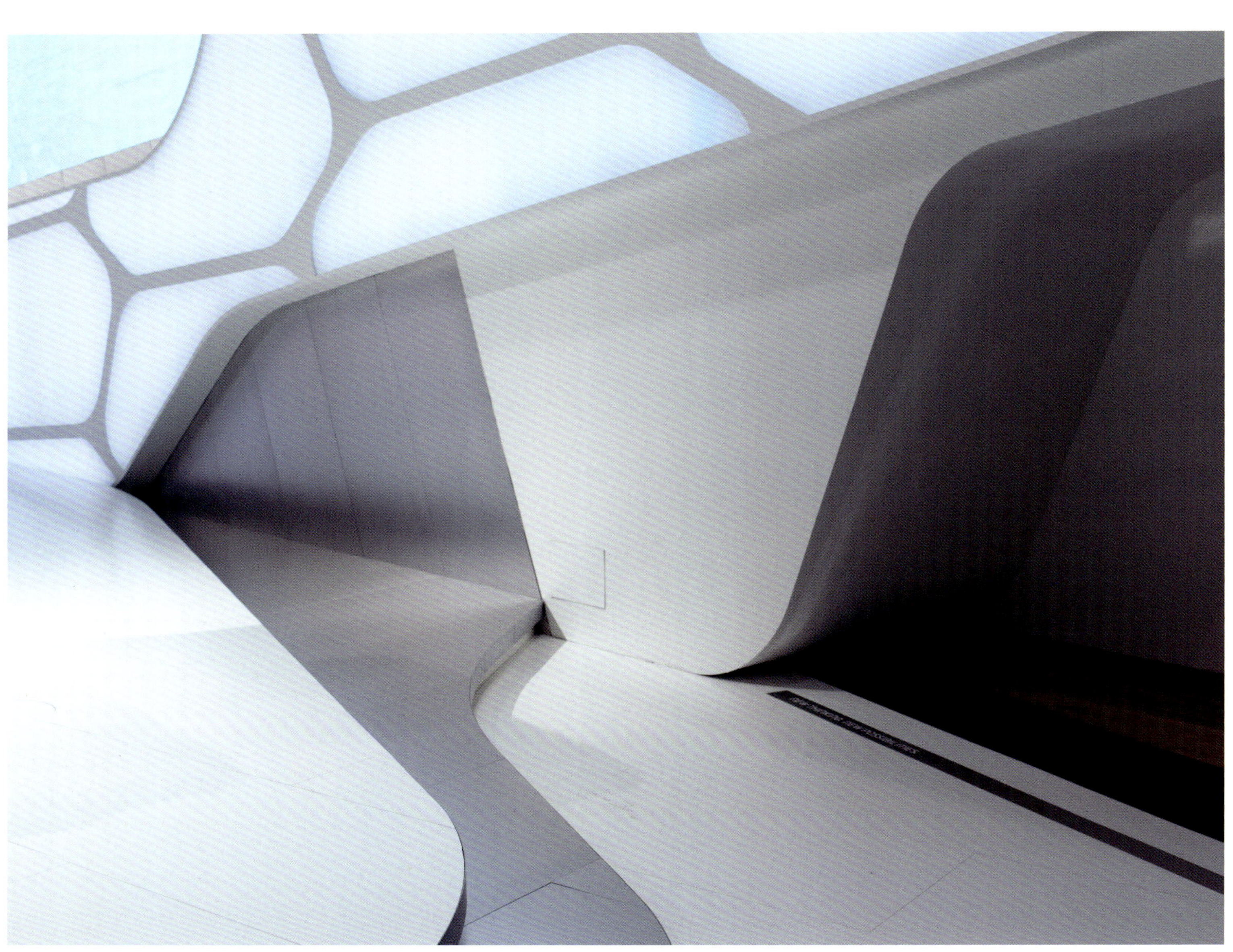

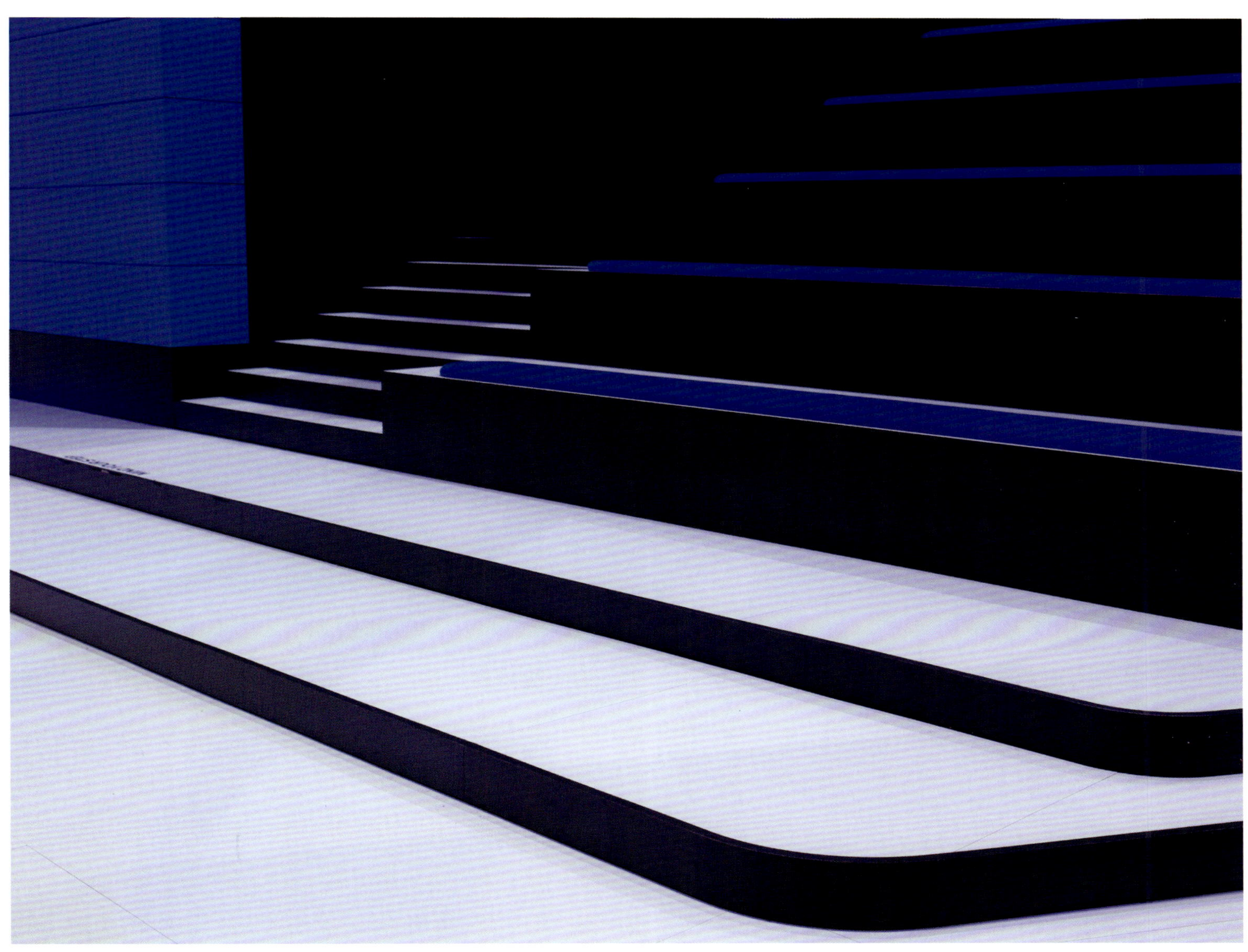

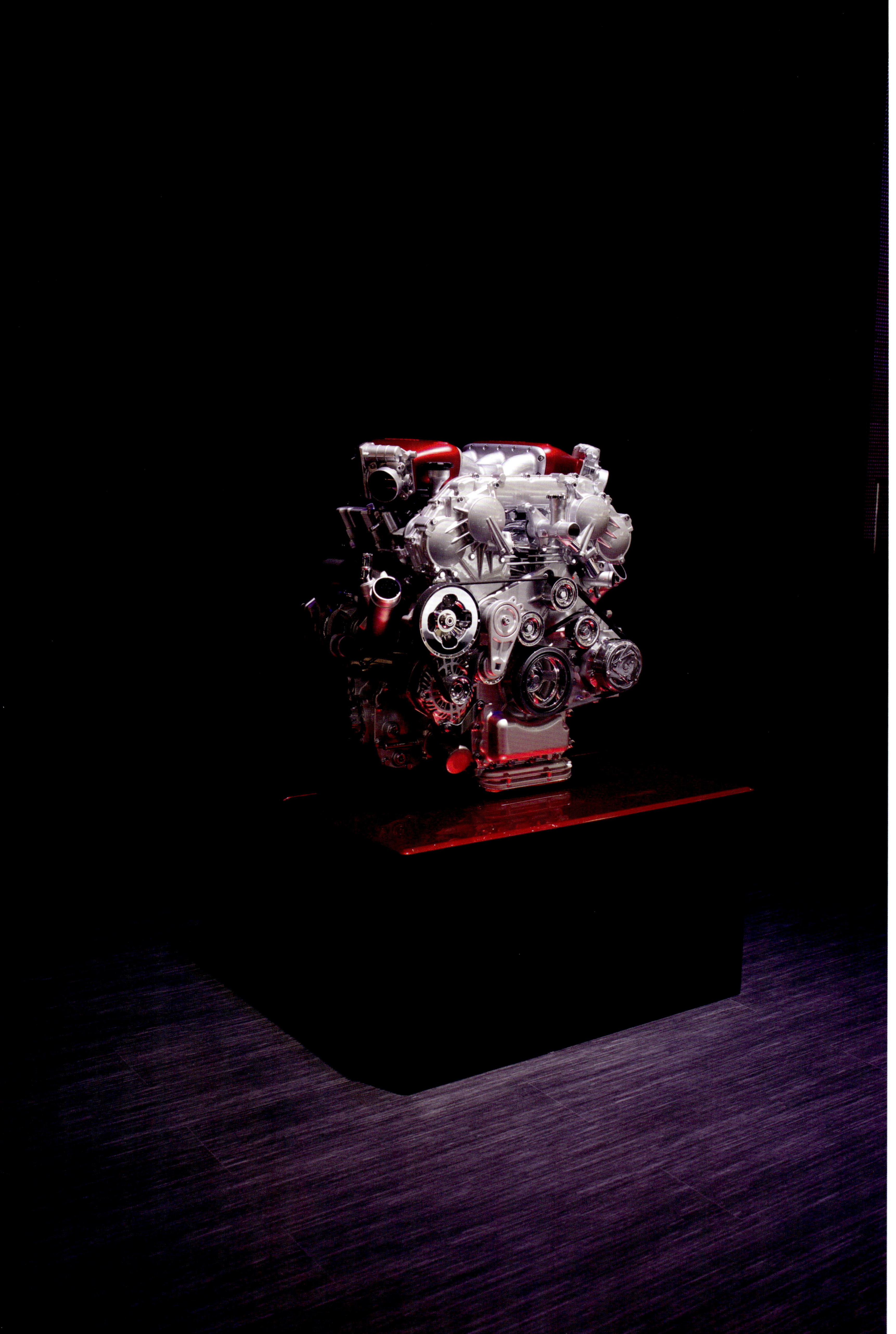

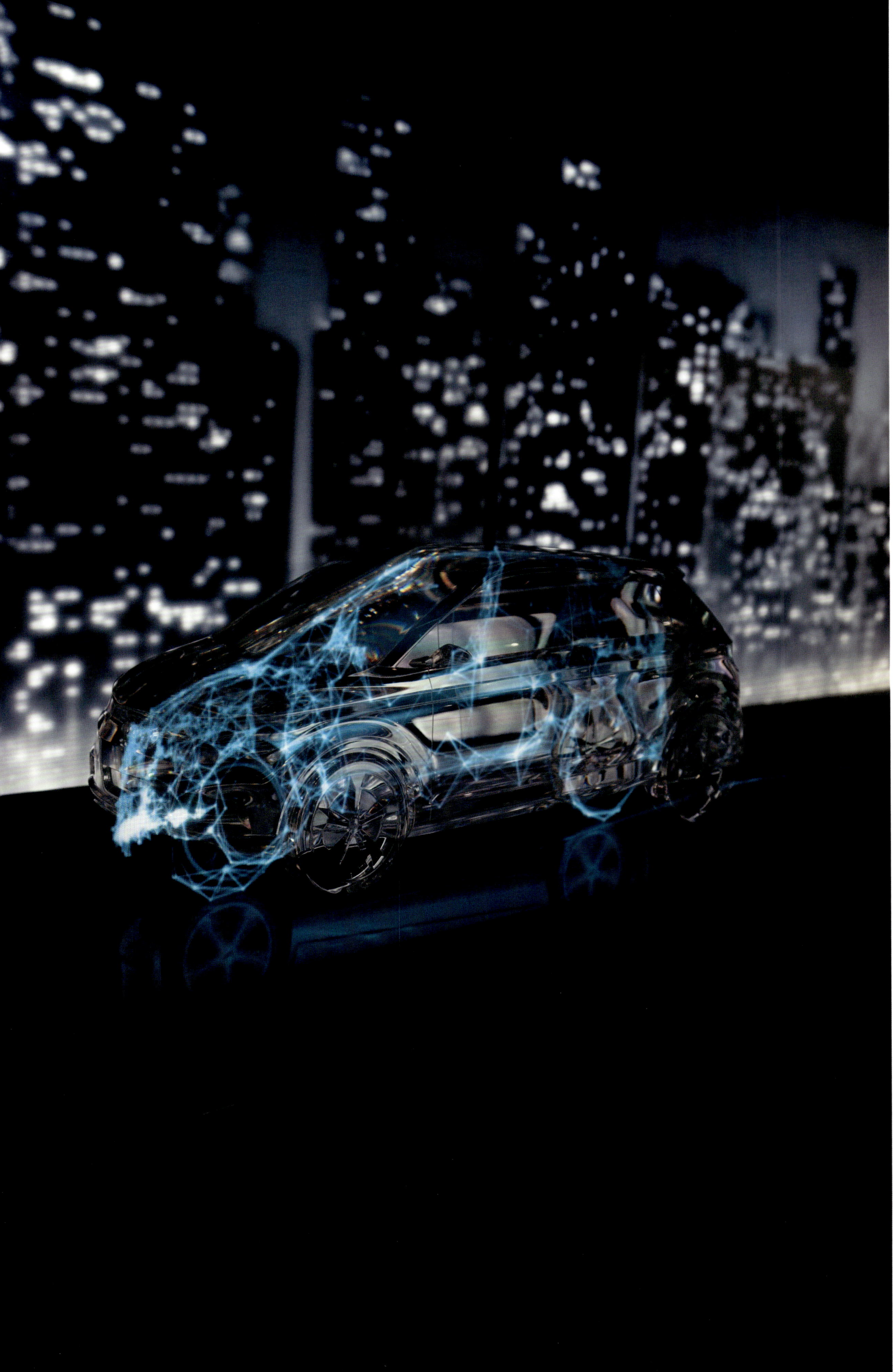

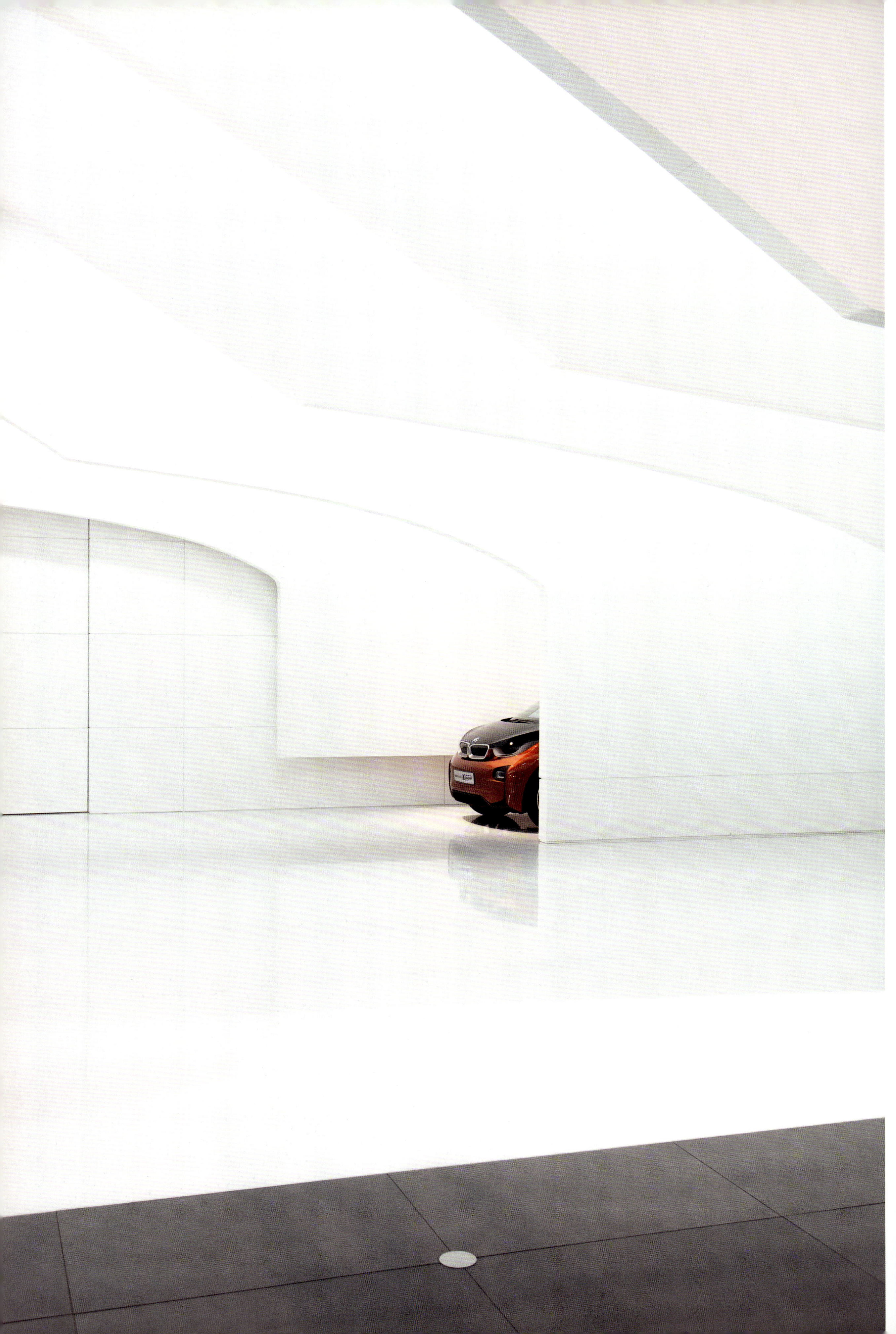

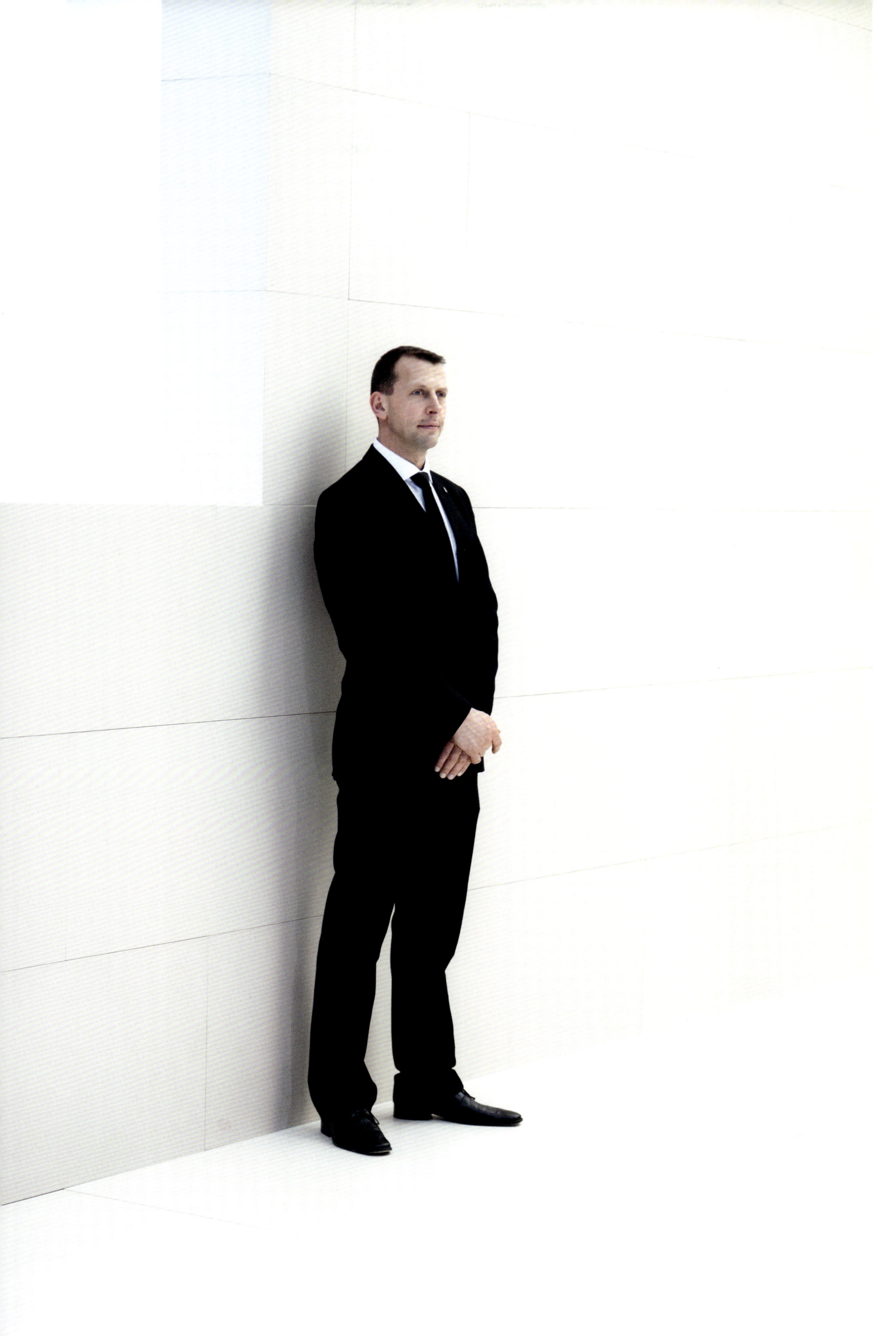

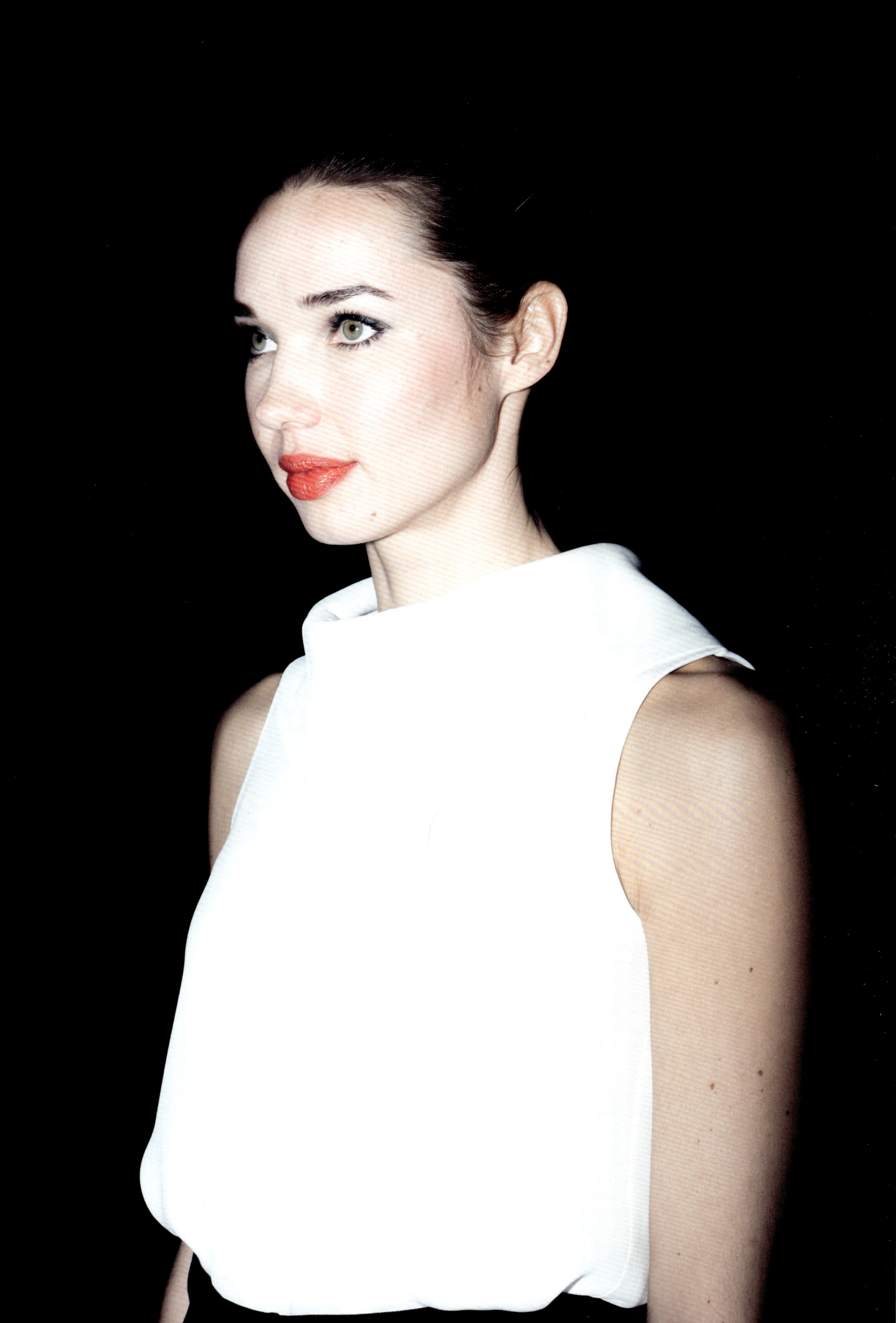

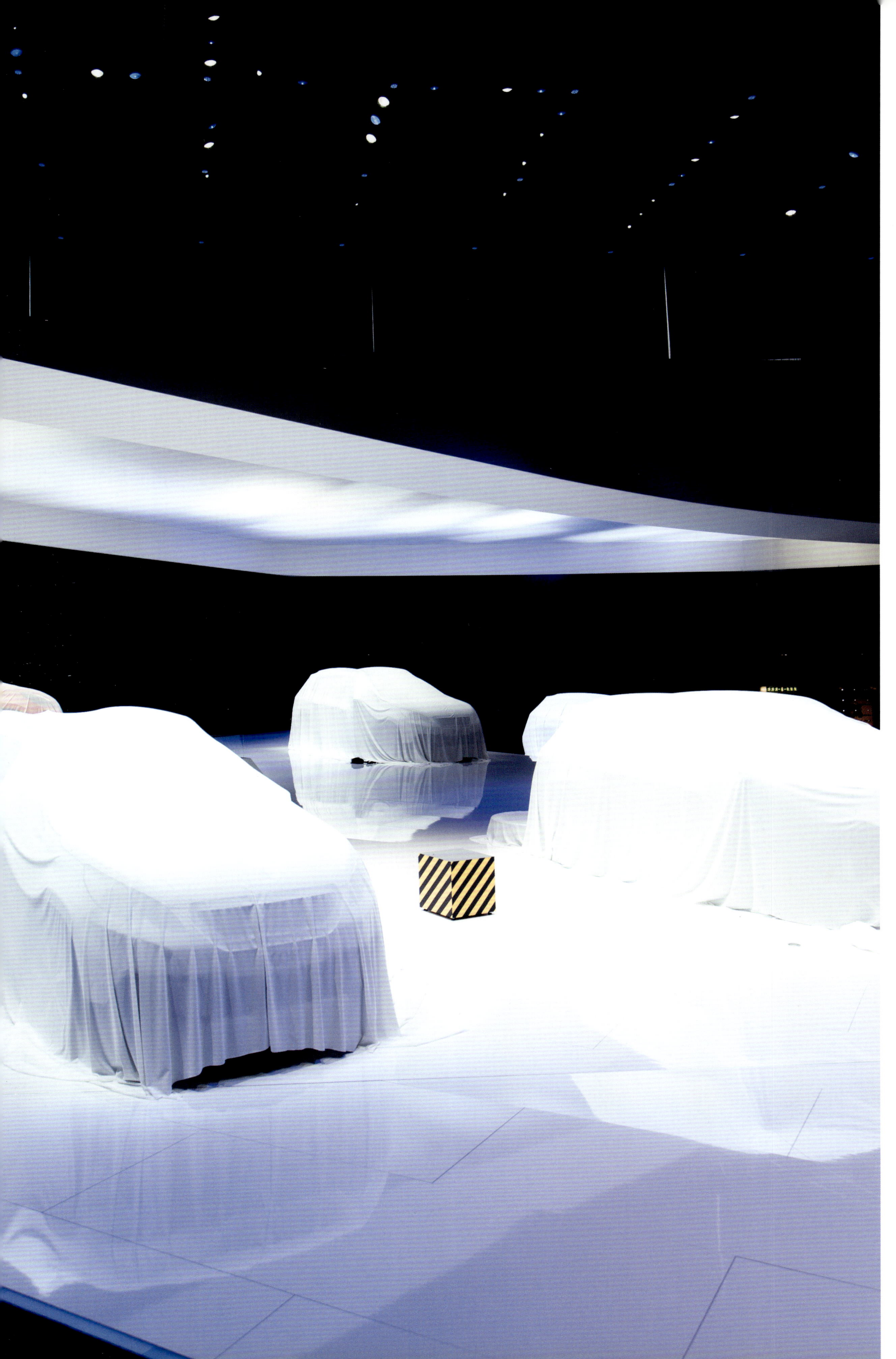

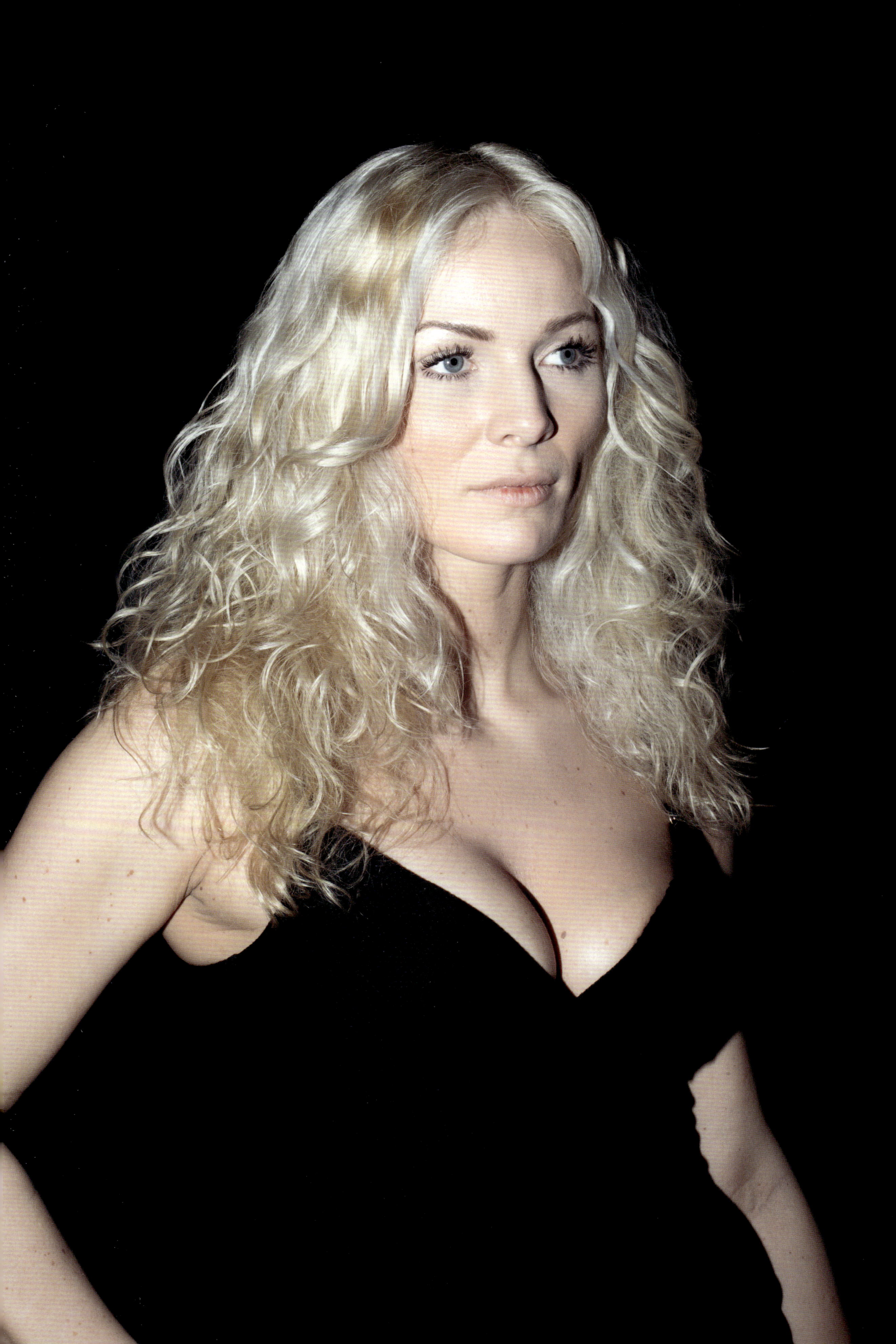

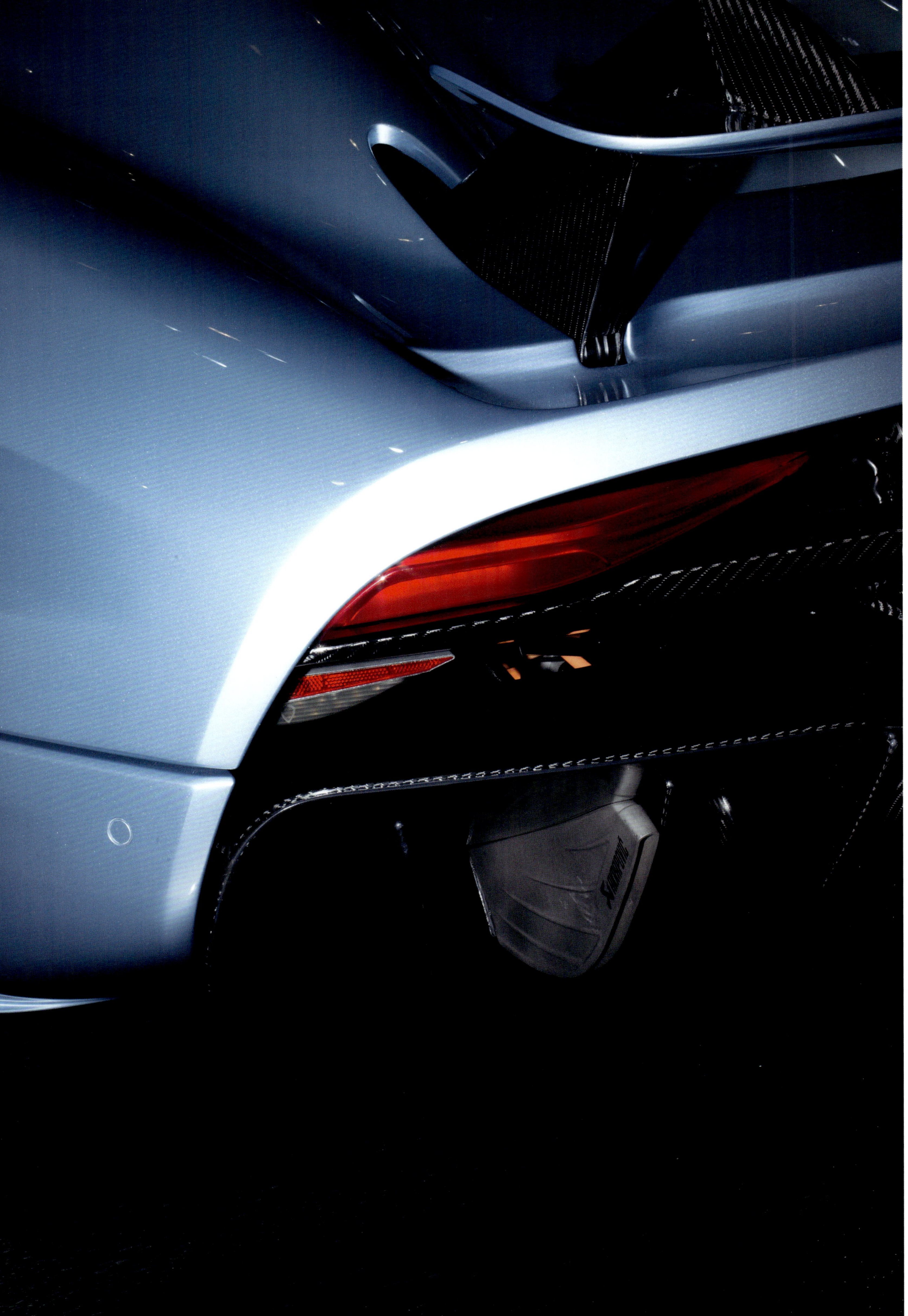

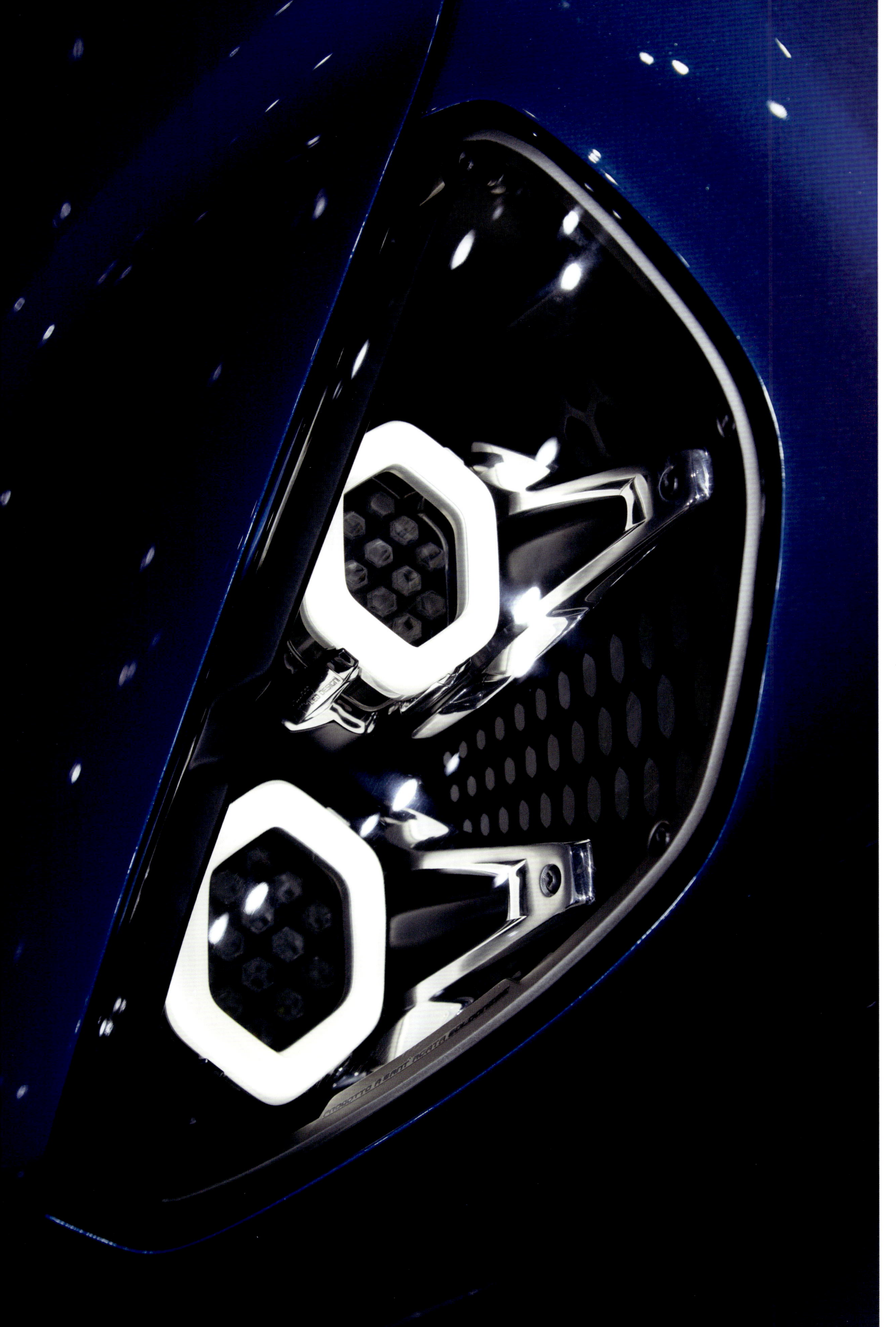

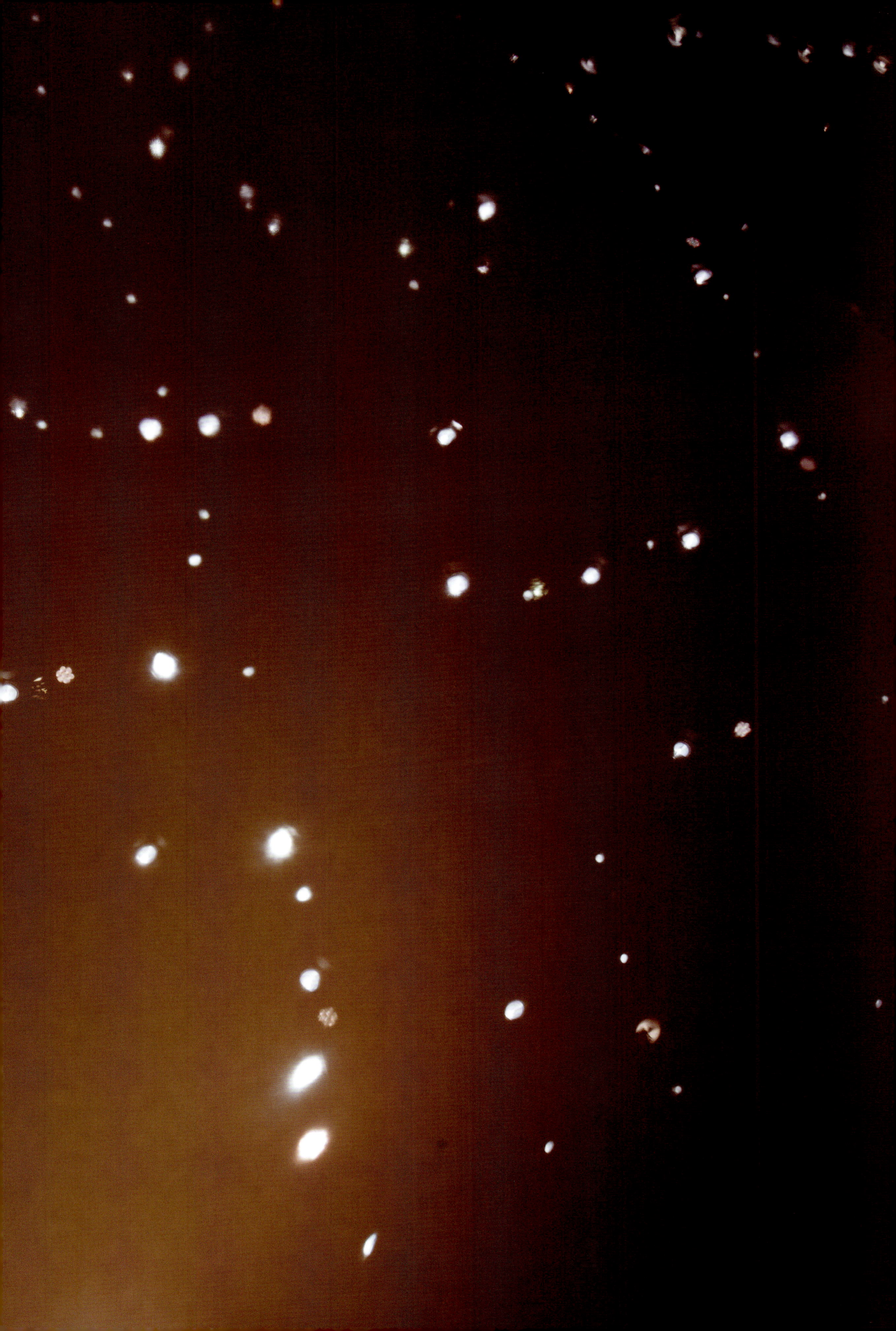

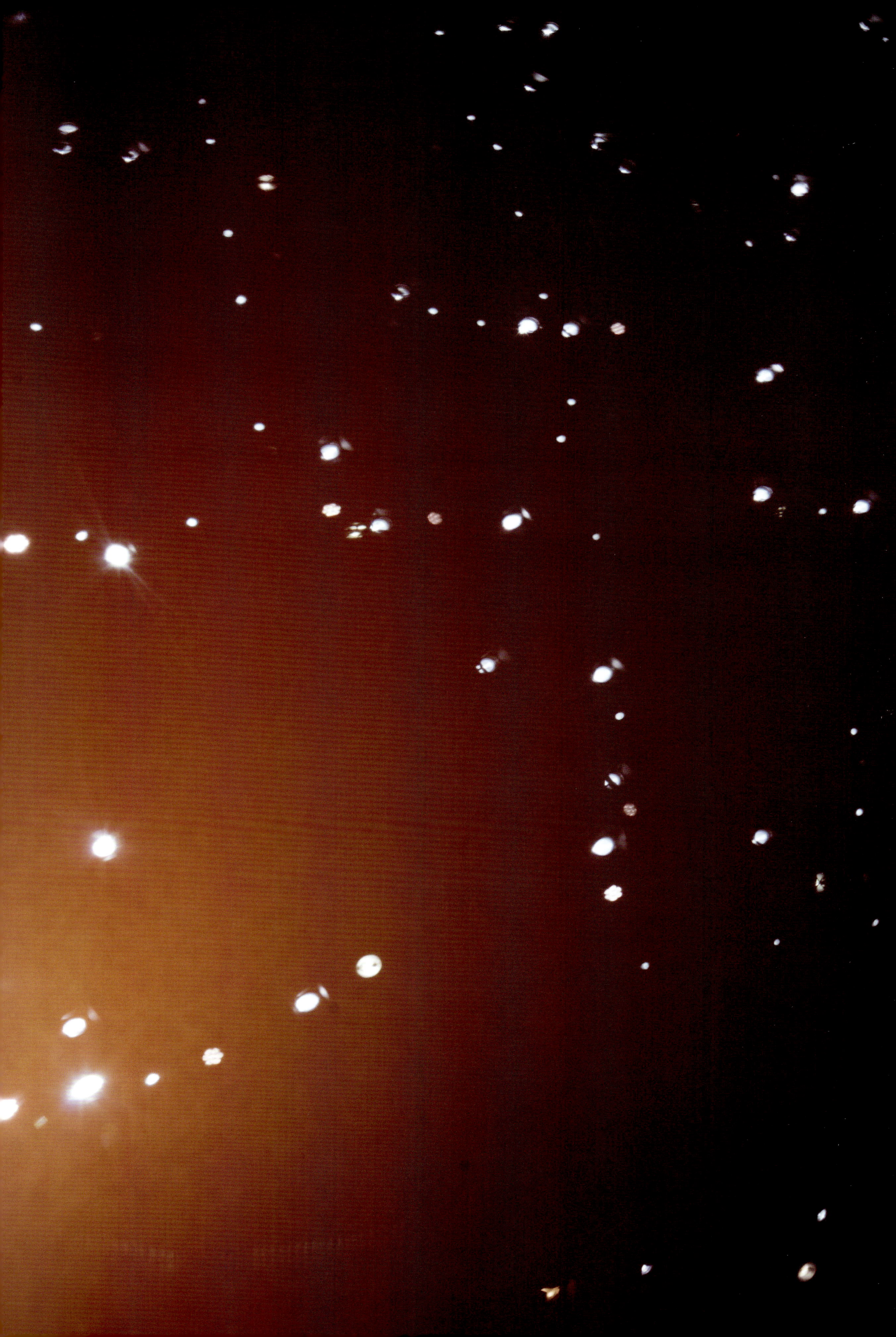

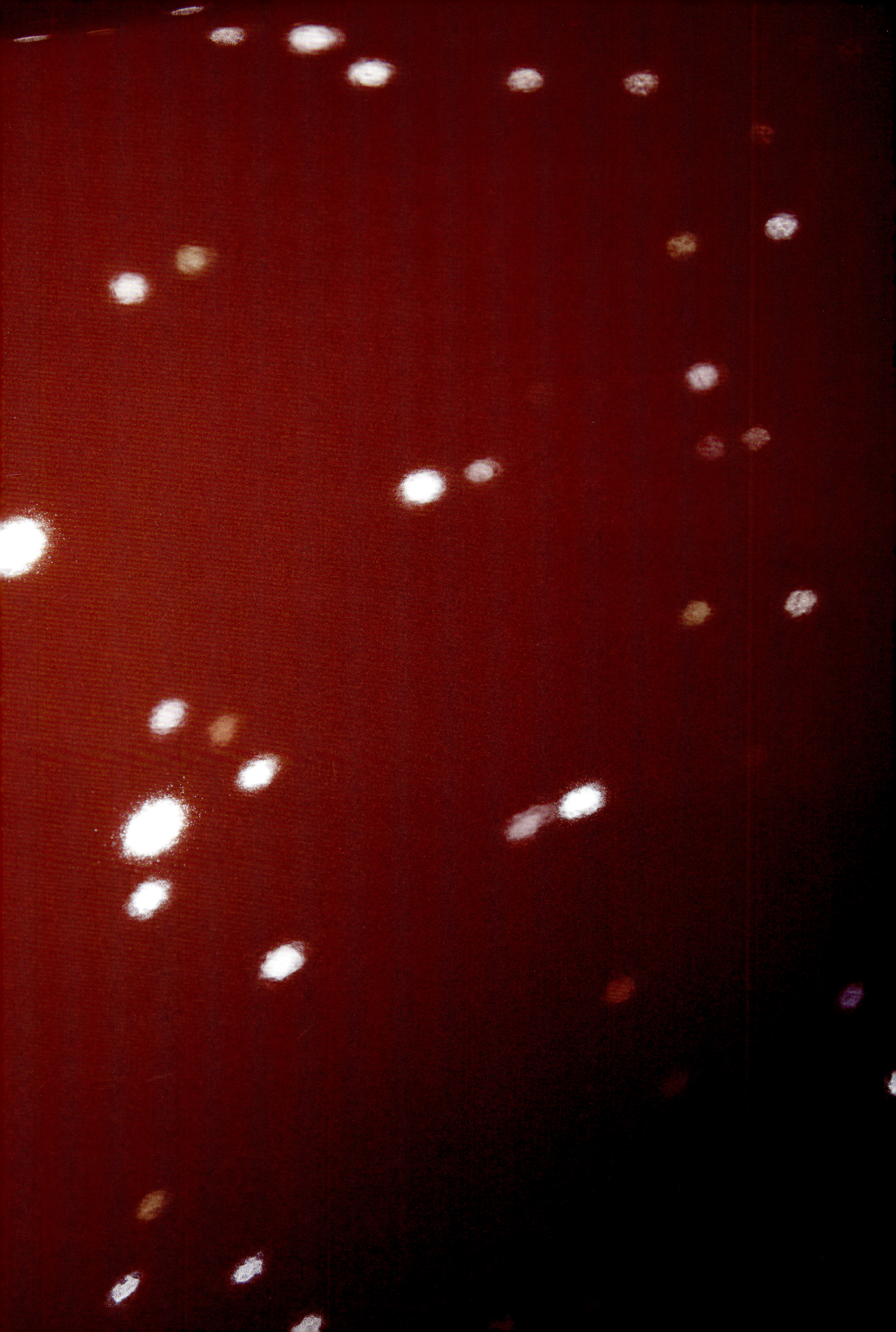

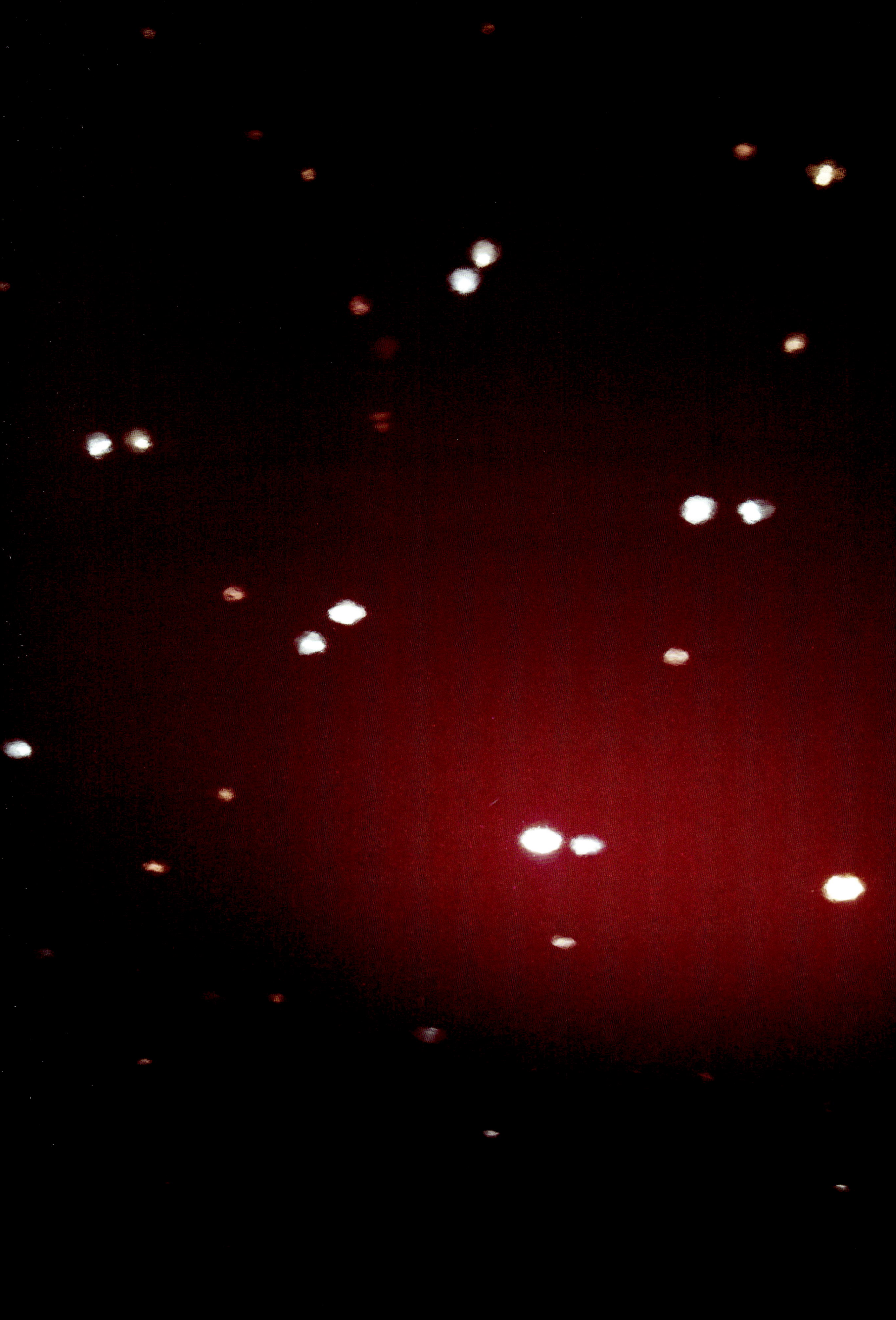

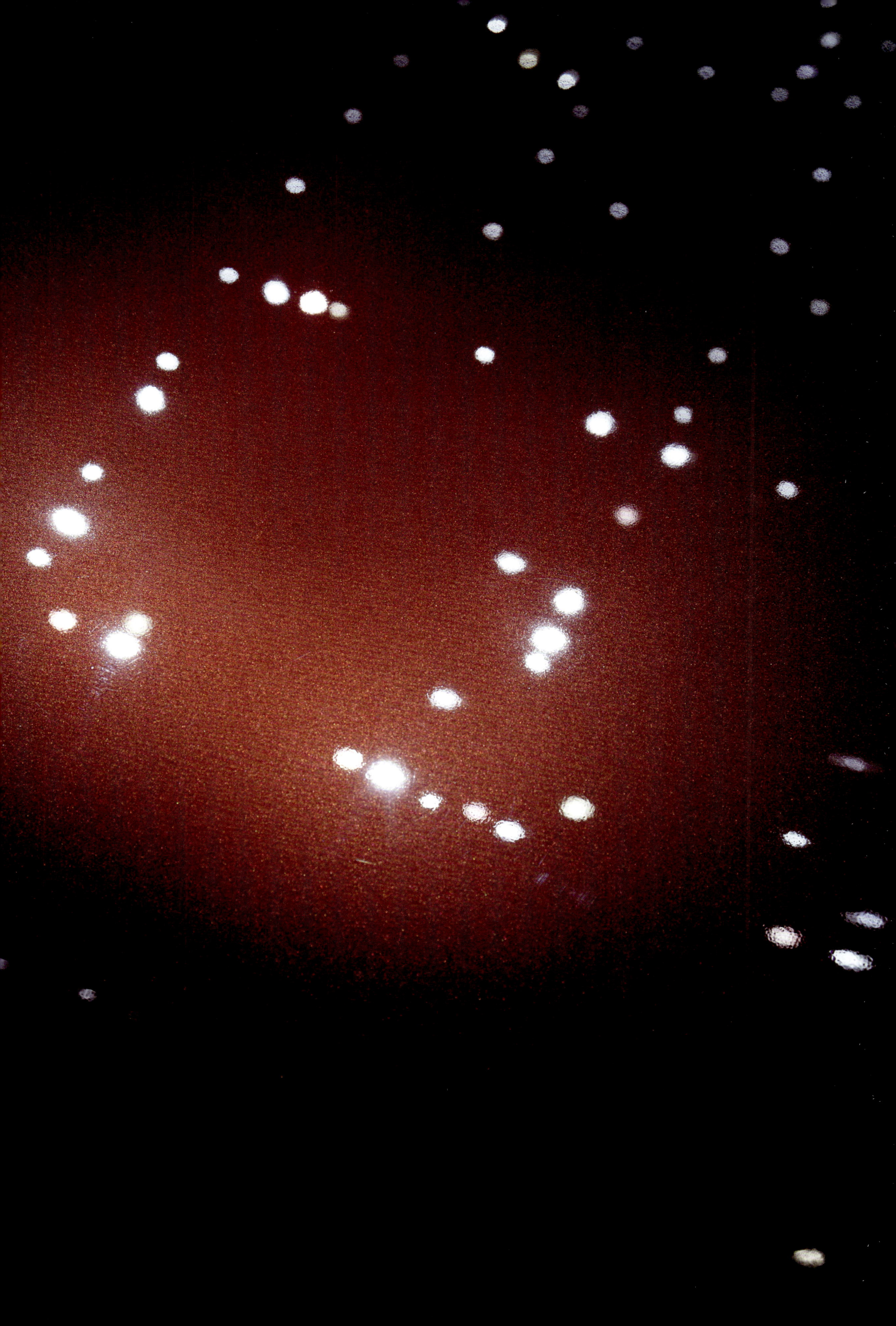

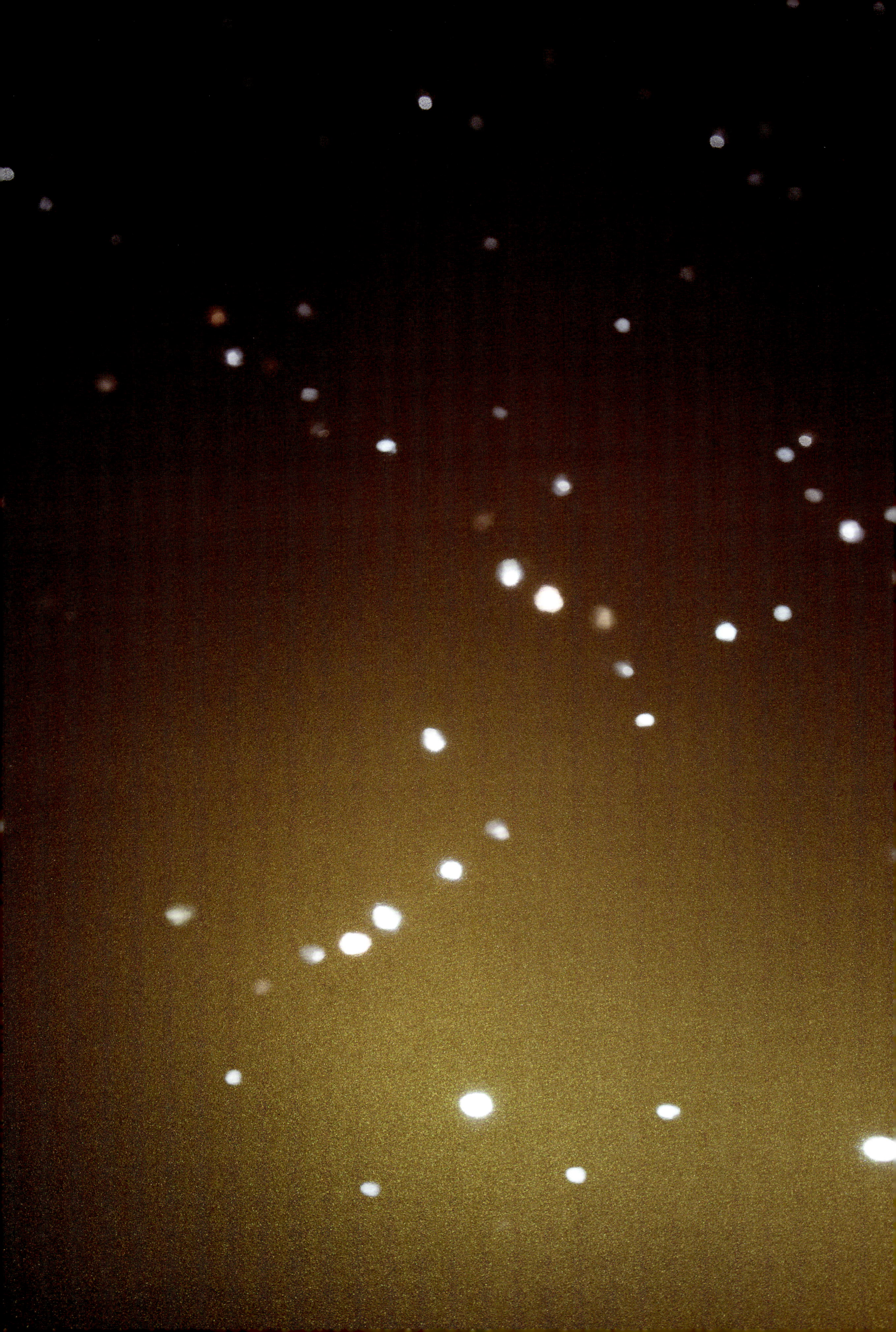

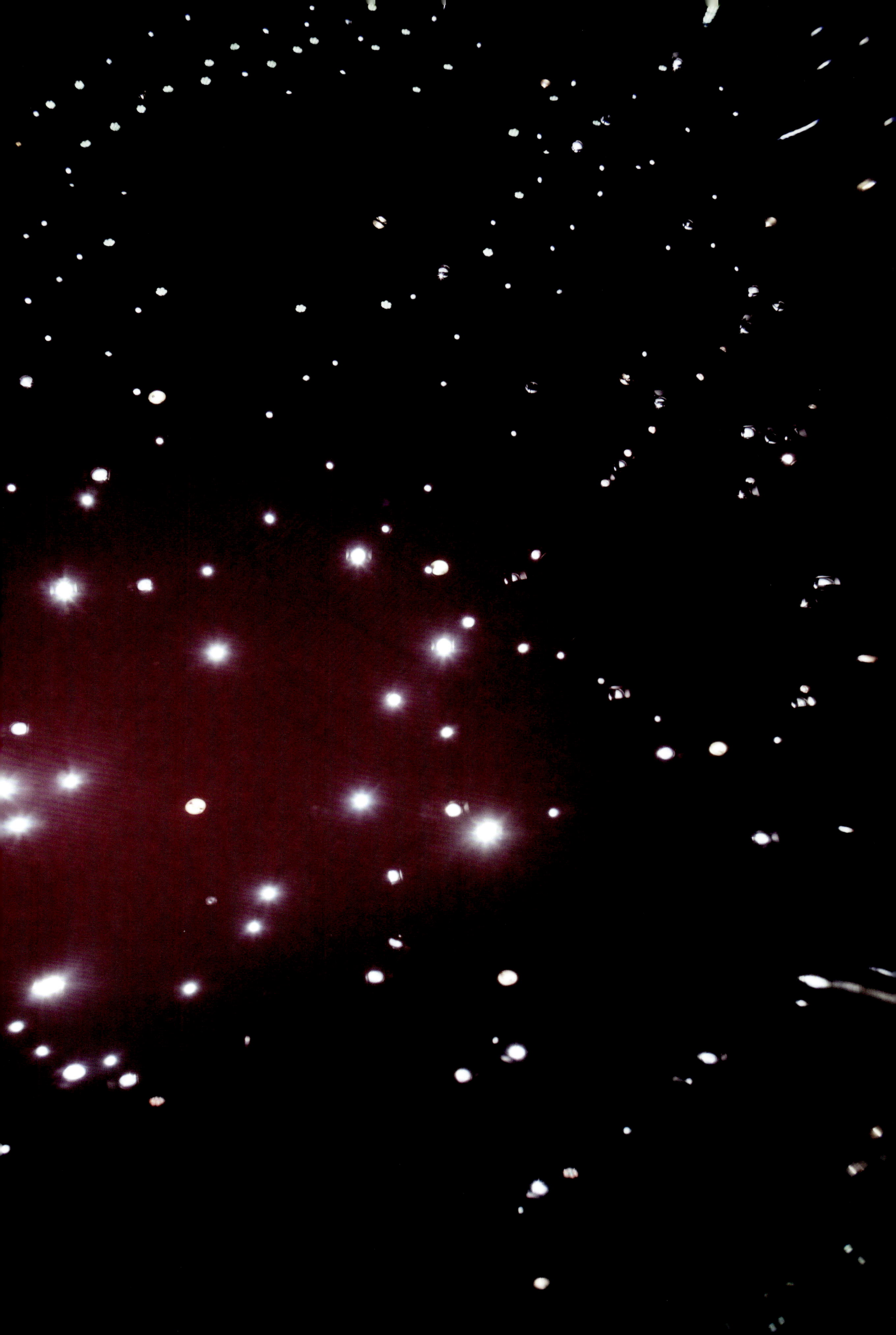

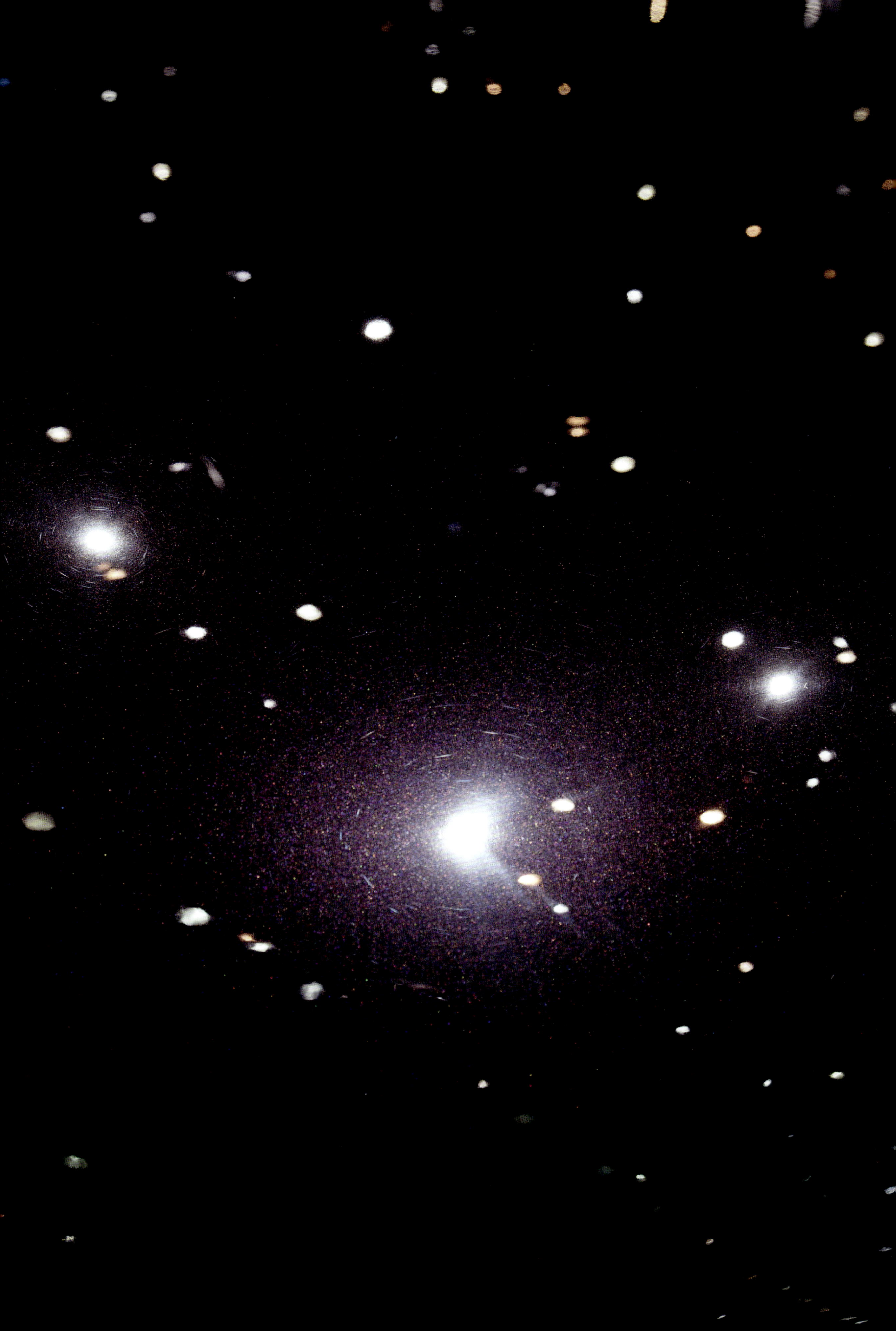

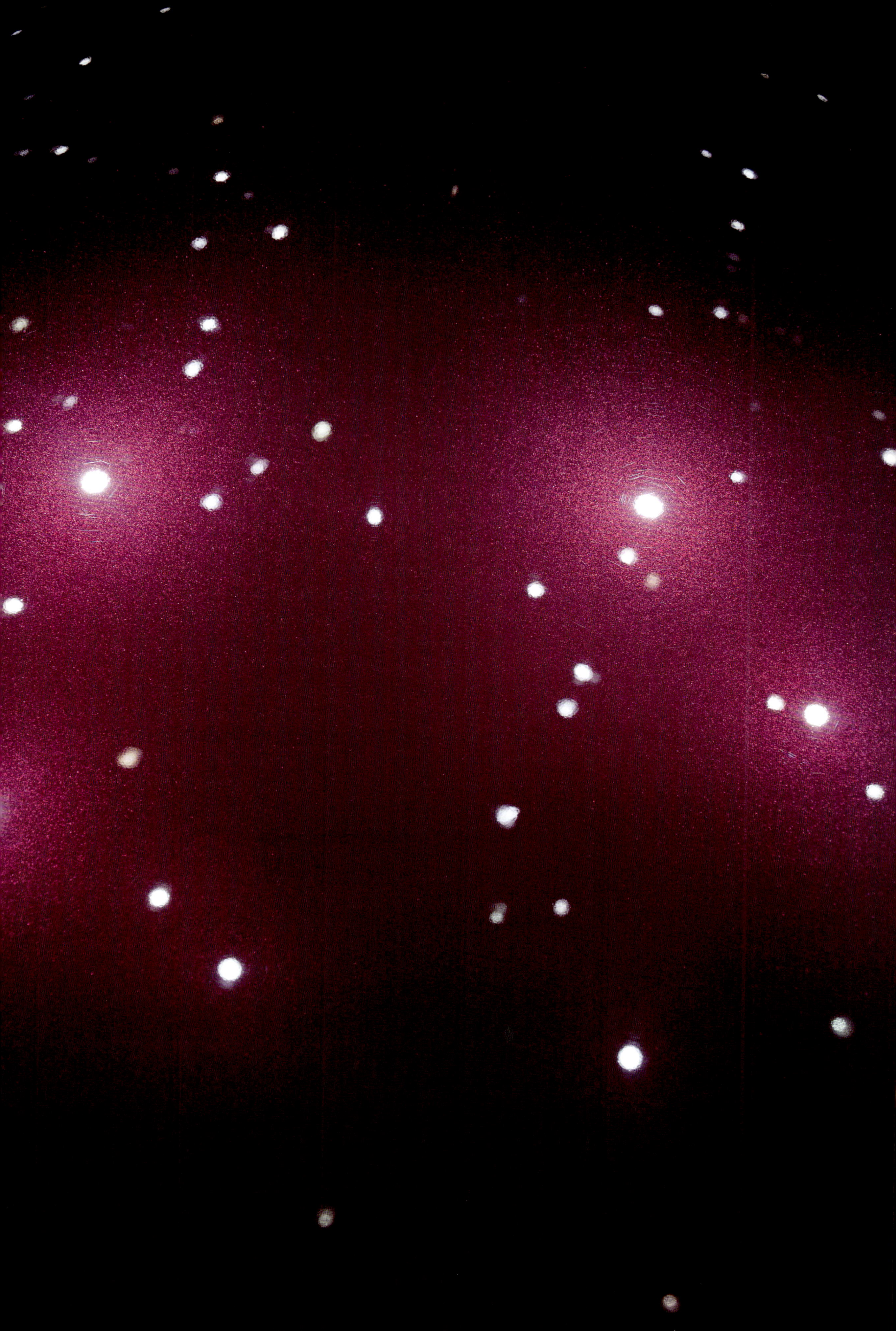

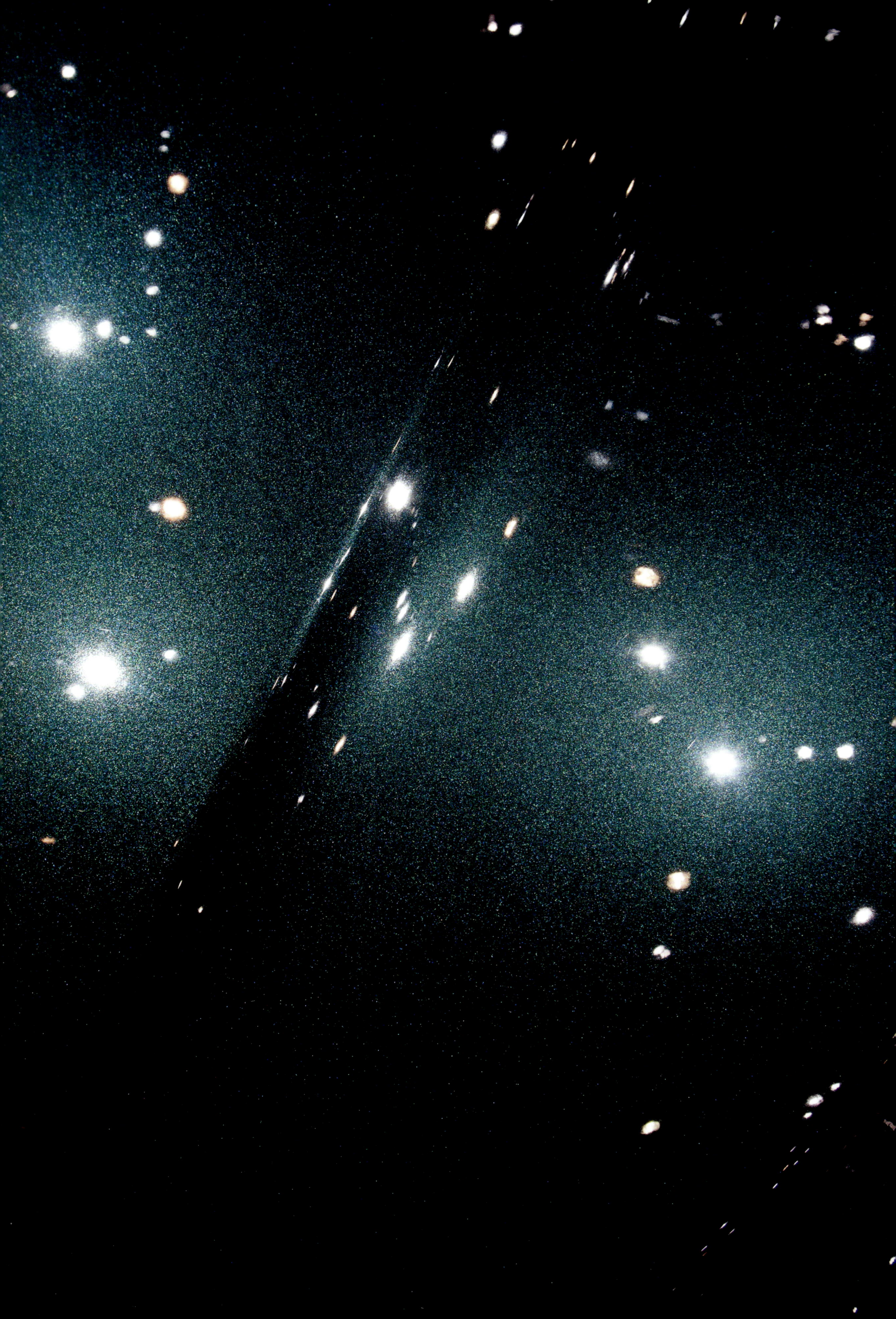

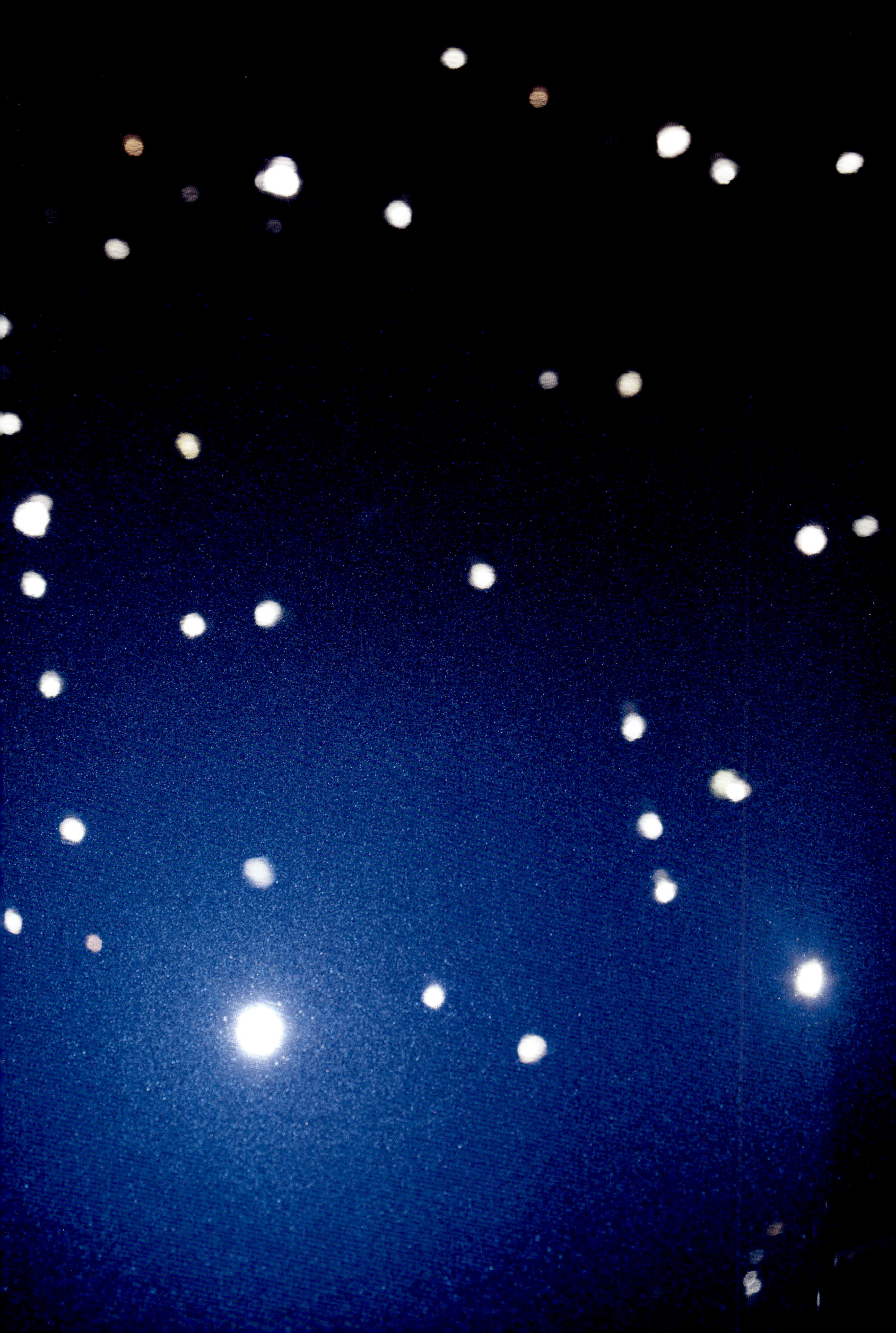

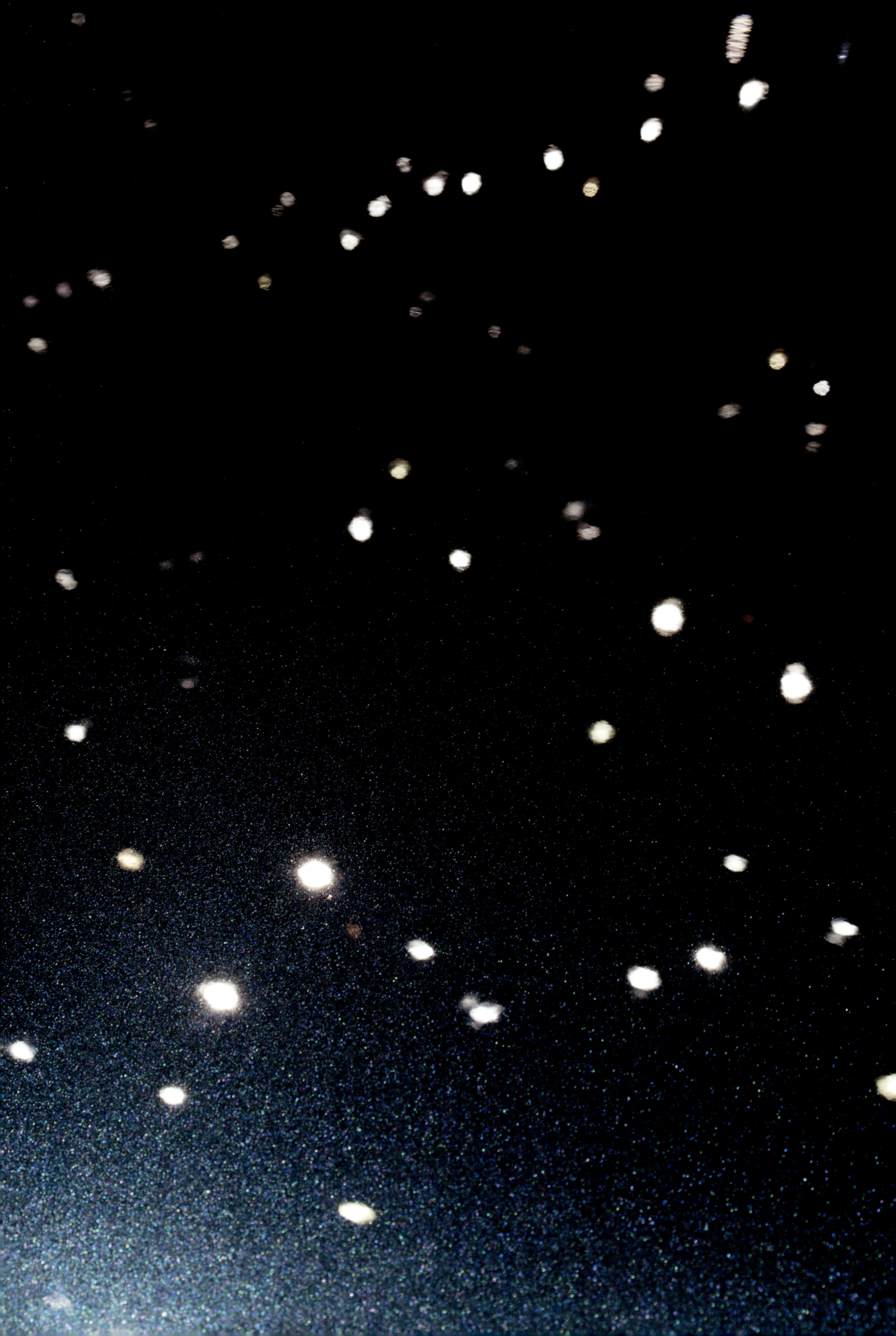

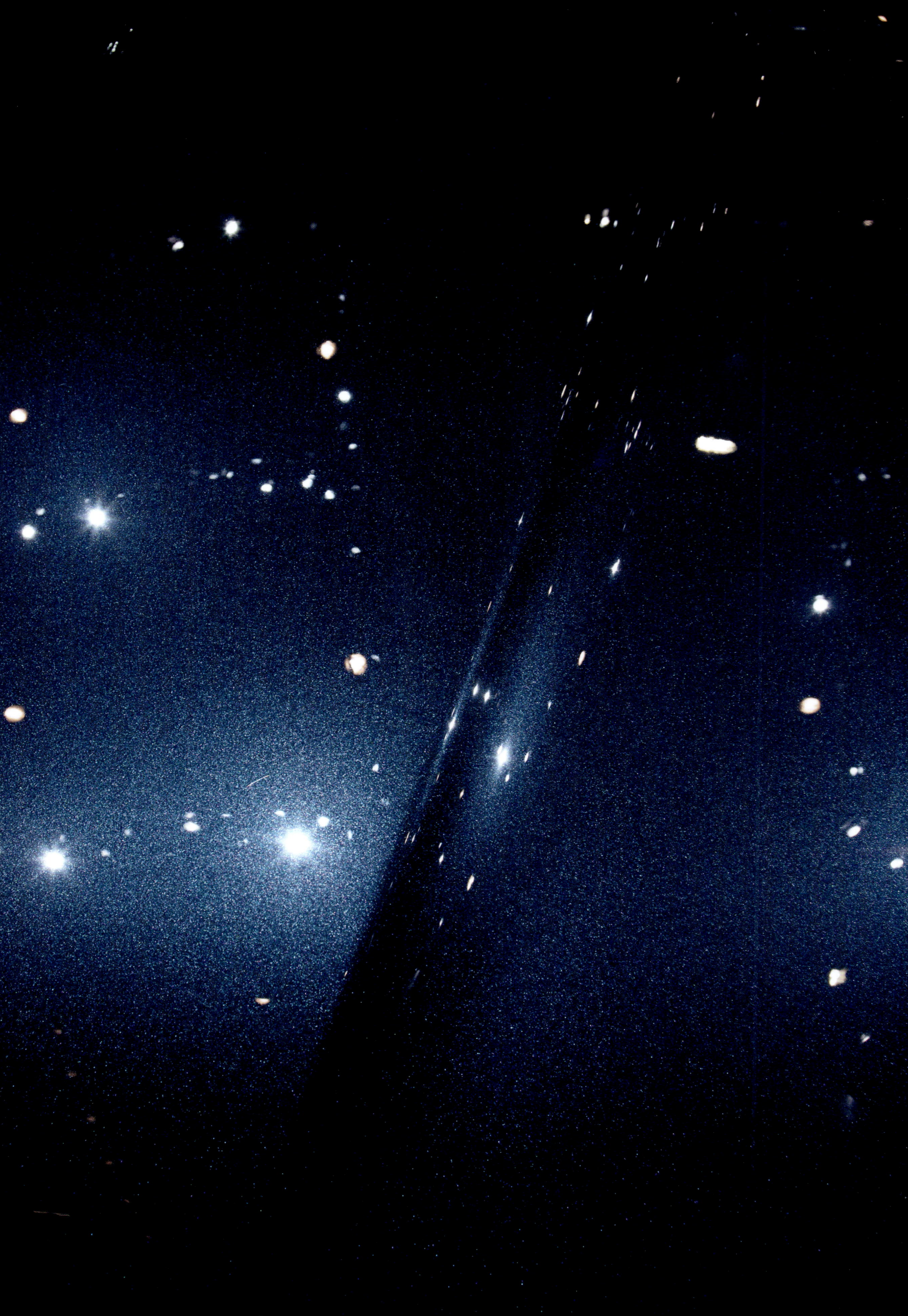

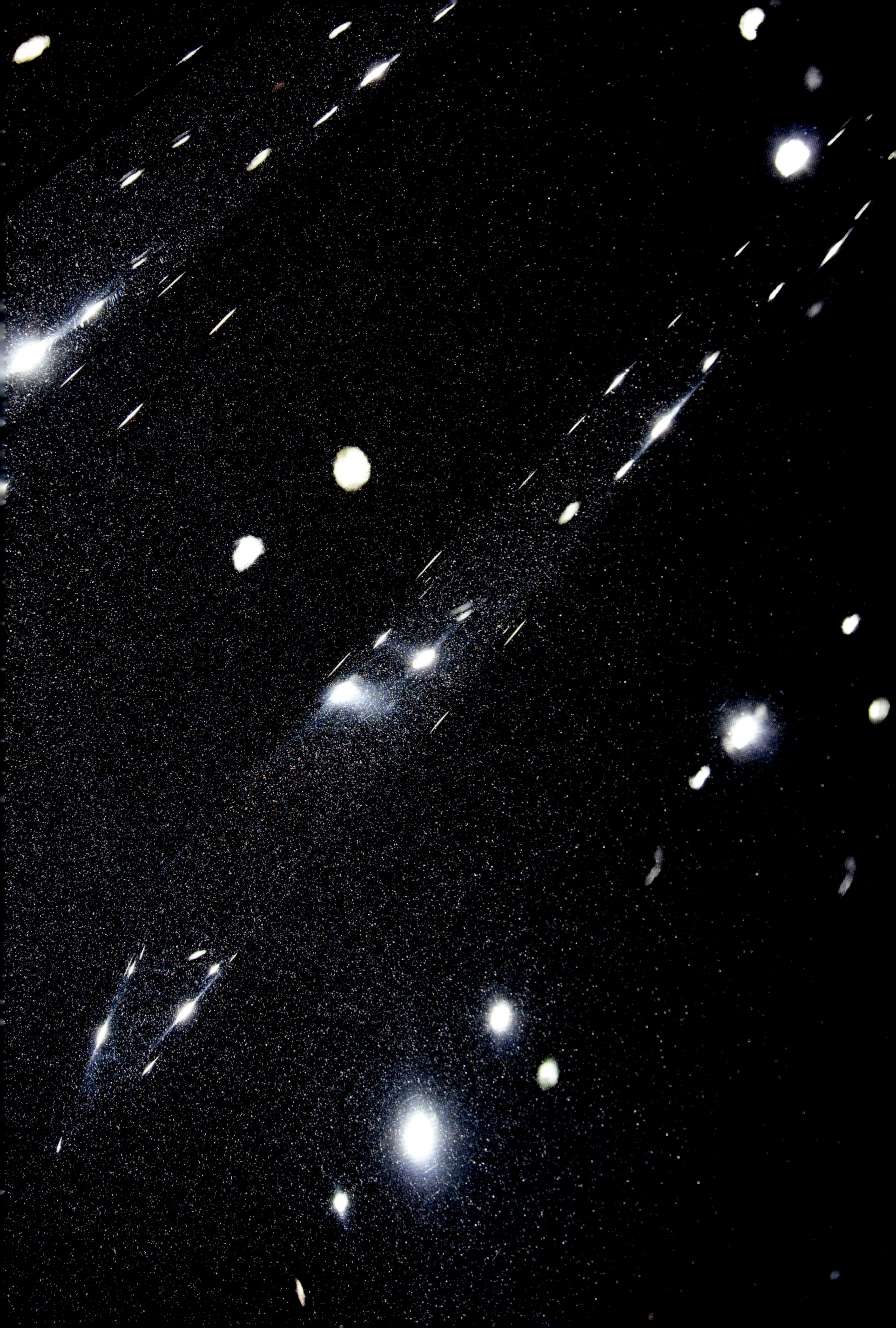

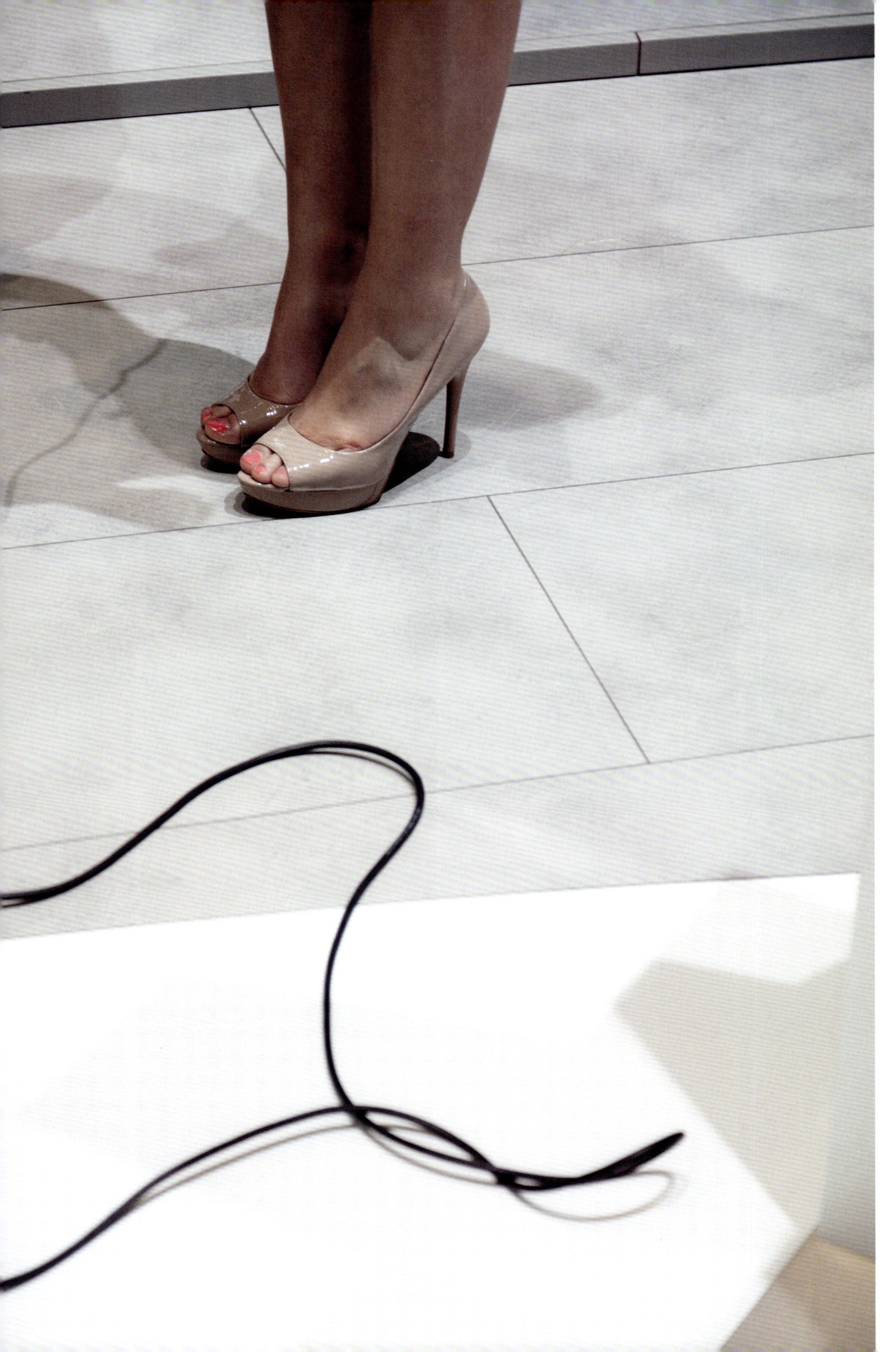

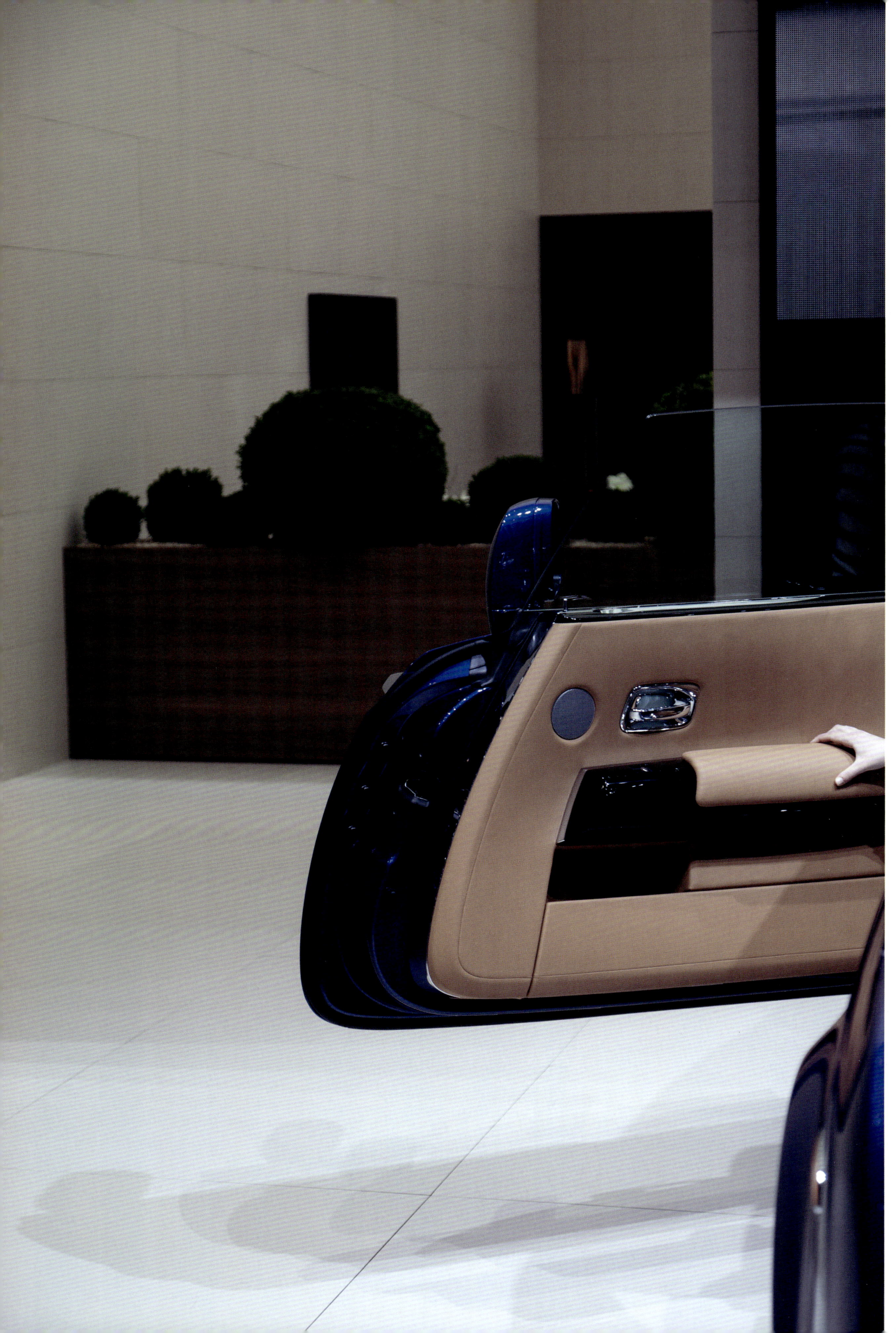

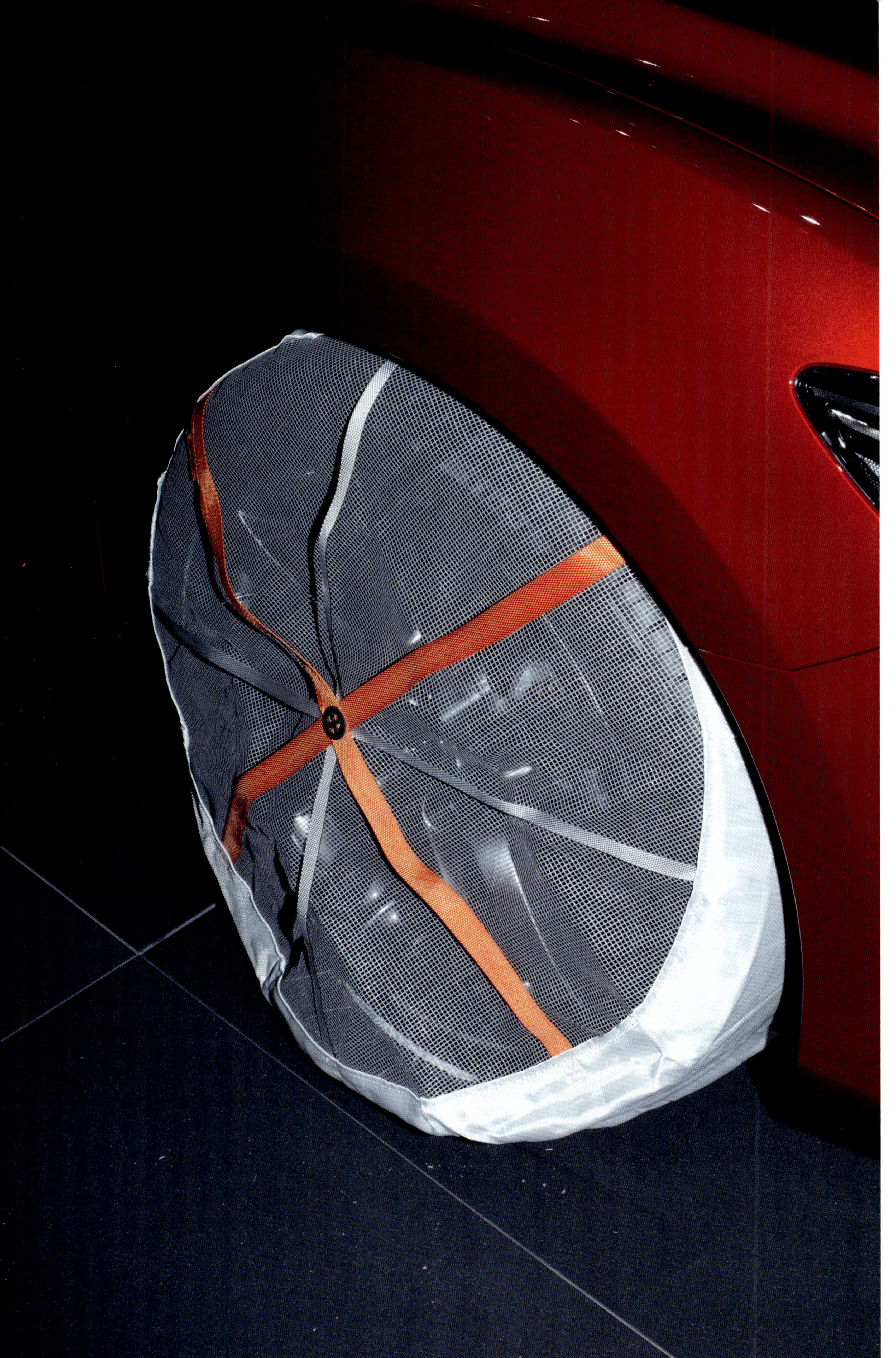

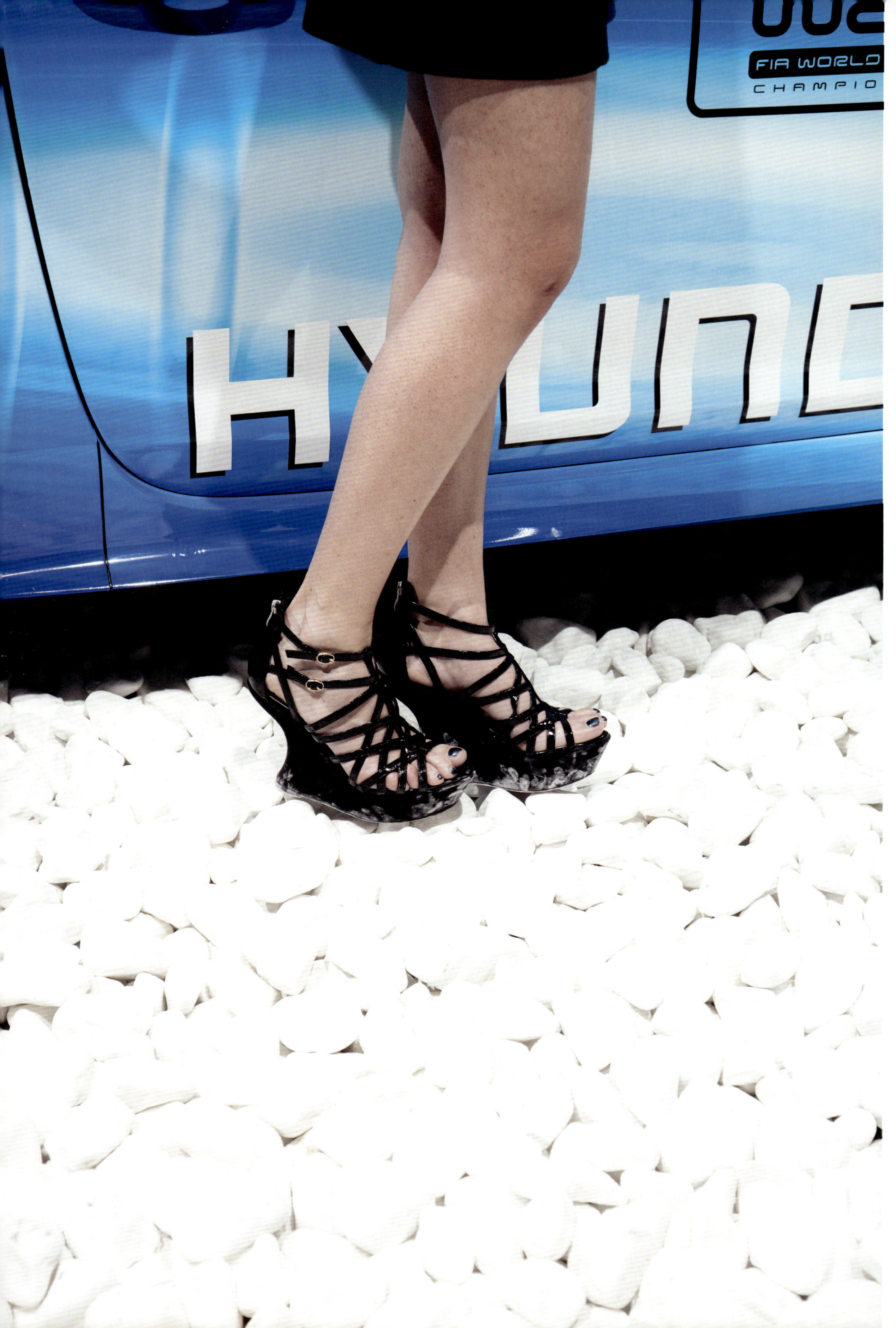
002
FIA WORLD
CHAMPIO
HYUND

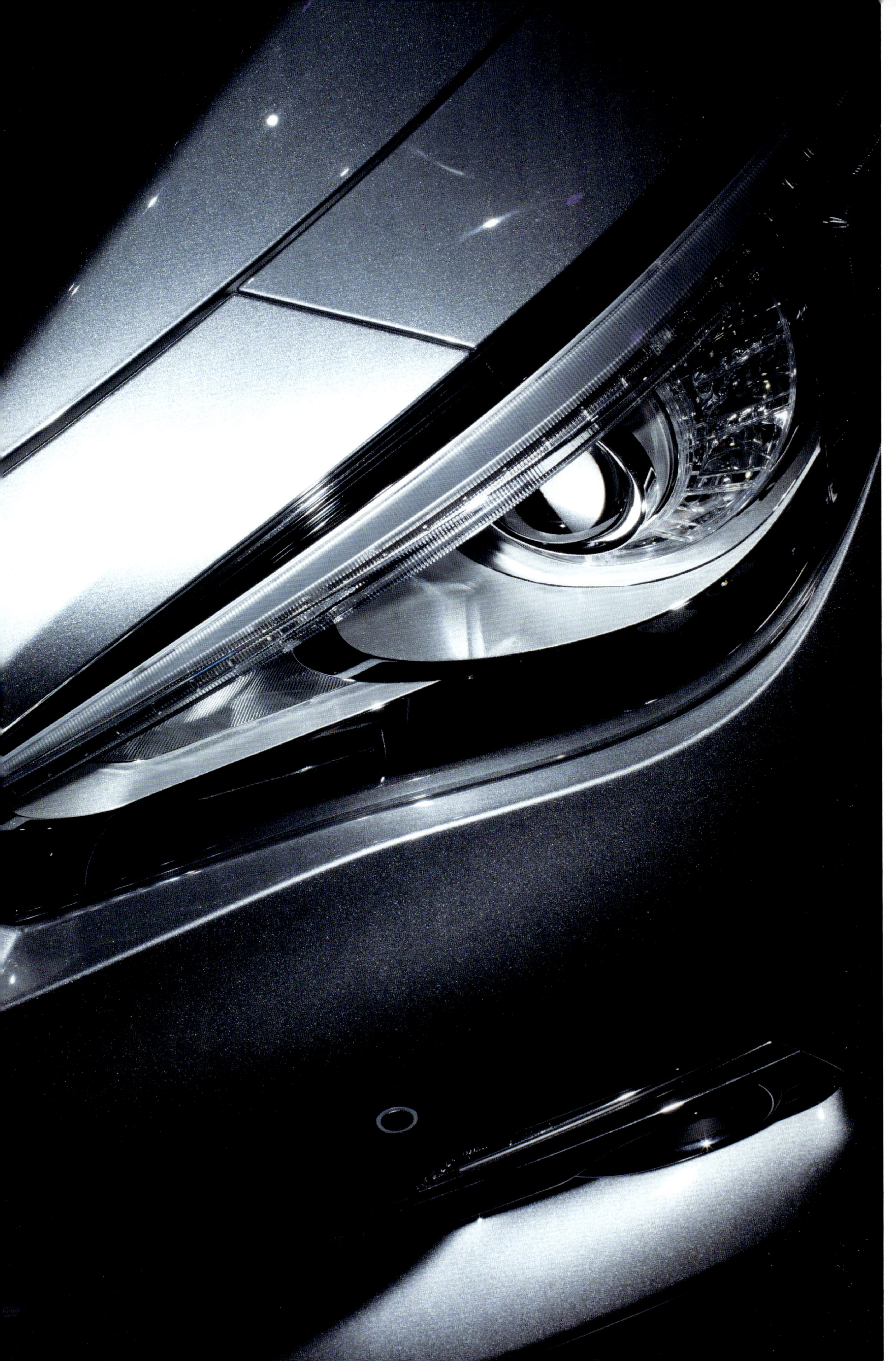

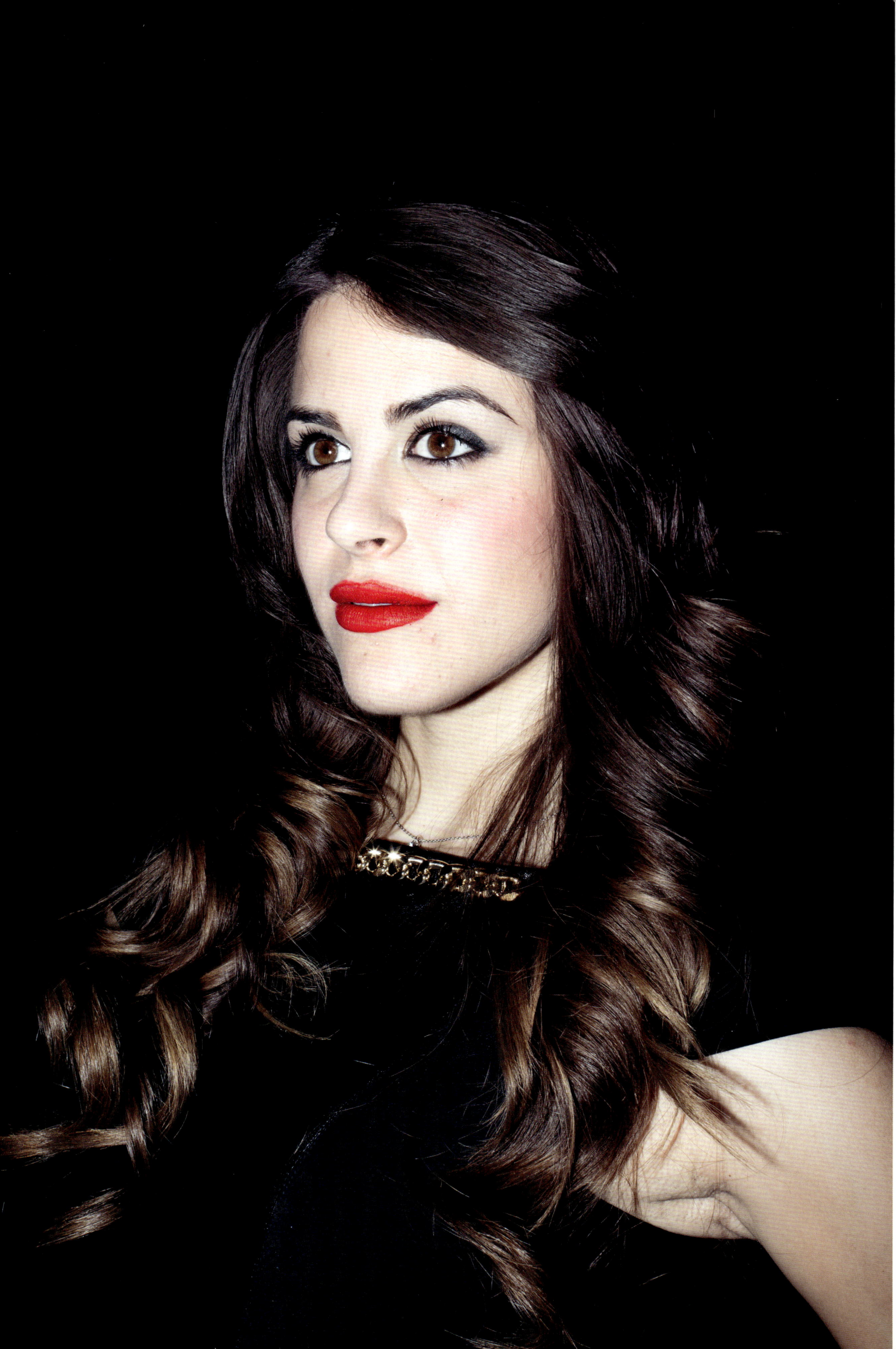

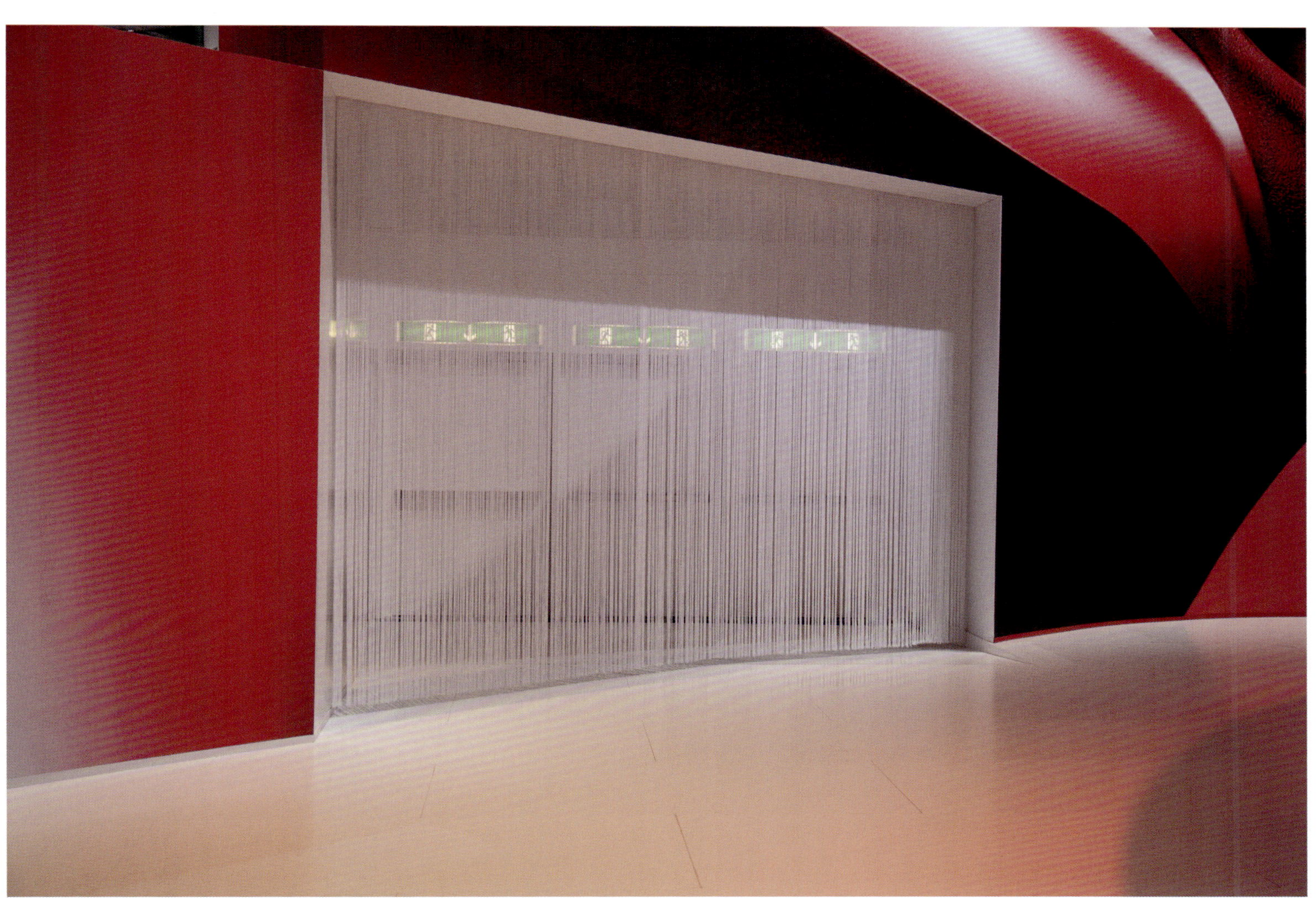

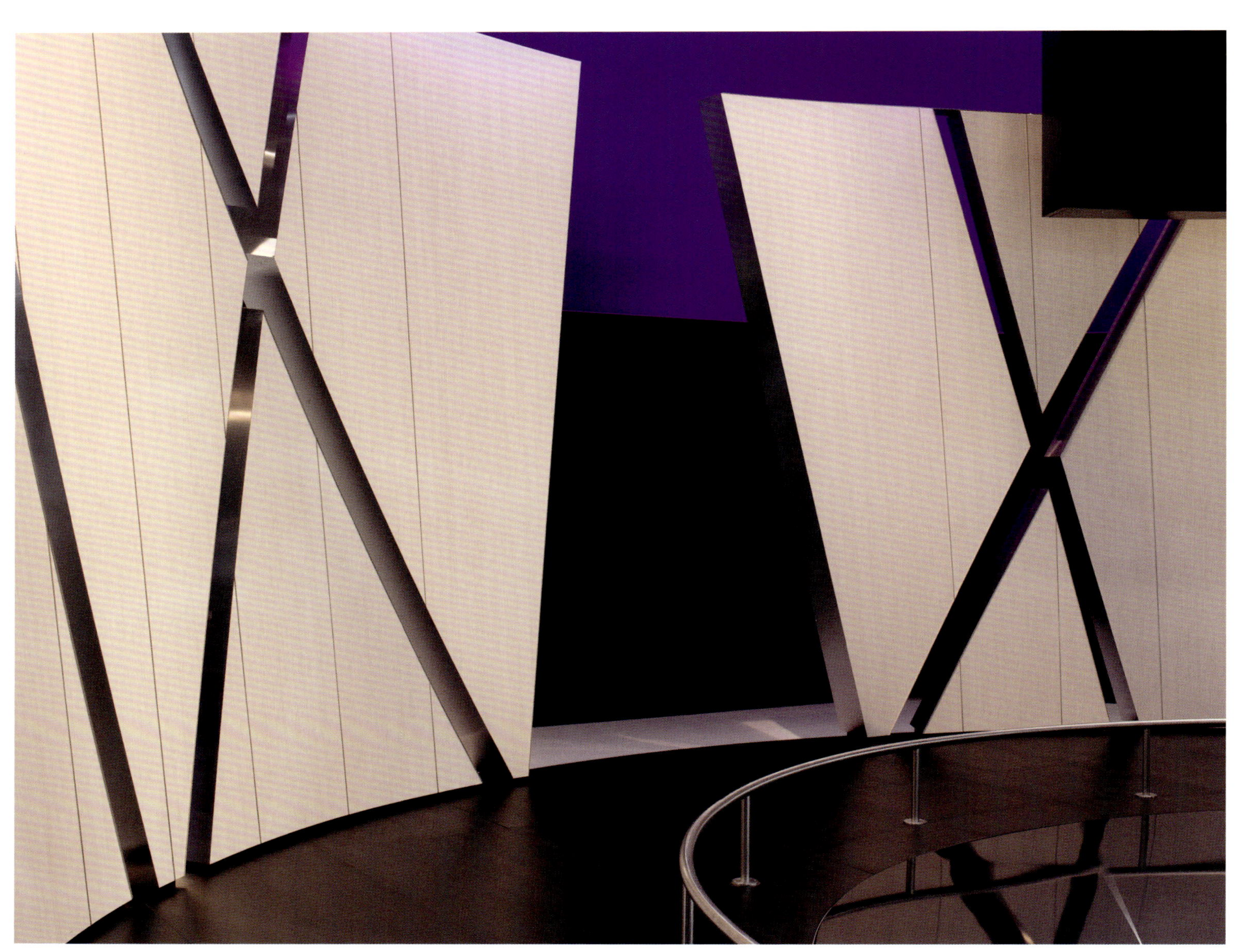

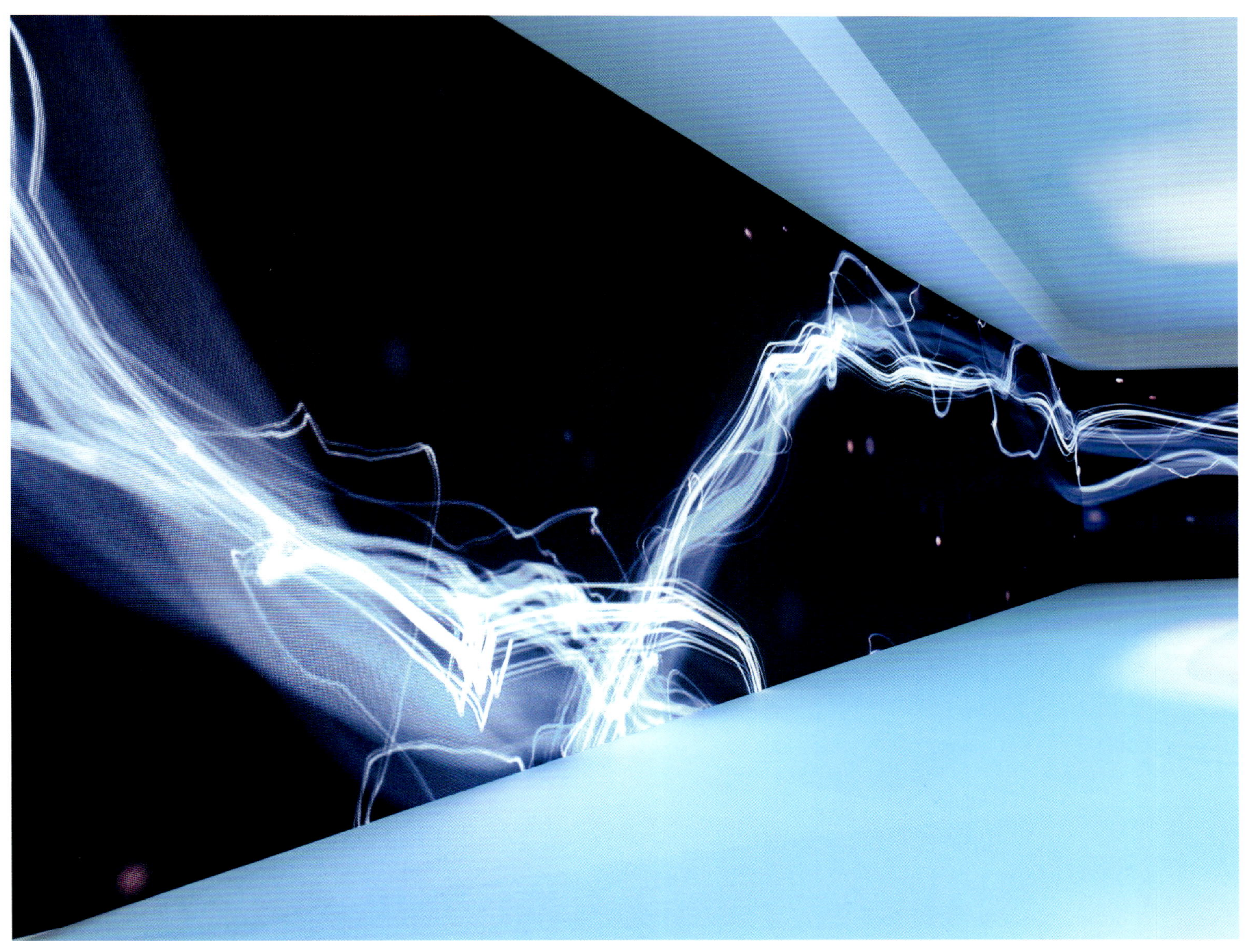

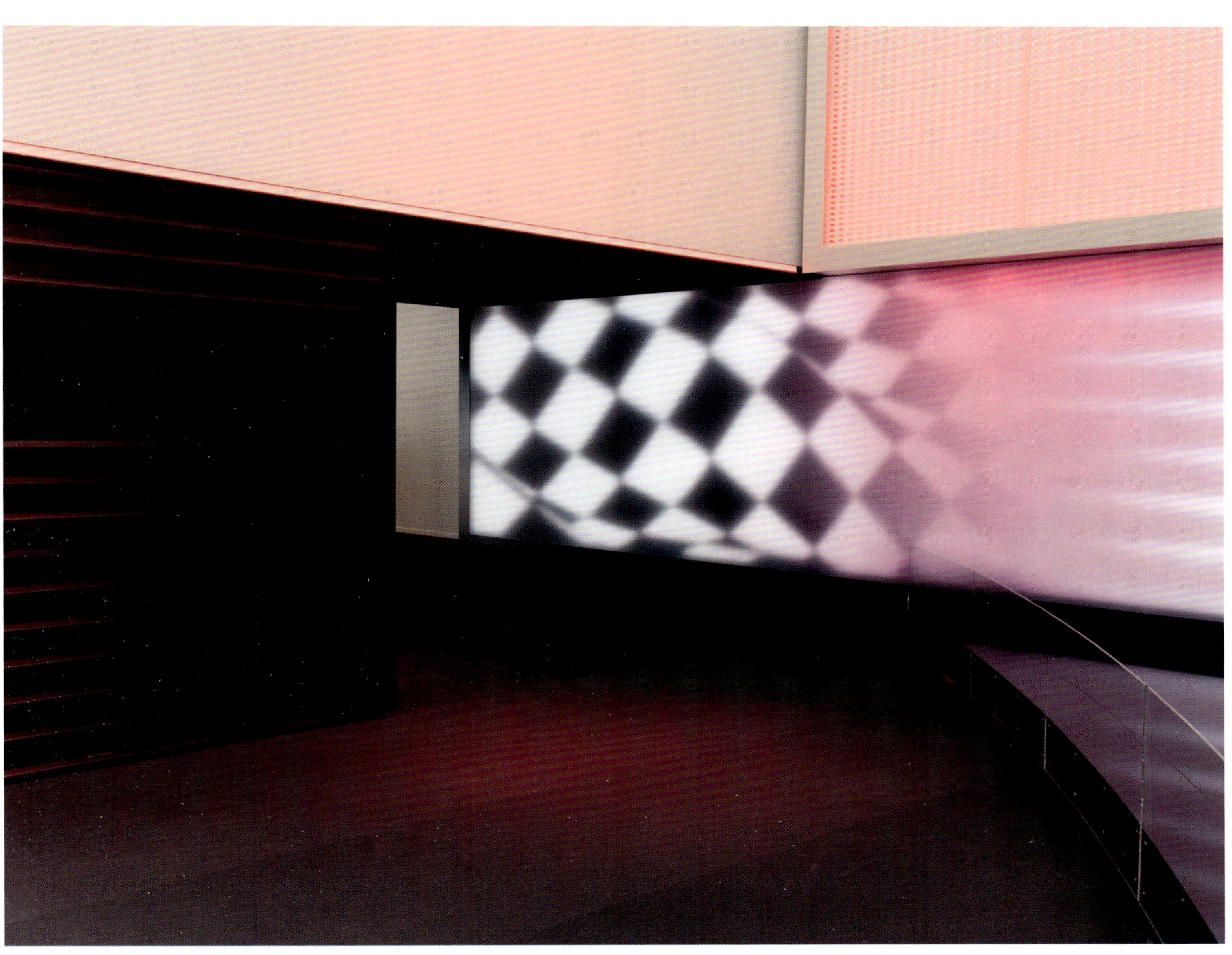

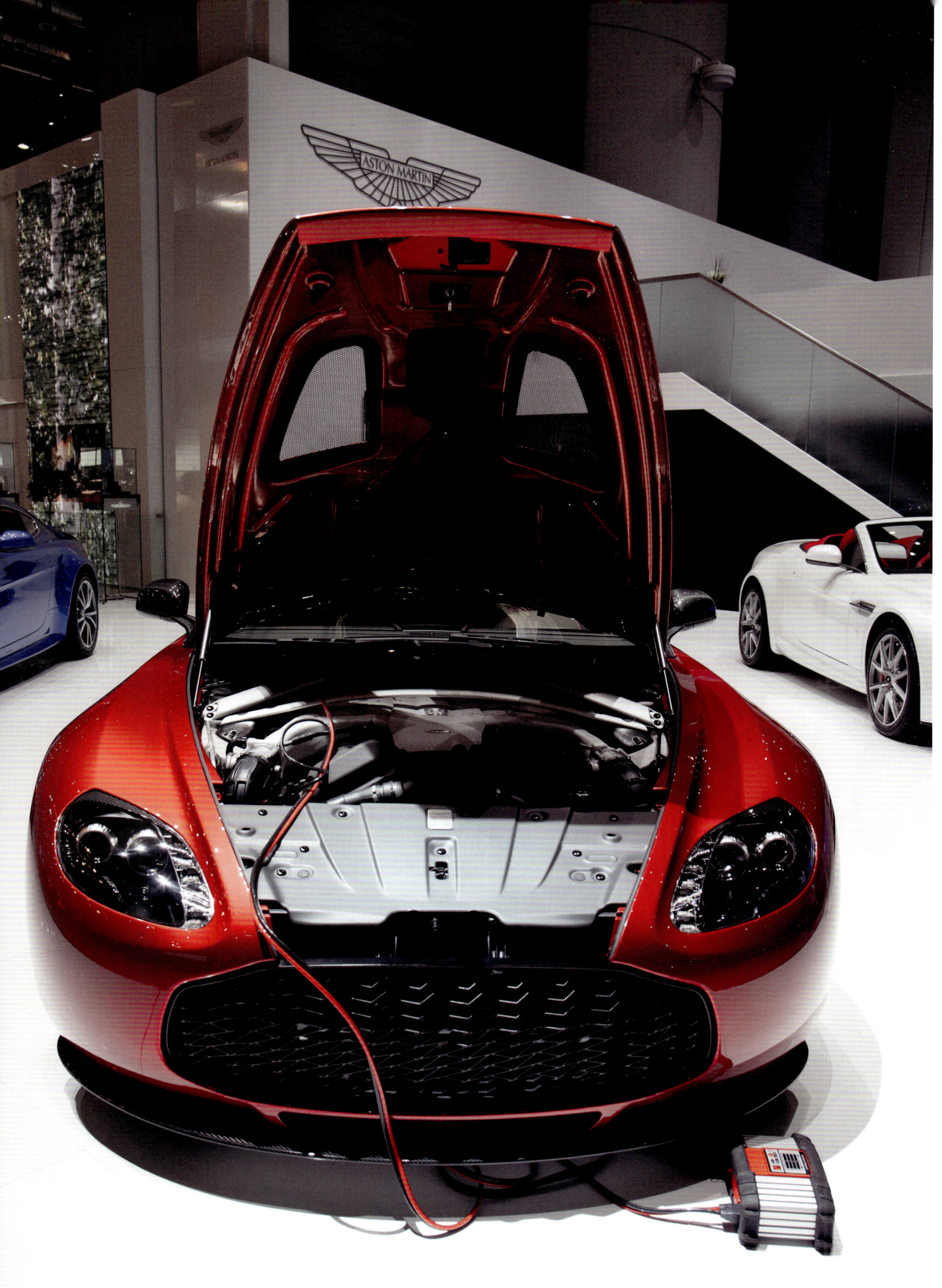

raffael waldner

salon

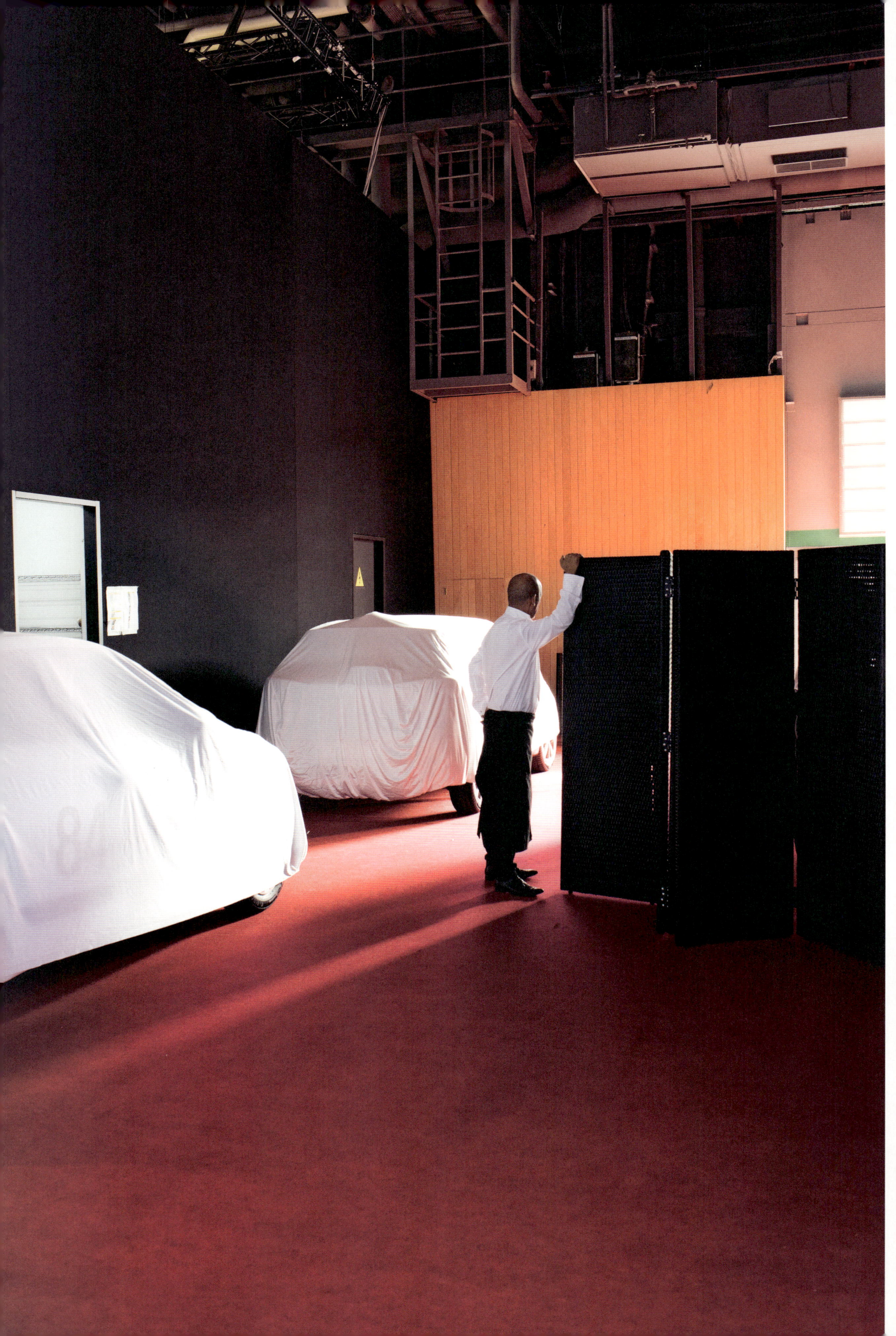

martin jaeggi

einleitung

Am Auto scheiden sich die Geister. Für die einen ist es Inbegriff von Komfort und Unabhängigkeit, eine beglückende Verbindung von Schönheit und Geschwindigkeit, von Design und Ingenieurskunst, ein untrügliches Ab Zeichen sozialen Status. Für die anderen ist es das Emblem des westlichen Konsumwahns und der damit einhergehenden Umweltzerstörung schlechthin, lebensgefährliches Spielzeug bornierter Vorstädter und testosterongesteuerter Raser, die sich den demokratischen Segnungen des öffentlichen Verkehrs verweigern. Die Widersprüche und Ambiguitäten einer ebenso technologiebesessenen wie -abhängigen Gegenwart scheinen sich exemplarisch zu verdichten in der Autokultur, ihren Phantasmen und Realitäten und bildhaft fassbar zu werden. Diesen Instanzen spürt Waldner in fotografischen Langzeitprojekten nach.

Ausgangspunkt dieser Recherche war 2005 die Arbeit *Sites*, die nächtliche Unfallorte nach dem Abtransport der verunglückten Fahrzeuge zeigt – gespenstisch leere Strassenstücke, auf denen nur Schleif- und Bremsspuren, auf den Boden gesprayte Markierungen, Ölschlieren und vereinzelte zurückgebliebene Gegenstände vom Unfall zeugen, nüchtern indexikalische Platzhalter des Schreckens, Vorboten der juristischen und versicherungsrechtlichen Abwicklung der Geschehnisse. Die Serie *Car Crash Studies*, an der Waldner von 2001 bis 2010 arbeitete, zeigt leere Unfallwracks auf Schrottplätzen, nachts aufgeblitzt aufgenommen, Umgebung und Kontext sind nur andeutungsweise sichtbar. Die Bilder wirken kühl und abstrakt skulptural; gerade so tritt aber im Kontrast die Wucht und Gewalttätigkeit des Unfalls hervor. Sie lassen die in der Technik immer schon angelegte Katastrophe augenscheinlich werden, den Tod als Fluchtpunkt der Exzesse des Materialismus. Es sind Chiffren für Vergänglichkeit, Vergeblichkeit und menschliche Hybris, Vanitas-Bilder für das 21. Jahrhundert.

Hat in den *Car Crash Studies* die Katastrophe die Versprechungen des Autos erbarmungslos kassiert, zeigt Waldner in *Salon* (2011–2016) nun spiegelbildlich das Auto als reines Ideal und Fetisch, der Wirklichkeit gänzlich entrückt. Er greift dabei wiederum auf Strategien der Reduktion zurück. Waldner fotografierte in Autosalons vor der Eröffnung, das Publikum bleibt unsichtbar, der jahrmarktartige Rummel wird ausgeblendet, wir sehen fast menschen-

martin jaeggi

foreword

There are two schools of thought when it comes to cars: for some, they are the epitome of convenience and independence, a felicitous combination of speed and beauty, design and engineering skill, an infallible token of social status; for others, they symbolize par excellence the West's mania for consumption and the accompanying destruction of the environment, and are nothing less than the lethal toys of small-minded suburbanites and testosterone-fuelled speed merchants who eschew the democratic benefits of public transport. The contradictions and ambiguities of the modern age, obsessed with – yet equally dependent upon – technology, seem to be summarized in exemplary fashion by the car culture, its phantasms and realities, and thus become comprehensible from a visual perspective. Raffael Waldner investigates these phenomena in his long-term photographic projects.

The starting point for this examination was the 2005 work entitled *Sites*, which shows the locations of nighttime accidents once the vehicles involved in the crash have been taken away. Eerily empty stretches of road where the only things to bear witness to these misfortunes are skid marks and gouges in the tarmac, lines sprayed on the ground, streaks of oil, and occasional objects that remain after the accident: soberly indicative placeholders of horror, harbingers of the legal and insurance complexities that these events have set in train. The series *Car Crash Studies*, which Waldner worked on from 2001 to 2010, shows empty write-offs in junkyards, taken by flashlight at night, with the context and surroundings only vaguely hinted at. The images come across as cold and abstractly sculptural; however, it is particularly by way of this contrast that the impact and violence of the accident becomes evident. The photographs reveal the disaster that has always been lurking within the technology, death as the vanishing point of the excesses of materialism. They are ciphers for transience, futility, and hubris, vanitas paintings for the 21st century.

In *Car Crash Studies*, disaster has mercilessly repudiated the promises made by cars; *Salon* (2011–2016) now shows us its mirror image, namely the car purely as an ideal

leere Hallen und Stände. Die Autos oder Teile davon sind oft noch mit Schutzstoffen verhüllt wie Götzenbilder, die dem Blick der Gläubigen ausschliesslich an hohen Festtagen preisgegeben werden. Er zeigt nur Teilansichten der Fahrzeuge und ihres Innenlebens – gleissend, glänzend, glatt, perfekt ausgearbeitet bis ins Detail, Preziosen der Ingenieurskunst. Die verführerischen Oberflächen der Autos finden ihre Fortsetzung in den schimmernden Kunststoffoberflächen der raumschiffartigen Ausstellungsarchitektur, die die abgerundeten aerodynamischen Formen der Fahrzeuge wieder aufnimmt – ein hermetisch in sich geschlossenes visuelles System, in dem nichts mehr an Natur erinnert, nicht einmal die in Gewächshäusern gezüchteten Blumenarrangements. Nichts lässt an den Verkehr und seine alltäglichen Widrigkeiten denken, an das Ende der Autos auf dem Schrottplatz als sinnentleertes Material ohne symbolischen Mehrwert – das Auto wird als zweckfreie Skulptur inszeniert, als rein ästhetisches Phänomen.

Dazwischen streut Waldner Bilder der Hostessen, die die Besucher empfangen – junge Frauen, gepflegt und perfekt geschminkt, in eleganten Kleidern und hochhackigen Schuhen. Jede von ihnen entspricht den von Werbung, Massenmedien und Modemagazinen hochgehaltenen Schönheitsidealen – als seien sie in einem genetischen Laboratorium entworfen und hergestellt worden, biologische Entsprechungen der ausgestellten Autos. Sie strahlen eine unnahbare, sterile Erotik aus, die auf der harten Arbeit unablässiger Körperoptimierung beruht. Sie richten sich als Objekte für den männlichen Blick her, als potenzielle Statussymbole wie die Autos, deren Ideal von Perfektion sie durch ihr Auftreten unterstreichen. Gleichzeitig lässt sie ihre normkonforme Schönheit so ersetzbar und verfügbar wie Autos erscheinen. Fast macht es den Anschein, als würde Waldner den Tempel eines futuristischen Phalluskults zeigen, mit dem Auto als Talisman ewiger Potenz und den Hostessen als dessen unnahbare Priesterinnen. Wir sehen eine perfekt dargebotene Männerphantasie, ein uneinlösbares Versprechen von Oberflächenperfektion, das in Frustration enden wird – der Lack wird bröckeln, das Metall rosten, das Fleisch altern. Die Unbarmherzigkeit der Zeit, die der Autosalon zugunsten einer Illusion makelloser Gegenwart auszublenden sucht, wird siegen – wiederum ein Vanitas-Motiv.

Zugleich stellen Waldners Bilder die Frage nach der Schönheit. Er untersucht eine besonders ausgeprägte Instanz des Schönheitskanons der Konsumkultur, ohne deren Versuchungen zu unterliegen, spielt mit ihr und hält sie zugleich auf Distanz. Er zeigt ein Labyrinth perfekter Oberflächen, das sich letzt-

and fetish, utterly divorced from reality. In doing so, Waldner once again resorts to strategies of reduction. His photographs were taken at motor shows before they opened: the visiting public remains invisible, the funfairlike razzmatazz has been edited out, and we see halls and stands that are almost devoid of human beings. The cars – or parts of them – are often veiled in protective coverings, like religious idols that are exclusively exposed to the adoring gaze of the faithful on high days and holidays. He shows only partial views of the vehicles and their interiors – gleaming, sparkling, smooth, perfectly finished to the very last detail, precious jewels of the art of engineering. The cars' seductive surfaces are continued in the shimmering plastic of the spacecraft-like architecture which mimics the rounded aerodynamic forms of the vehicles themselves: a hermetically sealed visual system in which nothing is reminiscent of nature, not even the flower arrangements that have been painstakingly cultivated in hothouses. There is nothing to remind us of traffic and its everyday trials and tribulations, of the final resting place of cars in the junkyard, where the materials of which they are composed lack any meaning or symbolic added value – the car is staged as sculpture for sculpture's sake, a purely aesthetic phenomenon.

Waldner intersperses this with pictures of the hostesses who greet visitors: young women, immaculately groomed and with perfect makeup, elegantly dressed, and wearing highheeled shoes. Each of them corresponds to the idealized beauty that is promulgated by advertising, fashion magazines, and the rest of the mass media, as if they had been designed and manufactured in a genetic laboratory, biological counterparts of the cars on show. They radiate an aloof and sterile eroticism that the hard labor of ceaseless body optimization has struggled to create. They pose as objects for men to stare at, potential status symbols just like the cars whose ideal of perfection they underscore by their appearance. At the same time, their ubiquitous availability and conformity to what is customarily perceived as beauty suggests they could be replaced in exactly the same way as the cars they adorn. We almost get the impression that Waldner is showing us the temple of a futuristic cult of the phallus, with the car as the talisman of eternal potency and the hostesses as its unapproachable priestesses. What we see here is a perfectly depicted male fantasy, an irredeemable promise of superficial flawlessness that will end in frustration: the paint

lich in Leere erschöpft, weil es die Zeit leugnet. Schönheit gerinnt hier zu blosser Formel und Norm. Implizit stellen die Bilder die Frage, worin eine andere Definition von Schönheit heute liegen könnte oder ob der Begriff sich in der Warenkultur erschöpft hat. Darin liegt ihre Sprengkraft.

will blister, the metal rust, and the flesh age. The ruthlessness of time, which the motor show endeavors to banish in favor of an immaculate yet illusory present, will ultimately triumph – yet another vanitas theme.

At the same time, Waldner's images question our notion of beauty. He examines a particularly pronounced example of what consumer culture typically considers to be beautiful, but without succumbing to its temptations; he plays with it and simultaneously keeps it at arm's length. He shows us a labyrinth of perfect surfaces that are ultimately doomed because they deny the march of time. This is where beauty loses its vitality and fluidity, becoming merely formulaic and standardized. The images implicitly ask where we might find a different definition of beauty today, or whether the term has lost all meaning in a culture that venerates consumer goods. This is what makes these photographs so explosive.

jürgen häusler

vom niedergang eines mythos

Raffael Waldners Fotografien rufen es uns augenblicklich ins Bewusstsein. Sobald wir auch nur eines ihrer Logos sehen, geschieht es. Selbst wenn wir ihre Formen nur erahnen, auch wenn wir lediglich gestalterische oder technische Details erhaschen, geschieht es: Menschen verfallen dem Mythos erfolgreicher Automobilmarken.

Diese Marken prägen die vergangenen 100 Jahre. Sie lassen den Traum der individuellen Mobilität träumen. Sie verkörpern die Freiheit des modernen Menschen. Sie schaffen persönliche Identitäten, sind unmittelbar wirkende Abbilder des jeweiligen sozialen Status. Sie vermitteln (vor allem Machos beiderlei Geschlechts) die Illusion des Herrschens in der eigenen Welt und des Beherrschens der feindlichen Umwelt. Sie verkörpern eine gesellschaftliche Grundstimmung: freie Fahrt für freie Bürger. Dynamischer Fahrspass für aufstrebende, wohlhabende Konsumenten. Grenzenlose Selbstbestimmung. Gleichberechtigte Teilhabe für alle. Ihre Fabrikationsstätten werden generationenübergreifend zu Herz und Seele von Regionen. Sie sind der Stolz ganzer Nationen.

An diesen Träumen, Wünschen, Hoffnungen und Assoziationen richten sich Markenexperten aus, wenn sie automobile Marken schaffen. Indem sie auf diese Kundenbedürfnisse oder -wünsche reagieren und sie mit den Vorstellungen und Interessen der Markeninhaber verbinden, definieren sie Markenvisionen, Markenmissionen, Markenwerte und Markenerlebnisse. Rein funktionale Produktleistungen wandeln sich so zu emotional ansprechenden Markenpositionierungen. Diese bringen Texter auf den Begriff und formulieren entsprechende Markenslogans. In Markenkampagnen adressieren Marketingmanager die identifizierten Bedürfnisse, Wünsche und Träume der relevanten Zielgruppen. Gestalter legen markenadäquate Ausdrucksmittel fest, von einer spezifischen Formensprache über entsprechende Materialien und Farben bis zu konformen Verhaltens- und Kleidungsregeln. Mitarbeiterinnen und Mitarbeiter werden so zu uniformierten Markenbotschaftern. Ausstellungsmacher schliesslich übersetzen Positionierungsaussagen und Gestaltungsregeln in umfassend gestaltete Räume und schaffen passende Erlebnisse und Inszenierungen.

Auf dieser Basis und mit diesen Vorgaben werden Automobilmarken in Ausstellungen rund um den

jürgen häusler

the twilight of a myth

Raffael Waldner's photographs are immediately evocative. And the minute we see just one of their logos, it happens. Even if we can only guess at their shapes, even if we merely catch a glimpse of their design or technical details, it happens: people fall for the myth perpetuated by successful automobile marques.

These marques – or brands if one prefers – have been an indelible feature of the past 100 years. They allow us to dream the dream of individual mobility. They embody the freedom enjoyed by people today. They create personal identities, and have a direct impact as reflections of our respective social status. Particularly in the eyes of overly assertive men (and women too), they foster the illusion of mastery within our own world and the domination of a hostile environment. They embody a prevailing social attitude, namely that a nation of free citizens should also be free of anything that might constrain its mobility. Dynamic driving fun for wealthy and aspiring consumers. Boundless self-determination. Equal participation for all. Across the generations, the factories that produce them have become the heart and soul of their respective regions. They constitute the pride of entire nations.

Brand experts focus on these self-same dreams, wishes, hopes, and associations whenever they create automobile brands. By reacting to what customers need and desire and then combining this with the brand owners' ideas and interests, they define brand visions, brand missions, brand values, and brand experiences. Purely functional product features are thus transformed into emotionally appealing brand positionings. Copywriters distil the essence of these positionings and come up with suitable brand slogans. Marketing managers use brand campaigns to address the needs, desires, and dreams of the relevant target groups. Designers opt for brand-appropriate means of expression, ranging from a specific language of form to corresponding materials and colors as well as consistently applied rules that dictate what one should wear and how one ought to behave. Employees thereby become uniformed brand ambassadors. Motor show

Globus entsprechend gefeiert. Geehrt werden sie dort wie einst gekrönte Häupter, inszeniert wird die Enthüllung neuer Modelle wie eine Götterhuldigung, platziert werden die Automobile auf Altären, umringt von Massen (und Models). Autosalons, die Kathedralen der Automobilmarken, sind meisterliche Gesamtkunstwerke. Darin ähneln sie den frühen Kaufhäusern als den Palästen der entstehenden Konsumgesellschaft oder den grossartigen Bahnhofsbauten als den Prachtbauten der kollektiven Mobilität. Immer wieder neu erschaffen werden sie im jährlichen Rhythmus (fast) ohne Rücksicht auf Kosten und Mühen.

Noch beeindruckender als anderswo verwandeln sich Marken im Rahmen von Ausstellungen zu Mythen. In lückenlos gestalteten Räumen werden präzise vorgegebene Welten geschaffen, Eindrücke erzeugt und Erlebnisse inszeniert – immer mit dem totalitär anmutenden Anspruch, alle Sinne der Besucher anzusprechen und ihre Gefühle wie ihren Verstand im Interesse der Marken zu erobern. Dort schaffen sie besonders grossartige und beeindruckende Bilder, erzählen ihre eigentlich stets gleichen Geschichten immer wieder spannend neu und werden in diesen weltweiten Pilgerstätten festlich gewürdigt. Wie in religiösen Pilgerstätten betrübt unter Umständen lediglich die Ambivalenz von gleichzeitiger Anbetung und Unerreichbarkeit.

So entstand und entsteht für nun bald 100 Jahre eine mythische Geschichte, die weltweit Menschen und Gesellschaften nachhaltig prägt. Aus dem Gebrauchsgut Automobil wurde so der Fetisch der Automobilität.

Die Fotos von Raffael Waldner klären auf. Sie zeigen das Davor und Danach der Inszenierung im Autosalon. In dieser Perspektive bedrängen die emotionale Leere der Hallen, die Unnahbarkeit und Kälte der Ausstellungsstücke und die degradierende Uniformierung des Personals.

Erleben wir gerade, wie die automobile Erfolgsgeschichte selbst zur Geschichte wird?

Also: Es war einmal …?

Vielfältige Bedenken trüben in jüngster Zeit das einst glänzende und glitzernde Bild. Neue und andersartige, sich als zeitgemäss preisende Haltungen, Einstellungen und Handlungen betreten die Bühne.

Kritische Vernunft hinterfragt gefühlsgetriebene Hingebung und verdirbt so die reine Fahrfreude. Ein schlechtes Gewissen verdrängt staunende Begeisterung und überschattet damit den befreiten Fahrspass.

organizers ultimately translate positioning statements and design guidelines into comprehensively designed spaces, and create appropriate experiences and mises-en-scène.

On this basis and with these stipulations, automobile brands are duly celebrated around the globe. They are venerated in a way that was once the prerogative of royalty; the unveiling of new models is staged like a homage to the gods, and the automobiles are placed upon altars, surrounded by crowds (and glamorous young women). Motor shows, the sacred temples of automobile brands, are imposing "Gesamtkunstwerke," i.e. fully integrated works of art. In this sense they resemble the early department stores that were palaces for the emerging consumer society, or the splendid railway stations whose magnificent edifices were dedicated to collective mobility. They are constantly recreated from year to year, without (almost) any regard for cost or effort.

Even more impressively than elsewhere, motor shows transform brands into myths. Precisely predetermined worlds are created in seamlessly designed spaces, impressions are generated and experiences are given a theatrical backdrop – always with the somewhat totalitarian goal of appealing to all the visitors' senses and subjugating their emotions as well as their reason at the service of these brands. This is where they assemble particularly sumptuous and impressive images, tell their stories – which are actually always the same – in a way that is constantly new and exciting, and are solemnly revered in these global sites of pilgrimage. As is the case with religious shrines, only the ambivalence of simultaneous worship and unattainability can sometimes cast a cloud over the proceedings.

Thus emerged – and has continued to do so for almost a century – a myth that has made a lasting impact on people and societies throughout the world. The automobile as a mere commodity has thus been transformed into the fetish of automobility.

Raffael Waldner's photographs are illuminating: they show the before and after of the mise-en-scène at the motor show. Viewed from this angle, one is oppressed by the emotional emptiness of the exhibition halls, the coldness and unapproachability of the exhibits themselves, and the degrading uniformity that has been imposed on the workforce.

Der sorgfältig kalkulierte globale Geschmacksdurchschnitt wird zum Mass der Dinge und verdrängt eigensinnige und liebenswerte Ikonen.

Weniger soll nun ernsthaft mehr sein. Kompaktheit gilt nicht mehr als ein bedauerliches Zeichen der Armut und des Mangels. Kompakt beschreibt neu eine attraktive Kategorie. Sparsamkeit und Verzichtbereitschaft steigen zu gefeierten Tugenden auf.

Bröckelt in diesen Tagen etwas? Verliert der automobile Mythos seinen Glanz, seine Bindungskraft und seine Deutungshoheit? Bildet sich der Warenfetisch zurück zum nackten Gebrauchswert des Gefährts?

Das müsste natürlich noch nicht das Ende der Geschichte des Automobils einläuten. Sie würde gleichwohl weniger glorreich ausfallen. Vieles deutet auf eine unschuldigere Zukunft hin. Nicht mehr die Sinne betäubend, die Gemüter berauschend und die Umwelt belastend. In dieser Welt sollte es zweckmässiger werden: elektrifiziert, online und selbstfahrend. Entlastet würde die Umwelt. Als Smartphone auf Rädern würden diese Fahrzeuge digital mit der Welt verbinden. Entlassen würde der Fahrer – nicht zuletzt aus der Verantwortung für die Konsequenzen seiner Hingebung an den Mythos.

Offensichtlich taugt eine solch karge, nüchterne und tugendhafte Zukunft nicht zum Mythos. Derart vollendet, würde das Fahrzeug lediglich den Alltag bereichern. So wie – zum Beispiel – der Kühlschrank. Und so wie dieser demütig seinen sinnvollen Platz in der Küche einnimmt, würde das Auto dann nicht mehr in Ausstellungen rund um die Welt zelebriert werden müssen und können. Die Kathedralen würden wieder zu Hallen werden und müssten ohne das Automobil auskommen. Sie würden – in jeder Hinsicht – leerer sein.

Und man würde dann nur noch – freudig oder wehmütig – erzählen können:

Es war einmal …

So gesehen, hält Raffael Waldner über die konkrete Welt der Autosalons hinaus einen Moment in der Lebensgeschichte des automobilen Mythos fest. Einen Moment, der im historischen Rückblick vielleicht einmal interpretiert werden wird als jene Phase, in der sich das Ende des Mythos ankündigte – wenn man nur genau genug beobachtet hätte. Vergleichbar darin jenen Familienfotos, auf denen die tödliche Krankheit des gefeierten Geburtstagskindes schon zu erkennen war – wenn man nur sensibel genug hingeschaut hätte.

Are we now witnessing how the automobile's success story is itself becoming history?

So: Once upon a time …?

A variety of reservations have recently been muddying the once shiny and sparkling image. New and different mindsets, attitudes and activities that pride themselves as befitting the times are now taking their place on the stage.

A critical and rational approach is questioning a type of devotion that is driven by emotions alone, and is thereby spoiling the sheer pleasure of driving. A guilty conscience is suppressing wide-eyed enthusiasm and thus overshadowing the enjoyment of driving which had hitherto been given free rein. The carefully calculated global consensus with regard to taste is becoming the dreary yardstick and is squeezing out lovable and idiosyncratic icons.

We are now encouraged to believe that less is more. Compactness is no longer seen as an unfortunate indication of poverty and deprivation. "Compact" now describes an attractive category. Thrift and a willingness to dispense with non-essentials are in the ascendant and are turning into much-lauded virtues.

Are things starting to fall apart? Is the myth of the automobile losing its luster, its power of attraction, and its exclusive right of interpretation? Is this fetishized commodity at risk of simply degenerating into the vehicle's trade-in value?

Of course this need not (yet) herald the end of the automobile's story, although it may well turn out to be less glorious. Many things indicate a more innocent future, no longer dazzling the senses, intoxicating the mind, and polluting the environment. In this brave new world, it ought to become more functional: powered by electricity, online, and self-driving. The environment would breathe a sigh of relief. Like a smartphone on wheels, these vehicles would connect digitally with the outside world. Drivers would be made redundant – not least of all because they are responsible for the consequences of their surrender to the myth.

It is obvious that such an austere, sober, and virtuous future provides unsuitable material for a myth. Executed in this way, the vehicle would merely make everyday life easier,

just like – for example – the refrigerator. And
just as the latter humbly occupies its rightful
place in the kitchen, the car would then no
longer have to – or be in a position to – be
celebrated at motor shows all over the world.
The temples would revert to exhibition halls
and would have to manage without the
automobile. They would – in every respect –
be emptier.

And one would then merely be able to –
joyfully or wistfully – tell their story:

Once upon a time …

Viewed in this way, Raffael Waldner is captur-
ing a moment in the biography of the automobile myth which transcends the concrete
world of the motor show; a moment that
with hindsight might one day be interpreted as
the phase in which the end of the myth was
announced – if only one's powers of observa-
tion had been sharp enough. In this sense
it is similar to that family photograph in which
the fatal illness of the beaming birthday
boy could already be detected – if only one
had studied it with enough sensitivity.

raffael waldner

Born	1972 Basel, Switzerland
	Lives and works in Bern, Switzerland
Education	
1999–2002	Zurich University of the Arts, Zurich, photography department
1995–1999	Hochschule für Grafik und Buchkunst, Leipzig, photography department

einzelausstellungen/ solo exhibitions

2010 Car Crash Studies, **Galerie Nicola von Senger, Zurich, CH***

2008 Cars, Motors & Traces, **Galerie Kenworthy-Ball, Zurich, CH**

Park, **Galerie Hobbyshop, Munich, DE**

2006 Crystal Peak, **Spielhaus Morrison Galerie, Berlin, DE**

Paradise Lost, **Ausstellungsraum 25, Zurich, CH**

ausgewählte gruppenausstellungen/ selected group exhibitions

2017 Photomobile, **Fondation Cartier pour l'art contemporain, Paris, FR***

2016 Catastrophe, **Albert Merola Gallery, Provincetown, USA**

2011 Project Ford Mustang: Engines, **Recyclart, Brussels, BE**

After Dark, **La Filature, Mulhouse, FR**

Zwischenlager, **Helmhaus, Zurich, CH**

Slippy Floor, **Pavlov's Dog Gallery, Berlin, DE**

2009 Darkside II, **Fotomuseum Winterthur, Winterthur, CH***

ReGeneration: 50 Photographers of Tomorrow (2005–2025), **Preus Fotomuseum, Horten, NO; Ronna and Eric Hoffman Gallery, Lewis & Clark College, Portland, USA; Alyce de Roulet Williamson Gallery, Pasadena, USA** (2007); **The Art Institute of Boston, Boston, USA** (2006); **Aperture Foundation, New York, USA** (2006); **Galleria Carla Sozzani, Milan, IT** (2005); **Musée de l'Elysée, Lausanne, CH** (2005)*

2008 F/Stop Photo Festival, **Leipzig, DE**

Veni Vidi Vicious, **Galerie Une, Neuchâtel, CH**

2007 Ingenuity, Photography, and Engineering (1846–2006), **Bozar, Brussels, BE; Fundação Calouste Gulbenkian, Lisbon, PT***

On the Road, **Musée-bibliothèque Pierre André Benoît/ PAB, Alès, FR***

2006 Cities and Conflicts, **Monat der Fotografie, Vienna, AT**

Mythkillers, **Galleria Klerkx, Milan, IT**

2005 Le Fil, **Ausstellungsraum 25, Zurich, CH**

Swiss Art Awards, **Art Basel, Basel, CH**

2004 The Lucky Number, **Ausstellungsraum 25, Zurich, CH**

Gridlock, **Govett-Brewster Art Gallery, New Plymouth, NZ**

Waldner/Augsburger, **Galerie Römerapotheke, Zurich, CH**

2003 We Love Art, **Ausstellungsraum 25, Zurich, CH**

10 Jahre Fotomuseum Winterthur, **Fotomuseum Winterthur, Winterthur, CH***

2001 Und da war noch ein Loch im Schwimmbad, **Kunstraum Walcheturm, Zurich, CH**

Kunst im Terrain der Werbung, Plakataktion im öffentlichen Raum/billboard campaign in public places, **Zurich, CH***

1999 Interventionen im Amt, **Kaspar-Escher-Haus, Zurich, CH**

1998 Accumulator, **Dogenhaus Galerie, Leipzig, DE**

1997 Labland, **Galerie Eigen+Art, Leipzig, DE***

öffentliche sammlungen/ public collections

Sammlung Deutsche Bank

Sammlung Kanton Zürich

Sammlung Stadt Zürich

Musée de l'Elysée, Lausanne

ausgewählte publikationen/ selected publications

2010 **Markus Bosshard** (ed.), Car Crash Studies (2001–2010), essays by Christoph Doswald and Maik Schlüter, **JRP|Ringier, Zurich**

2009 **Urs Stahel** (ed.), Darkside, Volume 2: Photographic Power and Photographed Violence, Disease, and Death, **Steidl, Göttingen**

2007 **Martin Jaeggi,** Photography Made in Zurich, **Scheidegger & Spiess, Zurich**

2005 **William A Ewing, Nathalie Herschdorfer, and Jean-Christophe Blaser,** ReGeneration: 50 Photographers of Tomorrow (2005–2025), **Thames & Hudson, London**

2001 Hors-Sol. Poster Actions in Switzerland, **Museum für Gestaltung Zürich & Lars Müller Publishers, Zurich**

www.raffaelwaldner.com

* Publikation/Publication

Alle Fotografien in diesem Buch gehören zur Serie *Salon*,
die Raffael Waldner in Paris, Frankfurt und Genf von 2011 bis 2016
realisiert hat.

All the photographs reproduced in this book belong
to the *Salon* series realized by Raffael Waldner in Paris,
Frankfurt, and Geneva, between 2011 and 2016.

bei codax publisher erschienen:
rineke dijkstra, beaches (1997)
ISBN 3-9521227-0-X
claudio moser, dedicated to the warmest flugelhorn tone (1998)
ISBN 3-9521227-1-8
teresa hubbard and alexander birchler, scene (1999)
ISBN 3-9521227-2-6
nobuyoshi araki, skyscapes (2000)
ISBN 3-9521227-3-4
smith/stewart, ahead (2001)
ISBN 3-9521227-4-2
shirana shahbazi, goftare nik (2002)
ISBN 3-9521227-5-0
julian opie, portraits (2003)
ISBN 3-9521227-6-9 (hardcover, not for trade)
walter niedermayr, titlis (2004)
ISBN 978-3-7757-1405-1 (buchhandel/trade)
ISBN 3-9521227-8-5 (not for trade)
bjørn melhus, auto center drive (2005)
ISBN 978-3-7757-1566-9 (buchhandel/trade)
ISBN 3-9521227-7-7 (not for trade)
daido moriyama, shinjuku 19XX–20XX (2006)
ISBN 978-3-7757-1729-8 (softcover, buchhandel/trade)
ISBN 3-9521227-9-3 (hardcover, not for trade)
walter pfeiffer, night and day (2007)
ISBN 3-9523070-0-9 (hardcover, not for trade)
ISBN 978-3-7757-1957-5 (softcover, buchhandel/trade)
david renggli, cage writes bird (2008)
ISBN 3-9523070-1-7 (hardcover, not for trade)
ISBN 978-3-905829-45-7 (softcover, buchhandel/trade)
charlie white, american minor (2009)
ISBN 978-3-9523070-4-1 (hardcover, not for trade)
ISBN 978-3-03764-003-6 (hardcover, buchhandel/trade)
gian paolo minelli, la piel de las ciudades – the skin of the cities (2010)
ISBN 978-3-9523070-5-X (hardcover, not for trade)
ISBN 978-3-03764-097-5 (hardcover, buchhandel/trade)
valérie belin, black eyed susan (2011)
ISBN 978-3-9523070-6-8 (hardcover, not for trade)
ISBN 978-3-03764-184-2 (hardcover, buchhandel/trade)
armin linke, srdjan jovanović weiss
socialist architecture: the vanishing act (2012)
ISBN 978-3-9523070-7-6 (hardcover, not for trade)
ISBN 978-3-03764-245-0 (hardcover, buchhandel/trade)
clegg & guttmann, modalities of portraiture (2013)
part I portraits and artworks, part II collaborative portraits
ISBN 978-3-9523070-8-4 (hardcover, not for trade)
ISBN 978-3-03764-317-4 (hardcover, buchhandel/trade)
jules spinatsch, snow management – complex (2014)
ISBN 978-3-9523070-9-2 (hardcover, not for trade)
ISBN 978-3-03764-355-6 (hardcover, buchhandel/trade)
erik steinbrecher, hits (2015)
ISBN 978-3-9524432-0-0 (hardcover, not for trade)
ISBN 978-3-03764-394-5 (hardcover, buchhandel/trade)
john stezaker, unassisted readymade (2016)
ISBN 978-3-9524432-1-7 (hardcover, not for trade)
ISBN 978-3-03764-449-2 (hardcover, buchhandel/trade)
raffael waldner, salon (2017)
ISBN 978-3-9524432-2-4 (hardcover, not for trade)
ISBN 978-3-03764-486-7 (hardcover, buchhandel/trade)

dank an:
jürg trösch, markus bosshard, clément dirié

herausgeber/editors:
markus bosshard, jürg trösch
grafische gestaltung/graphic design: markus bosshard
autoren/authors: jürgen häusler, martin jaeggi
übersetzung/translation: max kellermüller, editorial text,
www.editorial-text.com
lektorat/copyediting: linkgroup ag, zürich

satz und reproduktionen/
typesetting and reproductions:
linkgroup ag, zürich
druck/printing: linkgroup ag, zürich
www.linkgroup.ch

schrift/typeface: akzidenz
grotesk bq (g.g. lange, berthold)
papier/paper: dieses buch wurde
auf novatech satin fsc-mix 135 g/m^2
und olin regular high white fsc-mix
120 g/m^2 gedruckt. erhältlich bei
antalis ag, lupfig.
this book has been printed on
novatech satin fsc-mix 135 g/m^2 and
olin regular high white fsc-mix
120 g/m^2. available from antalis ag,
lupfig.

buchbinderei/binding: buchbinderei
burkhardt ag, mönchaltorf

© 2017 codax publisher, zürich
© 2017 für die abgebildeten werke
von/for the reproduced works by
raffael waldner

alle rechte der verbreitung, auch
durch film und elektronische
medien, fotomechanische wieder-
gabe, auszugsweisen nachdruck oder
einspeicherung und rückgewinnung
in datenverarbeitungsanlagen aller
art, sind vorbehalten bzw. nicht
gestattet. alle rechte vorbehalten/
all rights reserved.

verlegt von/published by:
codax publisher, zürich
mühlebachstrasse 52
postfach/p.o. box
ch-8032 zürich
schweiz/switzerland
tel. +41 44 268 12 12
fax   +41 44 268 12 13
www.codax-publisher.com

im vertrieb bei/distributed by:
jrp|ringier
limmatstrasse 270
ch-8005 zürich
tel. +41 43 311 27 50
fax   +41 43 311 27 51
E   info@jrp-ringier.com
www.jrp-ringier.com

jrp|ringier publications are available
internationally at selected bookstores
and from the following distribution
partners:

switzerland
ava verlagsauslieferung ag
centralweg 16
ch-8910 affoltern a.a.
verlagsservice@ava.ch
www.ava.ch

germany and austria
vice versa distribution gmbh
immanuelkirchstrasse 12
d-10405 berlin
info@vice-versa-distribution.com
www.vice-versa-distribution.com

france
les presses du réel
35, rue colson
f-21000 dijon
info@lespressesdureel.com
www.lespressesdureel.com

uk and other european countries
cornerhouse publications
home
2 tony wilson place
uk-manchester M15 4FN
publications@cornerhouse.org
www.cornerhousepublications.org

usa, canada, asia and australia
artbook|d.a.p.
155 six[th] avenue, 2nd floor
usa-new york, ny 10013
orders@dapinc.com
www.artbook.com

for a list of our partner bookshops or
for any general questions, please
contact jrp|ringier directly at
info@jrp-ringier.com, or visit our
homepage www.jrp-ringier.com
for further information about our
program.

ISBN 978-3-03764-486-7
gedruckt in der schweiz/
printed in switzerland

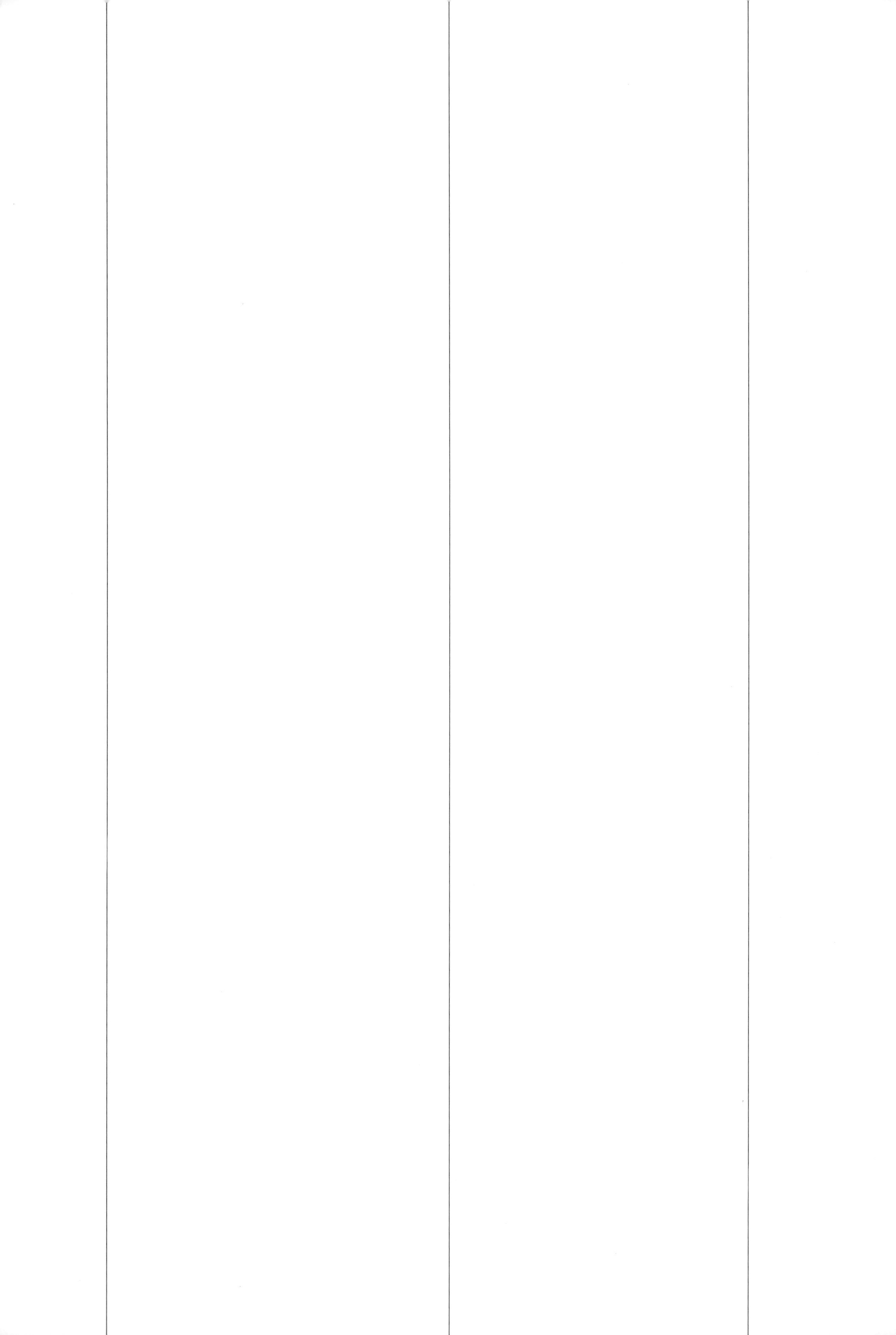